Lewis Ezra Hicks

A critique of design-arguments

A historical review and free examination of the methods of reasoning in natural

theology

Lewis Ezra Hicks

A critique of design-arguments
A historical review and free examination of the methods of reasoning in natural theology

ISBN/EAN: 9783337282721

Printed in Europe, USA, Canada, Australia, Japan

Cover: Foto ©Lupo / pixelio.de

More available books at **www.hansebooks.com**

OF

DESIGN-ARGUMENTS

A

HISTORICAL REVIEW AND FREE EXAMINATION
OF THE METHODS OF REASONING IN
NATURAL THEOLOGY

BY

L. E. HICKS

PROFESSOR OF GEOLOGY IN DENISON UNIVERSITY,
GRANVILLE, OHIO

NEW YORK
CHARLES SCRIBNER'S SONS
1883

PREFACE.

NOTWITHSTANDING the great bulk of the literature already produced upon the subject of Natural Theology, I have no apology to offer for this addition to it. This is not simply another book on a hackneyed theme in the same line with its predecessors. Instead of constructing a new design-argument, or revamping an old one, I have assumed the task of the reviewer and critic. Instead of heaping new material upon the mass, I have undertaken to sort out and label the elements of the heap which has already accumulated.

History and criticism are, therefore, the two dominant characteristics of this work. I take the liberty to offer a few words upon each of these points.

In the first place, respecting my historical sketch of Natural Theology, I do not wish it to be supposed that I regard it as a complete history, but only as a sketch, outline, or summary view of the work done and the progress made in this line of thought. It is not exhaustive, even as regards English writers, and is far from being so as regards Continental writers. The attempt to follow minutely the later developments of European thought upon this topic, would have been so large an undertaking that the publication must have been delayed for years. Besides, the task seemed to me not only formidable, but rather the reverse of inviting.

That part of it, especially, which relates to German meta-physics looked like a fathomless and misty sea. German natural theology is inextricably mingled and blended with German philosophy. He who would master either must patiently untangle both. If my present venture should prove fortunate, it is possible that I may trim my sails for a voyage upon that misty sea of German speculation.

But such as it is, — a mere sketch, — I conceive that the historical part of my work may be useful. It presents the salient points in the development of a certain phase of intellectual effort. By reason of this it may possess a degree of interest and profit for general readers, — all the more, perhaps, because it is a sketch, rather than a formal and elaborate history. Aside from this general utility, it may be of some special value to theologians. I cannot flatter myself that they will unanimously, or even generally, accept my conclusions; still, they may be thankful for my facts. My work does not constitute an exhaustive bibliography of Natural Theology, but it supplies considerable material for one. If any of my readers contemplate writing a "*Natural Theology*," I may be of service to them. This history reveals the fact, that a great many who formerly cherished such an ambition knew almost nothing of the work of their predecessors. If my book does not give information complete enough to guide future writers, and to preserve them from the reproach and wasted energy of doing over again what has been already done, I hope, at least, that it will provoke them to seek that complete information from other sources.

In the second place, as regards the critical portion of my work, my claim to originality will rest chiefly upon these four points : —

1. The fuller appreciation of the distinctness of the two sorts of reasoning in physico-theology. I have not only recognized the existence of two separate arguments, but I have endeavored to mark out their precise boundaries, and to fix and perpetuate the distinctions and differences which separate them, by giving to the argument from order a distinct name. It was necessary to coin a word for this purpose. My choice among the several Greek compounds which might have been considered as possible candidates for the honor, may not have been the happiest one; but I am sure it is not the worst. At all events, I present *eutaxiology* as a companion-word to teleology. The former designates the argument from order; the latter designates the argument from ends.

2. My criticism of the doctrine of *final causes*, and of the scholastic phrase upon which it is based. I am not the first to express dislike for the term "final cause," just as I am not the first to recognize an argument from order; but I have given careful and detailed reasons for my repugnance to this phrase, and shown the possibility of dispensing with it entirely.

3. My reasons for denying that the arguments of physico-theology are mere corollaries of the *causal* argument. The law of causation — *every event must have a cause* — can only conduct us to *some* cause. When we wish to reach a *specific* agent, such as intelligence or volition, we are obliged to leave the causal argument far behind us, instead of leaning upon it throughout. Thus, reasoning in eutaxiology, we may infer from the law of causality that order has some cause; but, in order to reach the conclusion that this cause is intelligence, we must rely upon the invariable conjunction

of order and intelligence as ascertained by induction, without any regard to causality. Reasoning in teleology, we may infer upon the basis of causation that there is some reason for the precise arrangement of causes in converging lines to produce a rational result; but, in order to reach the specific conclusion that this result is an *end* foreseen and chosen by an intelligent being, we must invoke some other law than that of cause and effect. Eutaxiology and teleology are, therefore, not only independent of the causal argument, but they are in advance of it and superior to it, in that they conduct us to higher and more specific conclusions.

4. My criticism of teleology. If my views are sustained, they will cause a radical change in the handling of this argument. I maintain that it has been hitherto uniformly taken in an *inverted* order. The attempt has been to conclude intelligence from ends, whereas the true and only valid form of the argument is to conclude, from intelligence as a premise, that ends exist in nature. I have shown that the old form of the argument involves its advocates in this dilemma : either their major premise is an identical proposition, or it is not true. The explanation of this dilemma is, that ends must be rational. Intelligence is the only mark which distinguishes them from simple effects. Hence, if you put ends in your subject, you have included intelligence in it, and thus made it identical with your predicate. For example, "Adaptation of means to ends implies intelligence" begs the question, because ends can only be distinguished from effects in so far as they are rational. The end must include intelligence by definition. Attempting to avoid this horn of the *teleological dilemma*, you may say, "The convergence of

many forces to produce a definite result implies intelligence."
But this is not true. Forces converge to all sorts of definite
results which are not ends because they are not rational;
i.e., not such as a rational being would choose. A railway
collision, a boiler explosion, a Chicago fire, a pestilence, a
Lisbon destroyed by an earthquake, are definite results for
the production of which many forces have coincided. Are
they therefore ends, or simply effects?

The topics discussed in this volume have claimed a share
of my thoughts for many years. Hence, during a few
months' residence in London, I eagerly availed myself of
the advantages afforded by the excellent library of the British Museum, where I found material for the historical review
of Natural Theology. My thanks are due, and are hereby
tendered, to the trustees of that institution for the facilities
there enjoyed while composing this work.

L. E. HICKS.

EDINBOROUGH, Sept. 6, 1882.

TABLE OF CONTENTS.

INTRODUCTION.

CHAPTER I.

CHAPTER II.

CHAPTER III.

CHAPTER IV.

CHAPTER V.

INTRODUCTION.

I.

MOST of the reasoning in natural theology falls under the head of what has been called *design*. If we inquire into the meaning of this word "design," we shall find that our ordinary conception of it grows out of its constant association with teleology. We think of design-arguments as teleological arguments. Not only do we so think of them in those moments when we are not making any studied effort to analyze them, or to think profoundly about them, but all writers on systematic theology have so classified them in those careful and elaborate treatises in which they have given us their best and deepest thoughts. They make all design-arguments teleological. I hope to be able to show that there are good grounds for a radical change in this classification. A teleological argument always has reference to the accomplishment of an *end* or *purpose* (τέλος). There are numerous appearances in nature, which, upon any ordinary principle of judging from appearances, are strongly indicative of an *intention* upon the part of the Creator to accomplish this or that result. Mankind have in all ages accepted these marks of de-

1

sign in good faith, and drawn certain conclusions from them. But the extent to which these indications of a purpose in nature have been suffered to guide the mind to an inference of the existence and attributes of a Supreme Ruler, has varied extremely in different periods of human history; as has also the extent of that field, or sphere of action, in nature wherein the play of special purposes and divine interpositions was supposed to be customary and legitimate.

In the youth of the world men looked upon all phenomena as direct products of a divine activity, specially directed to serve and bless, or to punish and destroy, mankind. *Every* natural event was an *end* foreseen, chosen, and brought to pass by suitable means. But with the birth of science many such teleological notions perished; and, as science has advanced, the phenomena of nature have been brought more and more under the reign of law, while the field of special interventions of a divinity for the purpose of achieving this or that result as an end has been constantly narrowed. At length the province of biology, the last stronghold of the old teleology, has been invaded by the theory of evolution, and, if not absolutely conquered, at least so far occupied, that teleology must either ally itself with evolution, or retire from the field. But, just as fast and as far as the field of teleology has been restricted by the advances of science, the range of another argument for the existence of God has been correspondingly enlarged. The reign of law is but another name for the *order* of nature. Physical law is merely a formula for the *orderly* movement of physical force. But order, and method, and the harmonious action and interaction of physical forces, are marks of intelligence, and prove the divine authorship of the cosmos just as conclusively as the use of means to accomplish an end proves it. As the reign of law has been extended over one after another of those provinces which were thought to be the special preserve of teleology, the argument from the order of nature has been progressively drawn into greater and greater prominence. This is also a *design*-argument, as well as the teleological argument. So that while teleology has been, as La Place remarked, pushed back more and more as science advanced, the order-argument having been at the same time brought to the front, the province of design-arguments has not suffered any restriction. On the contrary, it has been constantly enlarged, because the advances of science have created new fields for it, without infringing at all upon the sphere it formerly occupied.

It is not indeed historically true, that the order-argument has advanced *pari passu* with the retreat of teleology. All that can be said is, that it *ought* to have done so, and would have done so if natural theologians had been awake to their mission, and made good use of their opportunities. But it is only quite recently that reasoning from the order of nature, without regard to ends, has been recognized as an argument distinct from teleology, and quite as valid as that. In fact, it can hardly be said yet to be so recognized, only a few writers having employed it in such manner as to show that they clearly apprehended it as a distinct and independent line of reasoning. If the present treatise shall serve to set out the order-argument more clearly and prominently, an important object will be accomplished.

Dr. McCosh regards the order-argument in the light of a revival rather than a new invention. He says that natural theology has been chiefly occupied in this country for a century or two in displaying the external facts of nature instead of its internal principles of order, which the ancients attended to as well as the facts. Now "this branch of proof must come once more into prominence."[1] Professor Baden Powell also maintains, that design-arguments need a radical re-adjustment, such as to bring order to the front instead of utility, or useful ends accomplished.[2]

A clear proof that this is a very new argument, or else a very old one newly revived, is that it has not yet been named. As a distinct argument it deserves a name. Dr. McCosh has, indeed, suggested one: —

"Two great principles run through every part of the works of God. The one is the *principle of order*, or general plan, to which every given object is conformed with amazing skill. The other is the *principle of special adaptation*, by which each object, while formed after an ideal pattern, is at the same time, and by an equally wonderful skill, accommodated to the situation which it occupies, and the purpose which it has to serve. . . . The science which treats of the one might be called — were it not that the word has been so abused — cosmology; the science which treats of the other has an admirable phrase allotted to it in teleology."[8]

This suggestion is very cautiously advanced here, but repeated with greater confidence in his "Typical Forms and Special Ends in Creation," published six years later (1856). The doctor has not, however, followed his own suggestion. In his frequent references

[1] Method of the Div. Gov., p. 519. The first edition was published in 1850. Great Britain is meant by "this country."

[2] Unity of Worlds, p. 135; Order of Nature, p. 236. His second title is significant. "Unity of Worlds" was published in 1855; "Order of Nature," 1859.

[8] Meth. of Div. Gov., p. 158. The passage does not occur in the earlier editions: hence the more confident proposal of the name *cosmology* is probably *earlier* than the more cautious one, though it appears in a work published six years later.

to the principle of order in subsequent portions of these books, and in later publications, he describes it in other terms, avoiding the word "cosmology." Wolff, the famous German mathematician and philosopher, divided metaphysics into ontology, psychology, cosmology, and theology. Lewes adopts his division, except that he drops ontology. "There are three grand divisions of metaphysics; namely, psychology, cosmology, and theology."[1] This is a natural and convenient division. The terms might be briefly interpreted thus: psychology, the doctrine of the soul; theology, the doctrine of God; and cosmology, the doctrine of the cosmos, or the general metaphysical considerations respecting the universe. The meaning of the term seems to be too well fixed in this sense to admit of its being applied in the sense suggested by Dr. McCosh.

It is true it has been used in several other senses; and in order to judge fairly, and with all the evidence before us, whether it can be brought into physico-theology as a companion word to teleology, it may be worth while to notice some other examples of its use.

A quarter of a century before the publication of Wolff's "Transcendental Cosmology," which appeared in 1731, Nehemiah Grew, M.D., published in London his "Cosmologia Sacra." The greater part of this is in the ordinary style of apologetics, or a treatise upon the evidences of Christianity; and, so far as this part is concerned, the title, Sacred Cosmology, has no pertinence. But it also contains design-arguments, and a singular theory of a "vital principle" in matter generally, aside from vegetative and animal life, — a sort of hylozoism, or world-soul theory. So far it is cosmological, or treats of the cosmos.

[1] Hist. of Phi., I. lviii.

Twenty years after Wolff's book appeared in **Germany,** — that is, in 1751, — another cosmology was published in France [1] by Moreau de Maupertuis. His "Essai de Cosmologie" is an attempt to prove the existence of God by a novel method. Starting with a definition of the Supreme Being, he deduces from this, by rigid mathematical processes and formulas, the laws of the universe. Then comparing the laws so deduced with those actually found in nature, and finding them to be identical, he infers that the being from whom they were deduced must truly exist, and must be the author of the actual cosmos.

Still another cosmology appeared in 1861 in New York. This was the "Rational Cosmology" of Laurens P. Hickok, D.D. He attempts to reduce all phenomena under two forces, "antagonist and diremptive." "The principle of the generation of the material universe involved the agency of these two forces, and needed none other." [2] He seems to be trying to get at the *modus operandi* of creation *ex nihilo*, — a truly hazardous attempt.

Thus we have the transcendental cosmology of Wolff, the metaphysical cosmology of Lewes, the sacred cosmology of Grew, the mathematical cosmology of Maupertuis, and the rational cosmology of Hickok. Germany, France, England, and America have all had their tilt at the word. With good reason the canny Scotchman felt shy of attempting to appropriate it in a new and special sense after it had been thus bandied about. Besides, if life were not too short to be wasted in such an investigation, we might probably find still other varieties of cosmology. It is one of those handy Greek compounds, general in signification and convenient in

[1] It first appeared in Berlin in 1748.   [2] p. 384.

form, so that it is sure to be taken up and used in different senses by authors in different lines of research. Another objection to its use in theology is, that the adjective form of it, *cosmological*, is already appropriated for the argument for a First Cause.

The order-argument is therefore still unnamed. I propose to call it eutaxiological, from eutaxy (εὐταξία), *established order*. Eutaxiology will then be the sum of the reasonings from the order of nature respecting the existence of God.

In the following treatise I propose to deal with these two design-arguments, the eutaxiological and the teleological. But their relations to other arguments for the existence of God are so numerous and intricate, that it will be impossible to treat these fully without giving some attention to the others. And, in order that I may be clearly understood, it is desirable here in the beginning to set forth all these arguments in their mutual relations, and with their mutual limitations and boundaries, as I understand them.

First, there is the argument from intuitive conceptions of the necessary existence of a perfect Being, — the Ontological Argument.

Secondly, the argument which proceeds upon the principle of cause and effect, and seeks for an adequate First Cause, — the Causal Argument.

Thirdly, the argument from the mental and moral attributes of man, as implying the existence of God as a necessary complement to human faculties, — the Anthropological Argument.

The fourth and fifth are the two Design-Arguments.

The Ontological and Causal Arguments together constitute Rational, or, as Kant calls it, Transcendental Theology. The two Design-Arguments constitute

Physico-Theology; and the same, with the addition of the Anthropological Argument, constitute Natural Theology.

What I have called the causal argument is often called the cosmological argument, in accordance with Kant's scheme, I suppose. But Kant is not consistent with himself. In one place he applies the term " cosmological " to the causal argument alone; but in another place he includes under it the design-arguments of physico-theology, as well as the causal argument. A moment's consideration will suffice to enable us to see that the latter usage of the term is the more correct. The design-arguments are unquestionably cosmological. They draw their data from the cosmos just as much, or even more, than the causal argument; since the last may be based upon the existence of any single being, while design-arguments involve a wide survey of the universe. Indeed, they all draw their facts from nature; but each views its facts from its own peculiar standpoint. Teleology views them always in the relation of means and ends; eutaxiology, with reference to the principle of order; while the argument for a First Cause views them always in the relation of cause and effect. They are all cosmological; but as one is named *teleological* from its special ground-notion of an end, another *eutaxiological* from its special ground-notion of order, so ought the third to be named *causal* from its special ground-notion of cause and effect.

This would remove one objection to the use of the term " cosmology" as proposed by Dr. McCosh; namely, that the adjective " cosmological " was already appropriated to the argument for a First Cause. But it brings another objection into view at the same time that it removes the one. It would be as inappropriate to restrict the term to one of the design-arguments as to restrict it to the causal argument. Besides, the other objections to the doctor's suggestion are numerous enough without that.

The extent which I have given to the term "natural theology," making it include the argument drawn from the human intellect and conscience, has not been uniformly observed by writers upon this subject. The greater number, perhaps, have written about natural theology just as if it had to do only with design-arguments; and, as these were all included under *teleology*, the latter term was practically a synonyme of *natural theology*. The truth is, most of them did not stop either to analyze or define their terms and arguments; but, of those who did systematize their thoughts, the greater number include the anthropological argument under natural theology. Lord Brougham notably does so, and he further distinguishes between natural theology and natural religion. The first appeals to reason, endeavoring to convince men that there is a God; the second appeals to the moral sentiments, to the hopes and fears and reverence natural to man, as he contemplates his relation to the Deity so far as it is manifested to him by the light of nature.

II.

ANALYSIS OF THE TELEOLOGICAL ARGUMENT.

THERE is a degree of simplicity about teleological reasoning which in part accounts for its great strength as a popular argument. It has the advantage, that it can be gathered up into a single proposition, and hurled

like a solid shot at an adversary. Don't you believe
that feet were made for the purpose of walking? It is
difficult to make a blank denial, but the anti-teleologist *must* deny it. If he admits a purpose in this case,
he must do the same in a multitude of similar cases;
and, if he admits the existence of a purpose, he admits
the existence and dominance of mind in nature. There
is no such thing as a blind purpose. Purposes belong
to the realm of mind. Every conceivable sort of
purpose is an act of intelligence, though it may not
display wisdom. The most foolish aims of men presuppose an intellect to conceive and a will to execute
them. There are no foolish aims in nature; but, since
even a foolish purpose can only be entertained by a
being endowed with mind, how much more evident is
it that nature's purposes, provident and admirable as
they are, could not have been conceived and executed
by any other than an intelligent being!

This, I say, must be the conclusion if purpose is
admitted at all. The anti-teleologist must bolt on a
steel-plate armor of hard scepticism thick enough to
turn that first solid shot, or else make up his mind to
lower his flag sooner or later. He must speak out fair
and plain, without any mouthing or mincing, and say
that feet were somehow formed without any intention
that they should be used for walking.

In view of this fact, the reason of the popular strength
of teleology is not far to seek. Imagine two men de-
bating in public, one affirming and the other denying
that eyes were intended to see with! In the average,
intelligent, lecture-going audience, the man who would
plant himself squarely in the negative of that question
would be set down for a fool by half of his hearers the
moment he did so. Much more would he be set down

for a fool by the common crowd. This popular strength may be delusive, but it is a fact. Whatever fate this argument may meet at the hands of metaphysicians, the common sense of mankind will always gravitate mightily towards the belief that bodily organs were *intended* to perform the functions which they do perform.

It is implied in what has been said of the popular strength of teleology, that this strength is due to the simplicity of the reasoning. It is *apparently* very simple ; and, as compared with what Herbert Spencer calls "compound quantitative reasoning," it is really very simple. Still the analysis of it discloses a greater number of elements, and a greater complexity of relations, than would be suspected without analysis. Take a familiar example : The ear being well fitted for hearing, we infer that it was created, or evolved, for the purpose of hearing. In this the elements are, (1) the ear, a material object; (2) hearing, a physiological function, but just as real a thing as the material object; (3) a relation of fitness between the organ and its function ; (4) a mental conception of hearing as an end to be attained by means of the ear, — that is, a conception which includes all the first three elements, and forms a sort of duplicate of them ; (5) a volition or determination of the will to bring about hearing by means of the ear. The consideration that the end attained is a useful one is usually involved in the reasoning, and constitutes an additional element, making six in all. And these are simply the *conceptions* involved in teleological reasoning, without any reference to the logical processes involved in it. These will be carefully investigated in a subsequent chapter.

Thus the argument which looked so simple in its

concentrated form, looks much less simple when spread out by analysis into its elements. These are numerous enough; and their relations of dependence and likeness and unlikeness are intricate enough to furnish ground for two notable consequences. In the first place, there is a splendid chance for the advocates of teleology to get themselves tangled up, and involved in dangerous if not hopeless confusion, through the failure to keep each of these elements in its place, clear of entanglements with its neighbors or relatives to whom it bears a striking family resemblance. The sequel will show that they have made the most of this opportunity. Especially has there been a general failure to recognize the *duplication* of the elements of this argument. Hearing, for example, is one thing when regarded as the function of the ear, but quite another thing when it is regarded as an end. The one is a fact, the other a supposed mental conception of the Creator. The most cursory examination of physico-theological writings will reveal instances of the fallacy of an ambiguous middle term, arising from the fact that the author glided unconsciously from the function to the mental conception of it as an end.

In the second place, there is a splendid chance here for the enemies of teleology to throw these numerous elements into false relations and utter confusion; and they have not been slow to do it. They had this advantage, too, that they often gained their purpose through ignorance as well as through knowledge. They did not need to attain and hold fast to clear distinctions. All they wanted was to spoil the argument; and for that a small outfit of dialectic ingenuity was just as effective as, if not more so than, a thoroughly philosophical comprehension. And, in addition to their original capital of dialectic skill, their stock was always re-enforced by the blunders of the other side to an extent which enabled them to do a very respectable business in the argumentative line. The debaters on the affirmative side must comprehend their propositions through and through; but for those on the negative side a superficial treatment has certain advantages, especially if the affirmative position is inherently sound and strong.

But what if the affirmative is weak? Or, suppose it is apparently stronger than it is really, is it then the policy of its advocates to blink distinctions, and confuse relations, so as to conceal their weakness? That depends, of course, upon the question whether you love truth and righteousness. Now, in respect to the popular strength of teleology, I am constrained to make a remark which may be painful to my readers, because it is disparaging to that argument. But, besides being tolerably fond of truth and righteousness, I think I am doing a real service to any cause by ridding it of factitious and unreal elements of strength.

Now, the thing I am getting at is not so dreadful, after all, as you might suppose from such a solemn and formal introduction of it. It is simply this: the popular strength of teleology is partly due to a blinking of distinctions. Ask almost any ordinary person whether the eye was made for the purpose of seeing with it. He will say, " Yes, of course it was. Why should you ask such a foolish question?" But nine out of ten — nay, more likely, ninety-nine in a hundred — of such persons make that answer, and regard the question as a silly one, simply because they don't know, or, if they know, don't think of, the difference between *function* and *purpose*, — between seeing as a fact, and the mental, crea-

tive conception of vision as an end. The *function* of
the biceps muscle is to bend the arm at the elbow, is
one proposition; the *purpose* of the biceps muscle is
to bend the arm at the elbow, is a very different proposition. The first is a plain truth of physiology, to
which all who know the meaning of the terms will yield
a prompt and willing assent. The second is a teleological statement, to which no one who knows the full
import of the terms will subscribe, unless he is ready to
go the whole length of the teleological road, and accept
its uttermost conclusion. If the biceps muscle was
created, or evolved, for the purpose of bending the arm,
that was an act of intelligence, and the presence and
supremacy of mind in nature is established.

To the man who does not know or think of the distinction between use and end, between function and
purpose, between vision as a fact and the primitive
conception of it in creative thought, not only does the
affirmative answer seem a matter of course, but so much
a matter of course, that he adds to his "yes" the mental
if not audible comment, "What a silly question!" To
deny that ears were made for the purpose of hearing is,
to him, precisely equivalent to saying that they are not
used for hearing, and consequently are of no use at all.
That is why the anti-teleological debater would be set
down for a fool by the crowd, if he made a point-blank
denial that organs were intended for the functions appropriate to them.

The popular strength of teleology *is* delusive to this
extent at least, that it depends in part upon this obliri-
ousness to an actual distinction, — a distinction, too, so
fundamental that no teleological argument can be valid
which does not take it into account. The service rendered to the cause by pointing out this fallacy of con-

fusion is therefore a real one, since it lays the foundation for correct reasoning, and at the same time explains,
or does something towards explaining, the fact that
teleology has been so much stronger with the thought-
less masses than with the thoughtful few. If it stands
on such props alone, away with them, and let it fall!
but if, as I believe, it has other and better supports,
still away with these! Popular strength may be a
source of real weakness. It enables the other side to
say with a sneer, and a wag of the head, " Your argument will do for the multitude." Or it may lead the
defenders of a cause to repose in a false security while
enemies sap its foundations. But, worst of all, it fosters
the feeling, that an argument which is naturally so
strong can be easily and effectively handled by almost
any one whose fancy it is to make the trial. Teleology
has suffered untold mischief from this source. Not
only have incompetent bunglers taken it up because it
seemed so easy, but very able men writing upon it have
confided too much in its popular strength, and failed to
subject teleology in general, and their own presentation
of it in particular, to that severe analysis and criticism
which would have stripped off some of its fallacies.

Another remark of the same kind as the last, I have
to make, — like it, disparaging to teleology, but having
the same sort of defence. False pretensions are as
damaging to a cause as apparent but unreal elements of
strength. Now, it is a fact that a certain claim advanced by teleologists is a false one; and it has been
entered in behalf of their doctrine, and persistently
insisted upon, because of this very same blinking of distinctions mentioned in the previous remark. That is
to say, it has been asserted that teleology is a useful,
and even an indispensable, guide in physical, or still

more in biological, research. The case of Harvey's discovery of the circulation of the blood is cited; and, so far as he is individually concerned, there is some justice in the claim. He said to himself, "These valves all opening in the same direction are not here without a wise purpose;" and, thus reasoning teleologically, he was led on to his great discovery. But just make the reasoning non-teleological by substituting *function* for "wise purpose," and it works out the conclusion quite as well. Any rejecter of teleology, any Huxley or Haeckel with mere function as a guide, might have made the discovery just as well as Harvey did with "wise purpose" as a guide.

But not any better! The teleologist is not disqualified for scientific investigation by his belief, — only he has no private latch-key to the riddles of nature. He treads no royal road to discovery. Still, as he trudges along the common highway of science side by side with his unbelieving brother, is there not possibly some difference? As scientists they are on precisely the same level; but as men, as beings endowed with immortality, having a few other problems to solve besides those which can be attacked with scalpel, crucible, and balance, there may be just the difference that exists between a friendless orphan and a beloved child in his father's house.

III.

ANALYSIS OF THE EUTAXIOLOGICAL ARGUMENT.

At first view the teleological argument seems simple; but we find that it possesses a considerable degree of complexity. At first view the eutaxiological argument looks rather complex, but it is really very simple. The order of nature seems like a broad theme. To treat it exhaustively one would be obliged to survey the whole field of the physical sciences, and draw from each one of them its fundamental principles as illustrations of eutaxiology. Physical science is a classified knowledge of external nature; but the possibility of classification, and therefore of science, lies in the fact that there is first a natural, external *order*, whence arises the logical, internal order in the arrangement of facts and principles, which constitutes true science. The external order existed before the science which is based upon it. There was celestial harmony before the science of astronomy was constructed by formulating the laws and principles gathered from observation of the heavens. What, then, is this impressive fact of celestial harmony, — this majestic and orderly movement of vast bodies through boundless space, — what is it but a divine *thought* impressed upon the cosmos? Chemical combinations obey the law of definite and multiple proportions: can nature *count* then? Crystals present, some simple and complete, others modified and complex, geometrical forms: is nature a *geometrician?* Plants and inferior animals are built upon the radiate plan, the higher animals having, on the contrary, distinct right and left sides, dorsal and ventral aspects: is there any thought of symmetry in this? or any thought of symmetry and number both in the parts of flowers, and the fractional series in phyllotaxy? Then there are the "types of structure" in zoölogy, — a definite pattern or fashion running through whole classes and sub-kingdoms; a *plan* it would seem, and so the comparative anatomists call it.

Thus we might go on through all the sciences, and see, ever and anon, some new principle of order standing out like a creative thought. This eutaxiological argument, then, seems to have no end to it; for order is universal in nature. True, it is universal; and there is no end to the examples of it, but they are all essentially alike. Order in the heavens is the same principle as order in the setting of leaves on a tiny plant, or of the sparkling facets of a minute crystal. The illustrations of the principle of order are countless, but the argument based upon them is one.

The fundamental proposition of eutaxiology is, that order and harmony are marks of intelligence. They imply that there has been a preconceived plan, to which the phenomena in question have been made to conform. Let us take an illustration from the animal kingdom. Here eutaxiology takes the special form of morphology, or the doctrine of typical forms; that is, morphology is one of its phases, though not the only one. The orderly series of animals grouped into classes, orders, and genera, is another phase of eutaxiology; but we will draw upon morphology at present for an illustration.

In the sub-kingdom vertebrata the morphological type of a limb is, that there shall be first a *single* bone (*humerus* or *femur*), then *two* bones side by side (*radius* and *ulna* or *tibia* and *fibula*), then a number of small bones (wrist or ankle), then *five* bones side by side (*metacarpus* or *metatarsus*), and finally *five* digits (fingers or toes). This type, though not universal among vertebrated animals, prevails so widely, and is so often realized in different animals which are otherwise extremely unlike, that naturalists have no hesitation in accepting it as a type, and describing its elements with

all the minuteness and confidence which belong to the
description of real things. Is it not then a real thing?
Not in the sense of being material: it is simply an *idea*,
nothing more and nothing less. But an idea which has
moulded the form of the hand with which you hold this
book, and the wing of a bat, and the paw of a lion, and
a thousand other animal forms, all on the same pentamerous pattern, is considerable of an idea. It is quite a
real fact if it is not a material object. Call it a crea-
tion-idea or an evolution-idea, whichever you like best.
An idea it is at all events, — a veritable *plan* which only
an intelligent being could have conceived and executed.

The key-note of eutaxiology is *plan*, as that of teleology is *purpose*. "Plans and Purposes in Nature"
would be a comprehensive title for a treatise on
physico-theology.

The elements of the eutaxiological proof, or the fundamental conceptions involved in it, are, (1) the fact of
order in nature ; (2) the *plan*, or the mental conception
of that disposition of objects and that movement of
forces which constitute order and harmony.

This analysis shows that the eutaxiological is much
simpler than the teleological argument. There is no
such reduplication of the elements, and they are clearly
distinct and different ; so that there is not the same
danger of confounding similar elements as in teleology.
Eutaxiology is certainly simpler, but is it as forcible?
I shall not at present attempt to answer this question
in full. The critical estimation of both these arguments will be undertaken after I have given a historical
review of natural theology, and after that estimate will
be the time to institute the comparison.

But, without such careful examination, judging simply
by what lies upon the surface, it would seem that this

argument is at least equal to the other in effectiveness. Moreover, it is probable that a considerable part of the energy supposed to belong to teleology has really come from eutaxiology, seeing that they have always been lumped together under the head of *design*. When Napoleon, in reply to the fine-spun theories of the French atheists, pointed to the heavens and said, "But who made all these things?" his argument was eutaxiological, and there is no question but that it was forcible. It was a shot quite as solid as any which teleology can forge. The order, harmony, and beauty of the heavens speak a clear and universal language. "Their line is gone out through all the earth, and their words to the end of the world." The burden of their nightly song is the existence of a creative Intelligence. There is no thought of their utility, of an end for which they exist, — no complex relations of means and ends to be reasoned out before we can receive their sublime message. The lesson they teach is as simple as it is grand; and the argument based upon it is so plain, that neither bungling advocates nor captious critics can easily throw it into confusion.

If it should turn out that eutaxiology is as strong as teleology, the addition of an independent and valid proof of God's existence to those already in use would be a reason for separating this argument from teleology. But it may be that the latter is weakened by the separation. There ought to be solid reasons for it, aside from the mere increase in the number of arguments. There is a natural conservatism in human thought which will resent the change. Men who have become accustomed to associate the word "design" with teleology alone, will possibly feel reluctant to entertain the proposed division of design-arguments into two distinct species. Is there not a *purpose* in the order of nature? Why not leave that argument where it was before, under teleology? Are not all arguments from the order of nature really teleological, no matter how they are named?

Far be it from me to deny that there is a purpose in the admirable harmony of the universe. But the whole force of teleological reasoning consists in the fact, that not merely *some* purpose may be plausibly supposed to exist, but that the purpose is *unmistakable*, if it is a purpose at all. The purpose of the eye is vision, and no possibility of mistake about it, if it has any purpose whatever. Now, while the fact of order is plain enough, and the supposition of an underlying purpose is plausible enough, it is not so easy to say just what the purpose is. And teleology is certainly in a bad way, if, having set out to prove God's existence from the fact that special ends appear to have been chosen and wrought out in nature, its advocate is unable to specify what the end is, from the selection and accomplishment of which, as a premise, he hopes to reach his desired conclusion by legitimate reasoning.

But suppose we say that order is an end in itself? Very well: how, then, was it brought to pass? What are the means? Can you specify them minutely? Is not *order* too broad, and, so to speak, *diffuse* a thing to be of any teleological value? That argument is forcible only when structures and forces are, as it were, *focused* upon a definite result. But order is produced in a thousand different ways and places. Turn it about as you will, call it a means or call it an end, the notion of order sturdily refuses to shape itself as a valid teleological argument. But why grieve over that? Order is in itself a mark of intelligence just as clearly as the adaptation of means to an end. If by main force you thrust it under the relation of means and ends, it will give you but a halting and unwilling service. Why not leave it where it belongs? why so eager to spoil a good eutaxiological argument to make a bad teleological one?

But suppose that the advocate of the old teleology returns to the charge once more with the suggestion that *law* is the means by which order is maintained. That notion might be sound enough in political science, but not in physics or in physico-theology. Human laws are a means of preserving order, but nature's laws are a different affair altogether. Natural law, instead of being the cause of order, is merely one form of order: it is order itself under another name. Law is merely an expression of constancy in the operation of forces. It signifies that forces move in a regular, that is, an *orderly*, manner. Now, not only is it a difficult matter to point out the means by which other forms of order are brought about, and particularly so in the case of the orderly movement of forces, — who can tell why or by what means gravitation acts according to the law of inverse squares? — but when order appears under the form of law it is positively repugnant and hostile to the radical notion of teleology. Law is *unbending* and *universal;* teleology asserts that there has been a *bending*, a modification of structures directed to the evolution of a *special* result. Fixedness and universality are quite the opposites of adaptation and specialty.

We have already alluded to the constant encroachment of the province of eutaxiology upon that of teleology, — a diminution of the latter which has progressed just in proportion as men learned the lesson that God rules by fixed laws rather than by special interventions. The question whether there is any thing left of teleology, or, granting that it has some standing-room now, whether there will be any thing left of it after science has done its best or worst to reduce every thing under fixed laws, — that question is held in abeyance for the present. But, assuming that it may possibly receive an affirmative answer, that there is flexibility as well as fixedness in nature, that there are such numerous convergences of things and forces to a particular issue that any philosophical view of the whole system must take these into the account as well as the inflexible order of the cosmos, — then it is obvious, that, if there is such a thing as teleology, it is not only a thing quite distinct from eutaxiology, but the very opposite of it. Flexibility and specialty characterize the one, but fixedness and universality are the marks of the other. These opposite characteristics furnish ample ground for refusing to leave both together under the same name and in the same province of argument, — ample ground for the erection of eutaxiology into a distinct argument with a distinct name.

But, in thus emphasizing the sharp contrast between these two arguments for the purpose of justifying my classification and nomenclature, it may seem that I have so far overdone my task as to make them appear, not only distinct, but repugnant, hostile, irreconcilable, and mutually destructive the one to the other. It is therefore now in order to set forth their relations of harmony and likeness if they have any. Such relations do exist, and require but a moment's reflection to discover them. Radically different and even opposite in character as they are, still they are not opposed and hostile, but harmonious. Eutaxiology furnishes the general ground upon which teleology builds up definite results. If the scene which nature unfolds always presents certain hard and inflexible lines of order, and at the same time certain flexible lines which shape themselves into definite and graceful forms, the whole picture is none the less harmonious for that. There is unity of composition, notwithstanding the several elements are in sharp contrast.

Not only are these elements harmonious whenever they are found together, they are almost always together, almost inseparable in nature. Wherever the one is present, the other is more or less involved. In the analysis of teleology the divine element appears as a purpose; in eutaxiology it appears as a plan. The conception of a plan, type, or pattern realized in material forms is, indeed, quite distinct from the conception of an end accomplished by suitable means; but, though clearly distinct, it is entirely harmonious, and thus capable of co-existence in the same object, or in the same series of operations. General plans and special purposes are alike products of mind: they both alike and equally involve the notion of a foreseeing intelligence and a determining will. This brings them into a very close likeness, and the more when we observe that the presence of the one frequently involves the other in a greater or less degree. For instance, the conception of a given function as an end involves the conception of the plan of an organ as a means. Respiration involves the conception of lungs constructed upon some general pattern. Every clear case of teleology involves eutaxiological elements.

Is the converse equally true? Is there a purpose in every example of order? We have already seen that if there is, — and no one who admits any purposes at all in nature would feel competent to deny that there may be, — still it cannot, in many cases, be so specified as to base a teleological argument upon it. The typical vertebrate limb terminating in five digits is a plan realized in thousands of material forms; and it is probable there is a purpose in all this persistent exhibition of a morphological type, though it is not obvious what the purpose is, — at least not so obvious as in the case of organs in relation to their functions. Hence it appears that the converse is not true in the same sense and to the same extent.

In another sense, however, the teleological element is clearly present in all these cases. All the limbs built upon this general plan have some function, either walking or grasping or swimming or flying. But, the moment you turn your thought into this channel, it is the contrast and opposition of teleology and eutaxiology — or morphology, the biological phase of eutaxiology — that forces itself upon your notice. Teleology seizes the general pentamerous type which morphology presents, and plays all sorts of tricks with it; spreads it out into a paddle for swimming, or a wing for flying; swings round one or two of the digits to oppose the others for grasping; lops off one here, another there, or all but one of them for the sake of concentration and solidarity, as in the foot of the horse; in short, takes the greatest liberties with the general type, treating it as a sort of convenient platform, or stage, upon which to produce her ever-changing play of special ends.

IV.

THE USE AND ABUSE OF THE WORD "DESIGN."

WHAT is meant by *design* in natural theology? From the fact that it has been constantly associated with teleology, we might infer that it means *contrivance for a purpose*, or *adaptation of means to an end*.[1] That has undoubtedly been the thought of authors 'in the majority of places where they have written the word. But it is an ambiguous word: it has a number of other meanings. It may mean *preliminary sketch, outline, plan*, or *delineation*, as in drawing and architecture; or it may mean *scheme, plot, device, aim, intent*, or *purpose*. Any one who will examine the writings of design-advocates will easily find examples of gliding insensibly from the meaning usual with them, *contrivance for a purpose*, to some other of these numerous meanings. It is a pity that this ambiguous term should have so long held a foremost place in physico-theology; and, if this branch of theology is ever to have any pretensions to exactness and scientific method, the word "design" must either be wholly banished from its vocabulary, or at least remanded to a subordinate place, and used with extreme caution, in order not to mislead and confuse both author and reader.

---

[1] Whewell's definition of design. "We direct our thoughts to an action we are about to perform: we *intend* to do it; we make it our *aim*; we place it before us, and act with *purpose* (*propositum*) ; we *design* it, or mark it beforehand (*designo*)." Elements of Morality, I., i. 7. This would be a better definition of *designate* than *design*. He has been too much influenced by the force of the Latin original. Besides, the range of meaning of the noun is considerably different from that of the verb, and it is the noun with which we have to deal in teleology.

Although it would not be difficult to do so, it is not necessary to present an extended list of examples to show what abuses have arisen in the use of this word. The bare fact that teleology and eutaxiology have been lumped together as a single *design-argument* is enough to condemn it. How so? Are they not both concerned with the question of design in nature? Certainly they are; and that is just what I complain of, — that is to say, that design is so versatile in meaning that it can be applied to both of these arguments in spite of their radical distinctness and sharp contrasts. It has even caused a persistent ignoring of the fact that they were distinct. Were they not both design-arguments, and therefore one and the same argument?

Two considerable infelicities are involved in the use of the word "design." The first is rhetorical. Shall I say argument *from* design, argument *for* design, argument *of* design, argument *respecting* design? or shall I dodge the delicate question of preference among pretty little prepositions, and (as some men have died bachelors rather than grieve the other fair charmers by choosing one) bluntly say *design-argument?* What is the trouble about those prepositions? None whatever: the mischief lies in the word "design." There is some real difficulty or ambiguity about that, which has been at the bottom of all these variations in the phrase-form used as a synonyme of *teleology.* All the variations given above have been actually employed by different authors.

The reason of it is this: if your argument is teleological, then "design" means "adaptation of means to an end," and it is an argument *from* design; that is, from the fact of adaptation, as a premise, to an intelligent author of that adaptation as a conclusion. But, if your argument is eutaxiological, then "design" means "plan,"

and it is an argument *for* design; that is, the fact of
order in nature is your premise, from which you infer a
preconceived plan, or design, as a conclusion. So that
it is indeed true that both kinds of reasoning have to do
with *design*, but in very different senses of that word.

It turns out that none of those phrase-forms are correct. If we say *argument from design*, that might answer as a synonyme for teleology, were it not for a couple
of serious objections. One of these will appear presently; the other is, that, since *eutaxiology* has to do
with *design* as well as *teleology*, it is inexpedient to
incorporate the word "design" in the name of the latter.
The same objection lies against the phrase, "argument
for design," as a synonyme of eutaxiology. And if we
should attempt to deal out an even-handed justice to
both arguments by calling one the argument from design, and the other the argument for design, that would
involve the awkwardness of using *design* in opposite
senses in two closely related phrases in the same
science.

It is also inadmissible to speak of the design-argument, or the argument of design, or the argument respecting design; for in each case it is implied that there
is but one design-argument. These phrase-forms all
involve and imply a failure to perceive the distinction
between eutaxiology and teleology, and are indeed
largely responsible for that failure. It is, however, convenient sometimes, and always quite admissible, to use
these phrase-forms in the plural, — to speak of eutaxiology and teleology collectively as design-arguments. Or
we may speak of either one of them as *a* design-argument, but not properly as *the* design-argument. Design, with all its shortcomings, is too good a word, and
too firmly fixed by usage, to be wholly banished from

natural theology. And, if used at all, it may be conveniently employed in the general way indicated by the phrase *design-arguments*, or *arguments respecting design;* these phrases being understood as equivalent expressions for the sum of eutaxiological and teleological arguments. In this way, whatever convenience and utility there is in the word will be preserved, and at the same time its power to work mischief through ambiguity will be neutralized.

The second unhappy consequence involved in the old loose and indiscriminate employment of the word "design" was a logical one, and so disastrous that it would be an abuse of terms to call it a mere infelicity. *Design* is a cloak for numerous fallacies. Some of these have been pointed out by various writers; but it does not seem to be sufficient merely to *designate* "design" as a dangerous word, and to show that this or that fallacy has resulted from its use. The most effectual remedy would seem to be that of drawing hard and fast lines between eutaxiology and teleology, and showing in what sense *design* is used in each of these arguments. This I have done already; and a further safeguard against the ambiguities of design will be furnished by keeping each argument in its proper place, and applying it to its proper use, as I shall show in the sequel.

· One of these fallacies which has been frequently criticised is that involved in the proposition, "Design implies a designer." Irons, McCosh, Powell, and several others have noticed this fallacy, some of these criticisms being nearly half a century old; and yet we find that Dr. Hodge opens his discussion of teleology with this syllogism: "Design supposes a designer. The world everywhere exhibits marks of design. Therefore the world owes its existence to an intelligent author."[1] He goes on to explain design as including, "(1) The selection of an end to be attained. (2) The choice of suitable means for its attainment. (3) The actual application of those means for the accomplishment of the proposed end. Such being the nature of design, it is a self-evident truth, or even an identical proposition, that design is indicative of intelligence, will, and power."

Exactly so: the major premise is, as he says, an identical proposition. But, that being the case, the syllogism reduces to this form: A is A; B is A; therefore B is A. No valid syllogism can be constructed with only two terms. The truism contained in the major premise contributes nothing to legitimate reasoning, but serves only to cloak a fallacy.

V.

THE DOCTRINE OF FINAL CAUSES.

ANOTHER phrase which has been used as a synonyme of teleology is the "doctrine of final causes." To show that this is still more objectionable than any of the names containing the word "design," is the object of the following discussion.

Aristotle stands sponsor for final causes; also for the *dictum* that nature does nothing in vain, — two things which have done infinite mischief in physico-theology. Respecting any object in nature, the question may be asked, What is it good for? The answer to this question designates the Aristotelian so-called final cause of

[1] Systematic Theology, i. 215.

that object. What is a house good for? To dwell in: habitableness is therefore the final cause of a house.

Aristotle's statement of his fourth principle is,[1] *That on account of which a thing was to be and the good of it, for this is the* END *of all becoming and change.* It might easily be shown that modern teleologists have understood *final cause* somewhat differently from Aristotle's own interpretation of it. But that would be a waste of words, because the doctrine is vicious in any form, whether it be the primitive Aristotelian, or the perverted scholastic phase of it.

Ueberweg says, —

"Of the four principles, matter (ἡ ὕλη), form (τὸ εἶδος), moving cause (τὸ ὅθεν ἡ κίνησις), and end, or final cause (τὸ οὗ ἕνεκα), the three latter are often one and the same in fact; for essence (form) and end are in themselves identical, since the proximate end of every object consists in the full development of its proper form (i.e., the *immanent* end of every object, by the recognition of which the Aristotelian doctrine of finality is radically distinguished from the superficial utilitarian teleology of later philosophers), and the cause of motion is at least identical in kind with the essence and the end."[2]

From which it would seem that Aristotle's fourth principle was not the ultimate but the proximate end. But with teleologists the notion of final cause seems to be ultimate and exclusive cause, or end.

The schoolmen in the Middle Ages took up the phrase, and manipulated it in their peculiar fashion. From their commentatorial mills it sifted down into modern philosophy and theology. What sort of a

---

[1] τὸ οὗ ἕνεκα (ἦν εἶναι) καὶ τἀγαθόν, τέλος γὰρ γενέσεως καὶ κινήσεως πάσης τοῦτ' ἐστιν)

[2] Hist. of Phi., i. 162.

grist it has become may be gathered from Whewell's statement of it : —

"Thus we necessarily include in our idea of organization the notion of an End, a Purpose, a Design ; or, to use another phrase which has been peculiarly appropriated in this case, a *Final Cause.* This idea of a Final Cause is an essential condition in order to the pursuing our researches respecting organized bodies. This idea of Final Cause is not *deduced* from the phenomena by reasoning, but is *assumed* as the only condition under which we can reason on such subjects at all." [1]

He refers to his "History of Physiology," where, says he, —

"I have shown that those who studied the structure of animals were irresistibly led to the conviction that the parts of this structure have each its end or purpose ; that each member and organ not merely produces a certain effect or answers a certain use, but is so framed as to impress us with the persuasion that it was constructed *for* that use ; that it was *intended* to produce the effect. It was there seen that this persuasion was repeatedly expressed in the most emphatic manner by Galen ; that it directed the researches and led to the discoveries of Harvey ; that it has always been dwelt upon as a favorite contemplation, and followed as a certain guide, by the best anatomists ; and that it is inculcated by the physiologists of the profoundest views and most extensive knowledge of our own times. All these persons have deemed it a most certain and important principle of physiology, that in every organized structure, plant, or animal, each intelligible part has its allotted office ; each organ is designed for its appropriate function ; that nature, in these cases, produces nothing in vain ; that, in short, each portion of the whole arangement has its *final cause,* — an end

[1] Phi. of Ind. Sciences, B. ix. c. 6.

to which it is adapted, and in this end the reason that it is where and what it is.

"The use of every organ has been discovered by starting from the assumption that it must have *some* use. The doctrine of the circulation of the blood was, as we have seen, clearly and professedly due to the persuasion of a purpose in the circulatory apparatus." [1]

These statements involve all the principal vices of the doctrine of final causes, — the exaggerated pretension that, in "pursuing our researches respecting organized bodies," the idea of final cause "is assumed as the only condition under which we can reason on such subjects at all;" the ignoring of the distinction between *use* and *purpose*, which plainly appears in the unconsciousness with which he glides from the one to the other in the last quotation, and upon which fallacy of confusion his whole claim rests; the maxim that nature does nothing in vain; the notion of final cause as ultimate and exclusive, — "the reason why it (any organ) is where and what it is;" and the confounding of the two distinct notions of cause and effect, and means and ends. Let us examine some of these weak points in this doctrine, beginning with the last.

The trouble with final causes is, that while they are not causes at all, but ends or purposes, they take on the semblance of causes by reason of this name which is applied to them. Thus we have an inexcusable jumbling-up of two entirely distinct notions. Entirely distinct, I say, and so they are in close analysis; and yet they are sufficiently alike (here is where the trouble comes in) to lend themselves with great facility as instruments of confusion and mischief and mistaken identity, — in short, a whole "Comedy of Errors" when

[1] Hist. of Ind. Sciences, iii. 511.

they are set jigging and masquerading in each other's
clothes as they are in the doctrine of final causes.

Dr. Whewell distinctly admits this objection, but
does not regard it as fatal : —

" The idea of final cause, of end, purpose, design, intention, is altogether different from the idea of cause as efficient cause. . . . But, if the idea be clearly entertained and
steadily applied, the word is a question of subordinate importance. The term *final cause* has been long familiarly
used, and appears not likely to lead to confusion." [1]

In order to judge for ourselves of the extent of the
danger, which he admits does exist, that this term may
lead to confusion, let us look into it a little more
closely. The doctrine of final causes is clearly a teleological affair : hence we must recall the analysis of
teleology already given, in order to see whether any of
the elements of that argument can properly be called
a cause. We have in the example previously given,
that of hearing, (1) the ear, (2) hearing as a function,
(3) the relation of the first to the second, (4) the reduplication of all these three elements in creative
thought, (5) the determination of creative will.

If any one of these is a cause, it is certainly the last.
But in the doctrine of final causes the formula would
be, Hearing is the final cause of the ear. That is what
it is *good for*, in Aristotelian phraseology; that is "the
end to which it is adapted," "the reason that it is
where and what it is," in the phraseology of Whewell.
Let us see what consequences are likely to follow from
the proposition that hearing is the cause of the ear.
No one but a veteran teleologist ever thinks of cause
in any other sense than as efficient cause ; and even for

the teleologist it requires a special effort to think of it simply as an end or purpose. It looks very much as if Whewell himself mixed a little *efficient cause* into his notion of *final cause* when he spoke of it as the reason for any organ being such as it is and placed where it is. Whether he did or not, the ordinary reader would be sure to do it; and we will endeavor to see where it will lead him.

Hearing is the final cause of the ear; but is it hearing as a function, or hearing as an end? The latter of course, because *end* and *final cause* are synonymous. I say the latter of course; because, in the light of a clear analysis of teleology, there can be no possible doubt about it. But would it be a matter of course in the absence of that analysis? The old teleologists failed entirely to distinguish between *function* and *purpose*. This is notoriously true of Whewell: he glides from use to purpose, and skips back again to function, with a serene and guileless unconsciousness of any difference between them. If he had seen the distinction, it must instantly have opened his eyes to the monstrous fallacy of his pretension, that an apprehension of the idea of final cause was the only condition under which we can reason at all about organized beings. Turn back to the last quotation but one, and observe, that, if he had stuck to the word *use* all the way through, it would have given no support to his claim of the value of final causes; but in the very crisis of the statement he slips in the word *purpose* instead of *use*, just as if it were synonymous with it. If he used these words and the notions they represent so indiscriminately, it would be surprising if his readers were not still more confused about them. So that, when it is said that hearing is the cause of the ear, it is just as likely to be understood of the function as of the purpose. Suppose it is the latter, however: what follows? The statement will be, that the conception in creative thought of hearing as a desirable end was the cause of the ear. How would such a statement be commonly understood? If it conveyed any meaning at all, which is somewhat doubtful, it must be either, that, if God had not happily thought of hearing, the ear would never have existed; or that the conception acting as a *motive* was the cause of that volition which set in motion the whole train of agencies resulting in the production of the ear. The first alternative makes it a *condition* rather than a cause; and the second is almost blasphemous, because it implies a denial of the freedom of the will of the Almighty himself.

Suppose, then, it is hearing as a function that is the cause of the ear. Will the veteran teleologist subscribe to that opinion? If so, he surrenders his whole case. That is precisely what those evolutionists who deny all teleology assert. The utility of hearing, they say, even in the rudest beginnings of the ear, was so great, that, in the struggle for life, natural selection and inheritance carried the organ right up to perfection, without any purpose about it. The assertion that the physiological function of the ear was the cause of its present perfection at least, if not of its origin, would be received with applause; but the plaudits would come from the wrong quarter.

See where the devout teleologist is liable to be landed if he starts with the assertion that hearing is the cause of the ear. He is brought to face a dilemma of which one horn pushes him to the verge of blasphemy, and the other into the enemy's camp. That is what may come of playing fast and loose with words, and mixing up two distinct notions in one phrase. The safe course will be not to say that hearing is the cause of the ear at all: it is sure to be misunderstood, and there is no need of it. When we have good plain words to express the only legitimate meaning, — viz., that hearing is the purpose of the ear, — why should we resort to an obsolete scholastic phrase, and say that hearing is the final cause of the ear?

When you say *cause* you are supposed to mean it. There is but one kind of cause known to mankind in general, and that is *efficient cause*, — a cause that causes something. But the schoolmen were so much better off than mankind in general, that they had four kinds of causes, — the formal, the material, the efficient, and the final cause. They supposed that they got all these from Aristotle; but he probably regarded the first two, matter and form (ἡ ὕλη and τὸ εἶδος), as principles, or categories of existence rather than causes; and, whether he would agree to it or not, it is the real fact, that the fourth is not a cause any more than the first two. At all events, the notion of cause as efficient holds the common mind so firmly and exclusively, that confusion is sure to be the result of attempting to use the word "cause" in any other sense. There is no conceivable advantage in it which cannot be gained as well or better in some other way; and the dangers, difficulties, and objections involved in it are real, radical, and fatal.

It would be an interesting piece of knowledge, if it were attainable, to find out exactly what was the ordinary state of mind of a believer in final causes in respect to them and their relation to efficient cause; and whether they always succeeded in keeping them distinct, or sometimes themselves shared in the confusion which their use of terms was liable to produce in the minds of their readers. Just what was the "idea" of which Whewell speaks when he says, that, if it "be clearly entertained and steadily applied, the word in question is of subordinate importance"? Of course the answer to that is quite attainable: it was *end*, or *purpose*, though he called it *cause*. But his language implies some difficulty in holding on to this notion in its strictness, and yet calling it *a cause*. It is difficult. It requires a special and constant effort. The teleolo gist can manage it so long as his mental machinery is, so to speak, screwed up to it. But, as we often get a very different notion of a man by seeing him in church on Sunday from that obtained by a business transaction with him on Monday, the interesting point would be to get at the *every-day* conceptions of these men who believed in final causes.

In the first place, what did they ordinarily mean when they used the word *cause?* That, too, is a question easily answered. They meant *efficient cause*, just as mankind in general do, who know nothing about any other kind of cause but that. In his discussion of "The Idea of Cause," Dr. Whewell thus defines it: "By *cause* we mean some *quality*, *power*, or *efficacy*, by which a state of things produces a succeeding state."[1] He gives this simply as a general definition of *cause*, without specifying it as *efficient* cause. But he plainly meant that, though he left off the adjunct "efficient;" and he goes on through three chapters talking about *cause* just as if there were only one kind of cause in the world. He does not call it *efficient* cause in all those chapters, but simply cause. Subsequently, in the discussion of final cause, he brings in the term "efficient."

It was a matter of course with himself as well as his readers, that, when he said *cause*, he meant *efficient* cause.

The same is true of Dr. McCosh. In a long discussion of "cause and effect," he seems utterly oblivious of any other than *efficient causes*. Nevertheless, he uses elsewhere the term "final cause." It might be shown, that the advocates of the doctrine of final causes generally thought of cause as efficient. So far our attempt to get at their every-day thoughts of this matter have been reasonably successful. But in the further attempt to round out and complete this interesting piece of knowledge by inquiring whether they ever tripped, nodded, or got confused in respect to the two kinds of causes, and what was their notion of the relation of final to efficient cause, the path of this investigation is not so plain and easy.

It is not certain that Whewell always kept up a clear distinction in his own mind between final and efficient causes. As already hinted, his language about the reason of a thing being "where and what it is," smacks somewhat of efficient cause. If his thought was at all tinged with that notion, then he himself was weltering in the "confusion" to which he hoped the term "final cause" "was not likely to lead." However that may be, it is certain that another advocate of final causes was thoroughly confused. I mean Dr. Cudworth. His general notion seems to be, that all *mental* causes are final causes; and yet he speaks of the "wisdom and contrivance of the divine Architect" as "the true efficient cause." [1]

Upon the last point — that is, the relation of final to efficient cause — Kant's definition of *end* may give us

[1] See pp. 115–117 of this volume.

some light: "An end is the object of a conception, provided that this (the conception) is considered as the cause of that (the object), the real ground of its possibility." [1]

Here is a definition within a definition, and the incidental one is better than the principal one. An end need not be a material object, as seems to be implied here : but the incidental definition of *cause* is "the real ground of its (the object's) possibility." All the associations of this definition, as well as the definition itself, which would not well apply to efficient cause, show that Kant was speaking of final cause. The ground of possibility of a thing is of the nature of a *condition :* hence it appears that final cause was a conditional notion in the mind of the German philosopher. But each condition is a part of the efficient cause : it is one of the circumstances, all of which must be taken into the account in an exhaustive statement of the efficient cause ; so that here again we have a blending and mingling of the two notions, instead of a clean separation.

Not that Kant was to blame, however, for not making a clean separation of the two notions. It cannot be done, at least not without doing violence to nature and truth. He undoubtedly hit upon the correct statement of the relation when he made it conditional. We have previously encountered the same notion in this discussion. In speaking of the interpretations which might be placed upon the scholastic formula, — Hearing is the cause of the ear, — one alternative (and the only admissible one) was, that the conception of hearing as an end was a condition of the existence of the ear. Kant was

[1] Enquiry into the Grounds of Proof for the Existence of God, p. 79, note.

right in making the final cause a condition, because, in a true teleology emancipated from scholastic "finality," the conception of an end is of the nature of a condition.

But the vital consideration here again emerges, that the notion of an end is, though distinct, very closely related to the notion of efficient cause; that it is, in fact, a part of the cause. Hence the "Comedy of Errors." The twin brothers in the same dress — that is, both ideas clothed in the same word "cause" — make it a tough problem even for the veteran teleologist to distinguish them, and entirely too much for the "lay brethren" to manage.

Upon the whole, it appears that the advocates of final causes ordinarily thought of cause just as other people do. When they said cause they meant efficient cause. And so deep and strong was this current of their thought, that it was hard rowing for them to bring their minds up to the conception of final cause as simply purpose, — so hard that we find some of them in precarious shallows, and others actually aground upon the mudbanks of error and confusion. Hence it seems highly inexpedient, as it is wholly unnecessary, to use the word "cause" in any other than the commonly accepted sense of efficient cause.

But we have as yet dealt with only one-half of the phrase "final cause." The word "final" is no less objectionable than "cause." Its proper function in the phrase is to direct the mind to an end (*finis*); and, if it stopped there, all would be well, — at least, not so bad as it is. It would, indeed, be a self-stultifying phrase even then; for one end of it is a plain "end," and the other a fine, wire-drawn, metaphysical "cause." The two opposite notions might, however, neutralize each other, and less harm be done. But "final" does not

stop short and conclude its meaning when it has designated an end — or cause (?)   (I am really in doubt which
word would give the orthodox finish to that sentence.
In this "Comedy of Errors," where "causes" and
"ends" — Dromios and Antipholuses — are cantering
indistinguishable about the stage, one is very liable to
salute the wrong person as his dear friend who owes
him money.)   It goes on to describe it as the *ultimate*
and *exclusive* end, or cause.   When you have given the
final cause of a thing, there is no more to be said.
That's the *end* of it.   You have given *the* reason for its
being "where and what it is."

Now nothing could be more aside from the true·aim
and intent of teleology than such a notion as that.   The
purpose of any organ is always proximate and subordinate, not ultimate, not *final*.   Lungs exist for the purpose of respiration: but that is subordinate to the
existence and well-being of the animal; that possibly
is subordinate to the utility of the animal to man, to
plough his fields for example; that to the raising of
grain; and so on through a long series of proximate
ends, all subordinate to some ultimate divine purpose.
This word *final* throws a tremendous load upon the
teleologist, and a wholly needless one.   It places him
in the attitude of attempting to demonstrate, not merely
a purpose, but *the* purpose, the only, the ultimate, the
exclusive, the *final* intention of the Creator in respect
to each structure.   It has been objected to teleological
reasoning, that it is presumptuous in man to ascribe any
intention whatever to the Deity.[1]   How much more presumptuous to assume that we have entered so far into

---

[1] "I take care not to ascribe to God any intention." — Geoffroy St.
Hillaire: Phil. Zoöl., 10.   Des Cartes expressed himself substantially to
the same effect long before.

the divine counsels as to discern the one purpose which is exhaustive of his whole thought!

It may be said, that the advocates of this doctrine never meant any such thing by "final," whatever force that adjective may have acquired in popular use. With them it meant only what the etymology indicates. It is derived from *finis*, end; and its whole force and function is to describe cause as that peculiar sort of cause which is not a cause, but an end (*finis*).

I am quite desirous to put the case as favorably as possible for this "consecrated"[1] doctrine of final causes. But really it is hard for me to defend it in any of its phases without seeming to make fun of it, as witness that last sentence of the preceding paragraph. Let it be granted that the trained advocates of this doctrine never tripped on the precise teleological force of "final:" it would not follow that the rank and file of their readers did not. The English force of the word would be very likely to get the better of the Latin force of it in the common mind; and that would be a valid objection to it, no matter how rigidly teleologists might keep to the technical meaning.

A third element of difficulty in the doctrine of final causes is the Aristotelian maxim, that nature does nothing in vain. On this point I might content myself with saying, that, in the first place, the maxim is not true; and, in the second place, that, while it has stubbornly held its place as an inseparable element of the doctrine of final causes, it is no part of a true teleology. But such brevity might be misunderstood. To be more explicit, then, the maxim is true in one sense, though false in the sense intended by Whewell and the teleologists

---

[1] Dugald Stewart speaks of the term *final cause* as being "consecrated in the writings of Newton."

of the last century. It is not true, that "in every organized structure, plant, or animal, each intelligible part has its allotted office." There are abortive and rudimentary organs. These are "in vain" as regards their utility to the plant or animal to which they belong, though not in vain as tokens of morphological symmetry. The general *plan*, or *type*, of structure is often adhered to, even at the cost of making the creature carry about rudiments of organs which are of no manner of use to it. Such facts thrust themselves very disagreeably in the face of an advocate of the doctrine of final causes, but give no concern whatever to the true teleologist. He can assert, that the stomach was intended to digest food without being at all shaken in this conclusion by the consideration that farther down the alimentary tract there is a worm-like appendage to the cæcum which has no function at all. Instead of these rudiments disturbing him in the least, he seizes upon them as materials for eutaxiology, — an argument wholly distinct from teleology, but none the less valid for that. Those ideas of a plan in nature so forcibly brought home to the mind by the occurrence of abortive organs are very conclusive tokens of intelligence, although they have no relation whatever to the adapting of means to an end.

There are ample reasons why the term *final cause* ought to be summarily thrust out, and forever excluded, not only from physics, in which province Bacon regarded it as an intruder,[1] but also from metaphysics and theology.

---

[1] *Causarum finalium inquisitio sterilis est, et tanquam virgo Deo consecrata, nihil parit.* In view of the numerous progeny of fallacies and errors trailing in the wake of these "*virgines consecratæ*," a different sort of charge than that of sterility is liable to be brought against them.

Notwithstanding these ample reasons, the term "final cause" will cut an important figure in the following pages; but that is only because teleology has generally assumed the form of a doctrine of final causes, and in the historical review this term cannot be avoided. In the subsequent chapters it will not appear, unless it steals in as the ghost of a defunct fallacy.

CRITIQUE OF DESIGN-ARGUMENTS.

CHAPTER I.

THE NATURAL THEOLOGY OF THE GREEKS AND ROMANS: SOCRATES, CICERO, AND GALEN.

"For by the primitive and very ancient men,' it has been handed down in the form of myths, that the *Divine* it is which holds together all nature." — ARISTOTLE: *Metaphys.*, xi. 8, 19.

IT is impossible to fix a time when men had not already begun to draw inferences respecting the gods from the natural events and appearances which surrounded them. As young rustics in a great city, with wide-open eyes and eager ears, drink in all sights and sounds with ever-increasing amazement and mystery, so mankind in early ages, unable to rise to any conception of nature as a settled and orderly system, looked upon every striking phenomenon as the manifestation of a being or of beings of whom they could just dimly comprehend that they were mighty, mysterious, and awe-inspiring.

Such sentiments existed and crystallized into a firm conviction of the existence of superior beings long before men began to philosophize about them. The period of reflection, deliberation, argument, was long subsequent to that of childish emotion and open-eyed wonder.

Kant says, —

"In our humble opinion this cosmological proof is as old as the reason of man. It is so natural, so engaging, and enlarges our reflection so much with the progress of our insights, that it must last as long as there exists anywhere a rational creature who wishes to partake of the noble contemplation of knowing God by his works.[1]"

We have already seen, that Kant uses the term "cosmological" as a generic one for all proofs of God's existence drawn from nature, or, as indicated by the last words of this quotation, all discussions based upon that knowledge of God which may be obtained from his works. When he says that this argument "is as old as the reason of man," this statement, if admitted to be true, must be taken in a very general sense, so as to include those crude inferences, mingled with sentiments of wonder and awe, which characterized the youth of the world, as well as the more regular and philosophical reasonings of a later period which alone deserve the name of argument.

Among the ancient philosophers, Anaxagoras, born about five hundred years before the Christian era, distinctly recognized mind in nature. Dr. Hodge says, "Anaxagoras argued that νοῦς, *mind*, must be admitted as controlling every thing in the world, because every thing indicates design."[2]

But it seems rather, that, instead of arguing from the marks of contrivance to mind as their source, he fixed his attention upon the harmony and beauty of the cosmos, and assumed the existence of mind as a necessary hypothesis to account for the steady course and orderly sequences of nature. His notion of the νοῦς was that

---

[1] Enquiry into the Grounds of Proof for the Existence of God, p. 24.
[2] Sys. Theol., i. 226.

of a world-ordering force producing the broad and deep harmonies of the cosmos, rather, than that of a being directing events to special ends. That is, his argument was eutaxiological instead of teleological, and it stopped short of the inference of a personal God.

About the same time Zeno undertook to prove that the world is animated with intelligence. He framed a number of syllogisms for this purpose, of which the following is a sample: That which reasons is preferable to that which does not. Nothing is preferable to the world. Therefore the world reasons.

It is possible that this syllogism may once have convinced somebody, — at least, puzzled him; which, though less desirable than conviction, yet serves the same purpose in one respect, namely, to silence one's antagonist. But I fear it would not make much impression upon a modern materialist. This is the same Zeno who proved that Achilles can never catch the tortoise, because, as often as he reaches the place occupied by the tortoise at the previous moment, the latter has already left it.

Half a century later Socrates, for the first time, so far as we can learn from authentic sources, drew out the teleological argument in a clear and rational manner : —

" For observing that he (Aristodemus) neither prayed nor sacrificed to the gods, nor yet consulted any oracle, but, on the contrary, ridiculed and laughed at those who did, he said to him, —

" Tell me, Aristodemus, is there any man whom you admire on account of his merit?

" ARISTODEMUS. Many.

" SOCRATES. Name some of them, I pray you.

" ARISTODEMUS. I admire Homer for his epic poetry,

Melanippides for dithyrambics, Sophocles for tragedy, Poly-cletes for statuary, and Xeuxis for painting.

" SOCRATES. But which seems to you most worthy of ad-miration, Aristodemus? the artist who forms images devoid of motion and intelligence, or one who hath skill to produce animals that are endued, not only with activity, but under-standing?

" ARISTODEMUS. The latter, there can be no doubt; pro-vided the production was not the effect of chance, but of wisdom and contrivance.

" SOCRATES. But since there are many things, some of which we can easily see the use of, while we cannot say of others to what purpose they were produced, — which of these, Aristodemus, do you suppose the work of wisdom?

" ARISTODEMUS. It would seem most reasonable to affirm it of those whose fitness and utility are so evidently apparent.

" SOCRATES. But it is evidently apparent that he who at the beginning made man endued him with senses because they were good for him, eyes wherewith to behold whatever was visible, and ears to hear whatever was to be heard. For say, Aristodemus, to what purpose should odors be prepared if the sense of smelling had been denied? or why the dis-tinctions of bitter and sweet, of savory and unsavory, unless a palate had been likewise given, conveniently placed to arbi-trate between them, and declare the difference? Is not that providence, Aristodemus, in a most eminent manner con-spicuous, which, because the eye of man is so delicate in its contexture, hath therefore prepared eyelids like doors, where-by to screen it, which extend themselves whenever it is needful, and again close when sleep approaches? Are not these eyelids provided, as it were, with a fence on the edge of them, to keep off the wind, and guard the eye? Even the eyebrow itself is not without its office, but, as a pent-house, is prepared to turn off the sweat, which, falling from the forehead, might enter and annoy that no less tender than astonishing part of us. Is it not to be admired that the ears should take in sounds of every sort, and yet are not too much filled with them? that the fore-teeth of the animal should be formed in such a manner as is evidently best fitted for the cutting of its food, as those on the side for grinding it in pieces? that the mouth through which the food is conveyed should be placed so near the nose and eyes as to prevent the passage unnoticed of whatever is unfit for nourishment? while nature, on the contrary, hath set at a distance, and concealed from the senses, all that might disgust or in any way offend them? And canst thou still doubt, Aristodemus, whether a disposition of parts like this should be the work of chance, or of wisdom and contrivance?"[1]

The severe simplicity of this argument deserves high praise. As compared with the work of later writers, whose *beau idéal* of teleology seemed to be a huge, undigested mass of examples and illustrations, it is as a statue to a brick-kiln.

The reasoning is purely teleological; and in most of his examples the purpose, and the means of accomplishing it, are both obvious in their nature, and clearly specified by him. The peculiar Socratic method appears in the skill with which he drew from Aristodemus himself those admissions which he desired as a foundation for his argument; namely, that the works of nature are more admirable than those of art, and that fitness and utility are marks of wisdom and contrivance.

Yet his argument deserves some criticism as well as praise. If he did not fall bodily into that snare which caught the feet of so many modern teleologists, that of enlarging and expatiating and multiplying examples without discriminating the dubious from the good, perhaps even that negative excellence was due to the fact that he did not take the time to enlarge. He convinced

[1] Xenophon's Mem. of Socrates; Con. with Aristodemus.

Aristodcmus, and that was enough for his immediate purpose. But even in this brief argument he brings in examples of doubtful validity.

For instance, that case of the ear taking in sounds without being filled with them: the end contemplated is a negative one, that the ear should *not* be filled. The means are not specified: they could not be in his day; and, if modern physiologists can tell how the vibrations which produce the sensation of sound in the ear are stopped after they have done their work upon the auditory nerve, it is still true that the explanation is difficult, recondite, and conjectural to a degree which is damaging to any argument based upon it. He is to be commended, however, for leaving this result without explanation rather than to give a false one. Many teleologists have damaged their cause by inferring infinite wisdom from some explanation of phenomena which was totally at variance with the truth. And the remarkable thing about it is, that the true explanation being given, and being precisely opposite to that which was formerly supposed to be correct, the evidence of wisdom has been held to be equally good on either supposition. This is an interesting sort of paradox, to which I shall give some attention in a subsequent chapter.

But the most serious objection to this as an example of teleological reasoning remains to be stated. The reverberations of sound in the ear constitute a difficulty incident to the function of hearing. When men encounter difficulties, the contrivances which they employ to overcome them are good evidence of skill, because the difficulties overcome are inherent in matter, and thus beyond the power of man to remove, though he may surmount them or circumvent them by his ingenuity.

But the argument does not apply to the works of God. Having complete control of matter, he could remove the difficulty bodily, instead of getting around it in human fashion by contrivance. It is an unworthy conception of him to regard any thing in the light of a difficulty in his thought.

But if you insist upon doing so, and upon the inference of skill displayed in overcoming the difficulty, how can you avoid the counter-inference that the difficulty itself is a blemish in his work? An architect whose buildings invariably displayed bad acoustic properties would not escape the blame and loss of reputation incident to that fact by inventing an ingenious apparatus of curtains and wires to prevent the mischief. It is no evidence of wisdom, that the ear is *not* a bad structure acoustically. Its positive excellence, not its possible defects, is the rational ground for the teleological argument.

There is, nevertheless, a sort of fascination about just such vague and negative examples as this of the stoppage of reverberations in the ear. They awaken wonder and admiration in the common mind, all the more because they are vague, and the explanation difficult or wholly unattainable. For the purpose of arousing a sense of dumb wonderment akin to that with which men viewed all natural processes at first, they may have their uses. It is to be remembered, that the object of Socrates was not to prove God's existence, but his wisdom and power; and in that view the production of a sense of wonder in the face of unexplainable results was a point gained.

If it were not manifestly unfair to criticise an argument upon the ground of principles and discoveries wholly unknown to its author, many other weak points

might be specified in the reasoning of Socrates. But
all objections drawn from the development of modern
science must be ruled out as inapplicable to him individually. The effect of these upon teleology in general
will be carefully examined in the sequel; but in the
criticism of individuals the only questions raised will
be whether their arguments are internally self-consistent, and externally conformable to that degree of knowledge of nature which belonged to the age in which those
arguments were promulgated.

The point alluded to above — namely, that Socrates
aimed rather to show the Creator's wisdom and power
than to demonstrate his existence — is worthy of more
careful attention. Observe the steps of his argument.
First, the works of nature are more admirable than
those of art, unless, as suggested by Aristodemus, the
former are the products of chance. Now, the mark of
utility distinguishes the products of wisdom and contrivance from those of chance. "But it is obviously
apparent, that he who at the beginning made man
endued him with senses because they were *good* for
him." Socrates is laboring to cut off the hypothesis of
chance having produced the human form, by establishing the utility of its organs and their functions. There
is a suspicion of reasoning in a circle when he adduces
the utility of the senses on the one hand because they
enable us to perceive certain qualities of objects, and
then claims utility in those qualities on the other hand
because the senses are provided so as to distinguish
between them. But, granting that he makes out a good
case for utility, what are the resulting inferences?
Chance is ruled out in accordance with the axiom laid
down in the words of Aristodemus, that "it would seem
most reasonable to affirm it (wisdom) of those (things)

whose fitness and utility are so evidently apparent." The alternatives of chance are, that there is a personal being whose wisdom has been displayed in nature, or that there is an intelligent principle in nature itself. As Aristodemus did not suggest the latter alternative, both he and Socrates seem to have settled upon the former; and the conclusion of the argument is, that there is a wise and mighty Being to whose contrivance all these marvellous results are due.

Is it not therefore, after all, an argument for the existence of God? So it seems from its course and conclusion; and yet at the beginning Socrates distinctly assumed that point (at least he assumed the existence of a personal agent) by saying, "It is evidently apparent, that he who in the beginning made man endued him," etc. That is to say, if, as indicated by its course and conclusion, the aim of the argument was to establish God's existence, then Socrates begged the question at the start. And if, to save him from that reproach, we say that this was not his aim, but that he was simply illustrating the wisdom and goodness of God, then he ought to have adhered more strictly to that line of thought. The fact seems to be, that he had a kind of confused double aim, partly to show the wisdom of a creator whose existence was assumed, and partly to meet the denial of any creator at all.

This sort of confusion is not peculiar to Socrates, but appears in almost all teleological discussions. The conviction that there is a God, however it may have arisen, is a fact so fundamental in the human understanding, that it is extremely difficult to dismiss it long enough to get down plump and square upon an argumentative basis so constructed that this conviction forms no part of it. Besides this difficulty which confronts the initial steps of the advocate of teleology, his whole subsequent course is beset with temptations to wander from the severe and abstract logic of a demonstration of God's existence into the far easier and pleasanter paths of expatiating and indulging in pious reflections upon his wisdom, power, and goodness. These reflections are in no wise to be condemned or disparaged, but they ought to be sharply separated from pure argumentation. Each is good in its place; but the blending of the two makes the logic suspicious, at the same time that it detracts from that height of emotion and adoration to which a discourse entirely free from abstract reasoning might raise the mind of the reader.

Marcus Tullius Cicero, who was born in the year one hundred and five before Christ, devotes the greater part of his treatise, "*De Natura Deorum*," to the arguments for the existence of God, or rather of the gods. The book is a record of conversations between Velleius, Balbus, Cotta, and Cicero. The last two were Academicians, (disciples of Plato), Balbus was a Stoic, and Velleius an Epicurean. Balbus the Stoic delivers the teleological and eutaxiological arguments, with the manifest approval and support of Cicero and Cotta; while Velleius alone maintains that the world was produced by a "fortuitous concourse of atoms."

It would be a great mistake, however, to infer that Velleius was an atheist. He was just as firm a believer in the gods as Cotta or Balbus; only he insists that they did not create the world, and do not concern themselves at all in respect to man, or any thing else upon the earth : —

" For they do naught at all, are not entangled in any affairs, nor hammer out any *designs*, but are wholly taken up in the delight and contemplation of their own wisdom and virtue."

He thinks that such an opinion of the gods has manifest advantages over any other, especially in delivering
men from superstitious dread : —

"If we only sought piously to worship the gods, and be
delivered from vain apprehensions, here were enough said for
that end ; for our devotions are due to the godhead upon the
single score of its blessedness and immortality, because that
which is excellent exacts regard and veneration as its due.
But all superstitious dread of the power and anger of the
Deity is removed ; for hatred and love are alike held to be
separate from the blessed and immortal nature, and, they being once taken away, there can no longer be any cause to
stand in fear of those that are above us."

Velleius, who is here simply expounding the tenets
of his master Epicurus, thinks that the knowledge,
both of the existence and of the attributes of the gods,
is intuitive : —

"We cannot but be satisfied of the existence of a deity,
because all, as well fools as philosophers, are possessed with
ingrafted, or rather innate and connatural, apprehensions of
one. . . . And the same nature that furnished the notion
of their very existence engraved also in our minds an assur-
ance of their happiness and immortality."

Velleius was, of course, estopped from any inference
of the existence or attributes of the gods from nature,
because of the fundamental tenet of his sect, that the
world was neither created by them, nor do they now
give themselves the slightest concern about it. He
argues stoutly against the possibility of creation, and
especially against the Platonic view of it : —

"For with what eyes of the mind was your Plato able to
see that workhouse of such stupendous toil, in which he
makes the world to be modelled and built by God? What

materials, what tools, what bars, what machines, what assistants, were employed in so vast a work? How could the air, fire, water, and earth pay obedience and submit to the will of the architect? . . . What was it that incited the Deity to act the part of an ædile to illuminate and decorate the world? If it was because God might be the better accommodated in his habitation, why did he dwell such an infinite length of time before in darkness as in a dungeon?[1] Do we imagine that he could afterwards be delighted with that variety with which we see the heaven and the earth adorned? What entertainment could that be to the Deity? If it was any, he would not have been without it so long; or were these things made, as you almost say, by God for the sake of men?''

Plato had maintained that the earth itself is animated with intelligence. His doctrine on this subject is stated by Balbus in the following argument: —

'' That which is moved spontaneously is more divine than that which is moved by another power. This self-motion Plato places only in mind, and from thence concludes the first principle of motion is derived: therefore, since all motion arises from the heat of the world, and that heat not the effect of any external impulse, but of its own virtue, it must necessarily be a spirit or mind; from whence it follows that the world is animated.''

To this notion of the world itself being a sort of ''round and voluble deity,'' Velleius raises a novel objection: —

'' We see vast tracts of land uninhabitable and barren, — some because they are scorched by the too near approach of the sun; others because they are bound up with frost and

---

[1] In reply to the question, What was God doing before he made the world? Luther said, '' In the birch-grove cutting rods to punish impertinent questioners.'' — HASE: *Gnosis*, ii. s. 183.

snow through the great distance of it (the sun). Therefore, if the world is a deity, as these are parts of the world, some of the deity's limbs may be said to be scorched, and some frozen."

Cotta undertakes the task of answering Velleius. He resorts to ridicule in answer to the argument for the atomic theory : —

"You attribute the most absolute power and efficacy to atoms. Out of them you pretend every thing is made. But there are no atoms ; for there is nothing without body, nor is there any place which is not occupied by body : therefore there can be no vacuum, no individual. I advance these principles of the naturalists without knowing whether they are true or false ; yet they are more like truth than those absurdities you imbibed from Democritus, or before him from Leucippus, that there are certain light corpuscles, some smooth, some rough, some round, some square, some crooked and bent as bows ; which, by a fortuitous concourse, made heaven and earth without the influence of any natural power."

He is still more unsparing in his ridicule of the Epicurean conception of the gods. He claims that the ideal of happiness in the system of Epicurus was unchecked indulgence in sensual pleasures ; but, since the gods were deprived of these, they could not, from the Epicurean point of view, be happy : —

"But they are free from pain. Is that sufficient for beings who are supposed to enjoy all good things, and the most supreme felicity? The Deity, they say, is constantly meditating on his own happiness, having no other idea in his mind. Consider a little ; reflect what a figure the Deity would make, idly thinking of nothing through all eternity but, 'It is very well with me, and I am happy.' Nor do I see why this happy Deity should not fear being destroyed,

since without any intermission he is driven and agitated by
an everlasting incursion of atoms, and from him images are
constantly flowing. Your Deity, therefore, is neither happy
nor eternal.''

Balbus, too, has his shot at the fortuitous concourse
of atoms theory : —

    "Can I but wonder here that any one can persuade him-
self that certain solid and individual bodies should move by
their natural force and gravitation in such manner that a
world so beautifully adorned should be made by their fortuitous concourse? He who believes this possible may as well
believe, that if a great quantity of the one and twenty letters,
composed either of gold or any other matter, were thrown
upon the ground, they would fall into such order as legibly
to form the 'Annals of Ennius.' I doubt whether fortune
could make a single verse of them.''

This form of argument against the doctrine of chance
was a favorite one with the ancients; and we shall find
that it has been revived and much relied upon in modern
times as a method of attack upon the theory of evolution.

Cotta and Balbus having thus cleared the ground by
their destructive criticism of the systems of Democritus
and Epicurus, the Stoic proceeds to his constructive
task of framing arguments for the existence of the
gods : —

    "Our sect,'' says he, "divide the whole question concern-
ing the immortal gods into four parts, — first, that there are
gods ; secondly, what they are ; thirdly, that the universe is
governed by them ; and, lastly, that they regard mankind in
particular.''

But, although he starts with these clear distinctions,
he does not adhere to them closely, but blends the

several arguments together. Like Socrates, he seems unable to place himself fairly upon a platform of argument in which the existence of the gods is not assumed. He says that no one denies their existence; that it needs no proof, or, if it did, a glance at the heavens would be enough: "for, when we contemplate the celestial bodies, what can be so plain and evident as the existence of some supreme, divine intelligence by which they are governed?" Still, he goes on to recite many of the arguments of his sect to prove their existence.

In the first place, he claims that the gods exist because of the significance of "signs, portents, and prodigies:" —

"How great is the reputation of the augurs! Is not the art of the aruspices divine? Innumerable are the facts of this kind: who, then, can doubt the existence of the gods? They who have interpreters must certainly exist themselves. Now, there are interpreters of the gods: therefore we must allow there are gods.

"Cleanthes, one of our sect, imputes the idea of the gods, implanted in the minds of men, to four causes. The first is what I just now mentioned, a pre-knowledge of future things. The second is the great advantages we enjoy from the temperature of the air, the fertility of the soil, and the abundance of various kinds of benefits. The third, from the terror with which the mind is affected by thunder, tempests, storms, snow, hail, devastation, pestilence, earthquakes often attended with hideous noises, showers of stones, and rain like drops of blood; by rockings and sudden openings of the earth; by monstrous births of men and beasts; by meteors in the air, and blazing stars, the appearance of which in the late Octavian war was ominous of great calamities; by two suns, which, as I have heard my father say, happened in the consulship of Tuditanus and Aquillius, in which year also another sun (P. Africanus) was extinguished. These things have terrified mankind, and produced the notion of the existence of some celestial and divine power. His fourth cause, and that the strongest, is drawn from the regularity of the motion and revolution of the sun, the distinction, variety, beauty, and order of the heavens, the mere appearance of which is sufficient to convince us they are not the effects of chance; as when we enter into a house, a school, or court, and observe the exact order, discipline, and method therein, we cannot suppose they are so regulated without a cause, but must conclude there is some one who commands, and to whom obedience is paid: so we have much greater reason to think that such wonderful motions, revolutions, and order of those many and great bodies, no part of which is impaired by the lapse of countless ages, must be governed by some intelligent being.

"Let us proceed from celestial to terrestrial things. What is there in them which does not prove an intelligent nature? First, as to vegetables: they have roots to sustain their stems, and to draw from the earth a nourishing moisture. They are clothed with a rind or bark to secure them from heat and cold. The vines we see take hold on props with their tendrils as if with hands, and raise themselves as if they were animated. It is even said that they shun cabbages and coleworts as noxious and pestilential to them, and, if planted by them, will not touch any part.

"But what a vast variety is there of animals! and how wonderfully is every kind endowed with what is necessary for its preservation! Some are covered with hides, some clothed with fleeces, and some guarded with bristles; some are sheltered with feathers, and some with scales; some are armed with horns, and some are assisted with wings.

"Mankind likewise receives great advantages from different soils. The Nile waters Egypt; and, after having overflowed and covered it the whole summer, it retires, and leaves the fields softened and manured for the reception of seed.

The Euphrates fertilizes Mesopotamia, into which, as we may say, it carries yearly new fields. The Indus, which is the largest of all rivers, not only improves and cultivates the ground, but sows it also; for it is said to carry with it a great quantity of grain.

"But how bountiful is Nature, that has provided for us such various and delicious food, and this in different seasons, that we may be constantly pleased with change and with plenty! How seasonable and useful to man, to beasts, and even to plants, are the eastern winds she has bestowed, which moderate intemperate heat, and render navigation more sure and speedy!"

Then Balbus plunges into the subject of human anatomy, where we could not follow him in such manner as to do him justice without transcribing whole pages. He infers a divine purpose from the position and character of the cutting and grinding teeth, in which he was borrowing from Socrates; from the "sort of coverlid" (*epiglottis*) which guards the entrance to the "rough artery" (*trachea*), so that food may not fall into it and stop the respiration; from the functions of the stomach, lungs, and heart; from the bones and their joints; from the upright form, enabling us to contemplate the heavens, and attain a knowledge of the gods; from the commanding position of the senses in the highest part of the body; from the eyelids, eyebrows, and the bony walls of the sockets in which the eyes are lodged; from the fact that the ears and nostrils are always open, while the mouth and eyes may be closed; from the modulating power of the tongue and lips in articulate speech; and from the human hand, so nicely adapted for a multiplicity of uses.

"Thus, if we every way examine the universe, it is apparent from the greatest reason that the whole is admirably governed by a divine providence for the safety and preservation of all beings."

In the examination of these arguments which Cicero puts into the mouth of Balbus, two things strike us with astonishment, — first, the extent of his knowledge of human anatomy; and, secondly, the exhaustiveness with which he traversed the field of reasoning covered by the writings of modern teleologists. Scarcely any thing, either in the style of argument, or in the range of illustration used by them, but was anticipated by Cicero, and, before him, by I know not how many Greeks.

Like most of the modern teleologists, he constructed his argument by the method of analogy : —

"When you view an image or a picture, you imagine it is wrought by art; when you behold afar off a ship under sail, you judge it is steered by reason and art; when you see a dial or water-clock, you believe the hours are showed by art. and not by chance : can you then imagine that the universe, which contains all arts and the artificers, can be void of reason, void of understanding?

"If that sphere lately made by our friend Posidonius, which shows the course of the sun, moon, and five wandering stars (planets), as it is every day and night performed, were carried into Scythia or Britain, who in those barbarous countries would doubt that reason presided in that work? Yet these people (the Epicureans) doubt whether the universe, from whence all things arise and are made, is not the effect of chance or some necessity, rather than the work of reason and a divine mind. According to them Archimedes shows more knowledge in representing the motions of the celestial globe, than nature does in causing them, though the copy is so infinitely beneath the original."

Another of Cicero's books, the "*De Divinatione*," contains additional design-arguments : —

"Can any thing done by chance have all the marks of design? Four dice may by chance turn up four aces; but do you think that four hundred dice, thrown by chance, will turn up four hundred aces? Colors thrown upon canvas without design may have some similitude to a human face; but do you think they might make as beautiful a picture as that of the Coan Venus? A hog turning up the ground with his nose may make something of the form of the letter A; but do you think that a hog might describe on the ground the Andromache of Ennius? Carneades imagined, that, in the stone-quarries at Chios, he found, in a stone that was split, a representation of the head of a little Pan, or sylvan deity.[1] I believe he might find a figure not unlike, but surely not such a one as you would say had been formed by an excellent sculptor like Scopas; for so, verily, the case is, that chance never perfectly imitates design."

In comparing these arguments of Cicero with those of Socrates, we observe, in the first place, that, while the latter confined himself to teleology, the former gives equal prominence to eutaxiology. At least half of his reasoning is based upon the order of nature, especially the celestial harmonies. This justifies the remark of Dr. McCosh, that the ancients attended to the internal principles of order in the cosmos, as well as to the external facts of adaptation. So far as the proof of God's existence is concerned, Cicero seems to rely wholly upon eutaxiology. His teleological reasoning has for its sole aim the establishment of the proposition that the gods "regard mankind in particular." It is an argument for the providence of God, rather than for the existence of God.

[1] Some fossils are decidedly better looking than some of the old sylvan deities. This does not invalidate the argument, however; since the fossils are not the work of chance, as Cicero implies that the one in the quarry at Chios was.

In the second place, Cicero is at once more copious and more faulty than Socrates. The wide range of illustration in which he indulges has been a snare to him. Even in the quotations I have made, though I have selected the best specimens of his style, there are trivial examples and inconsequent reasonings. The antipathy of vines to cabbages is not a very solid corner-stone for an argument. An east wind may be a good thing in Italy, but quite the reverse elsewhere. Indeed, it may be said of atmospheric phenomena in general, that they are not good teleological material. Though one should believe ever so firmly that each wind and cloud were divinely guided, it would not be wise to select these as the means of convincing another who was sceptical about it, that there are special and kindly purposes underlying natural phenomena. Gentle winds and soft showers are beneficent enough, but hurricanes and water-spouts must be considered also.

In the third place, Socrates had much more positive convictions and worthier conceptions of the gods than Cicero. The latter seems to be floundering in a misty sea of heathen speculation, unable to settle upon any positive opinion as to the number or nature of the gods. Balbus maintains that each star is a deity as well as the earth. His expressions respecting the "intelligent nature" of plants show that he regarded mind in nature somewhat as Anaxagoras did; namely, as a principle embodied in matter, and ruling it, rather than as an attribute of a personal being. But this is explicitly asserted in the following quotation : —

" That universal nature which embraces all things is said by Zeno to be not only artificial, but the absolute artificer, ever thinking and providing all things proper ; and as every particular nature owes its rise and increase to its own proper seed, so universal nature has all her motions voluntary, has affections and desires productive of actions agreeable to them, like us who have sense and understanding to direct us."

His exaggerated polytheism is displayed in the following: —

" I have hitherto spoken of the universal world, and also of the stars : from whence it is apparent, that there is an almost infinite number of gods, always in action, but without labor or fatigue ; for they are not composed of nerves, veins, and bones. Their food and drink are not such as cause humors, too gross or too subtile. Their bodies are not subject to the fear of falls or blows, or in danger of diseases from a weariness of limbs. Epicurus, to secure his gods from such accidents, has made them only sketches of deities, thin, pellucid, and void of action ; but our gods of the most beautiful form (that of a sphere), and situated in the purest region of the heavens, dispose and rule their course in such a manner, that they seem to contribute to the support and preservation of all beings. Besides these (i.e., besides the stars, already ' almost infinite ' in number), there are many other natures which have with reason been deified by the wisest Grecians, and by our ancestors, in consideration of the benefits derived from them : for they were persuaded that whatever was of great utility to human kind must proceed from divine goodness ; and the name of the deity was applied to that which the deity produced, as when we call corn Ceres, and wine Bacchus."

Balbus then goes on through the whole calendar of heathen deities, taking it nearly all in good faith. It would be unjust to Cicero to take the opinions which he puts into the mouth of Balbus as his opinions in the same sense and to the same extent as if he had uttered them in his own name, though it is true that in general he and Cotta agreed with Balbus. But the latter, being a Stoic, was more positive than they in his convictions. And this leads at once to the consideration how far the contrast between Socrates and Cicero, and the indecis'on of the eloquent Roman orator respecting the gods, was due to the fact that he was an Academician. The enemies of that sect charged, that their fundamental tenet was "to be certain of nothing," — an accusation which is repeated by Velleius in this very conversation of which the *De Natura Deorum* is a record. Addressing Cicero and Cotta, Velleius says, "For you have both learned from the same Philo to be certain of nothing." The Academics, of course, repudiated this form of statement of their doctrine. What they claimed was, that the sources of doubt and error are so many, and so inextricably blended with the truth, that a judicial suspense of judgment is more rational than ill-grounded positive convictions. Cicero remarks, —

"The Academics are prudent in refusing their assent to things uncertain ; for what is more unbecoming in a wise man than to judge rashly? or what rashness so unworthy the gravity and stability of a philosopher as to conceive wrongly, or to defend absolutely, what he has not thoroughly examined, and does not clearly comprehend? . . . We do not assert that nothing has the appearance of truth; but we say that some falsehoods are so blended with all truths, and have so great a resemblance to them, that there is no certain rule of judging and assenting."

That last sentence goes near to justify the charge of their enemies, that they had learned to be certain of nothing. For if there are elements of falsehood in all truth, and "no certain rule of judging" by which we may separate the false from the true, then nothing remains for us but doubt and indecision on every possible question.

This sort of excessive philosophical caution was very different from that of Socrates. With him it took the form of intellectual humility. He said the justification of the oracle in pronouncing him the wisest of men was, that, while others thought they knew something, he had found out that he knew nothing. But his dialectic method did not stop with stripping off the masks of error, and dissecting away the semblances of knowledge: it went on to positive results. Intellectual humility is a very different thing from univeral scepticism.

Claudius Galen, born at Pergamos in Asia Minor in the year 130 A.D., was remarkable for his learning, and for his skill in medical practice. He was a walking encyclopædia of the knowledge of his own age, and the medical science of previous ages; and for twelve centuries after his death his authority in medicine was supreme, and "the veneration in which he was held was such that he was by many regarded as a god." Dr. Coxe stoutly maintains that he was well acquainted with the circulation of the blood; and consequently that Harvey's claim to the exclusive honor of that discovery is groundless. His knowledge of anatomy and physiology was certainly of surprising extent and accuracy.

In his book " Concerning the Use of the various Parts of the Body," he develops his teleological views : —

" Those weapons with which the lion is furnished are as appropriate to his nature as they would be useless to the timid hare, whose safety, depending entirely on flight, requires that swiftness of foot for which she is so remarkable. But to man, the only animal that partakes of divine intelligence, the Creator has given, in lieu of every other weapon or organ of defence, that instrument *the hand*, — an instrument applicable to every art and occasion, as well of peace as of war. Man therefore wants not a hoof or a horn or any other natural weapon, inasmuch as he is able with his hand to grasp a much more effective weapon, the sword or spear.''

With this he weaves the garment that protects him from summer's heat or winter's cold, forms nets and snares, the lyre and lute, altars and shrines, and with the pen "bequeathes to posterity in writing the intellectual treasures of his own divine imagination."

" Let us, then, scrutinize this member of our body, and inquire, not simply whether it be in itself useful for all the purposes of life, and adapted to an animal endued with the highest intelligence, but whether its entire structure be not such that it could not be improved by any conceivable alteration.''

He goes on to show its fitness for grasping by virtue of, (1) its division into digits; (2) co-operation of the two hands; (3) opposition of the thumb to the fingers; (4) softness, yet not too great softness, of the inner tips; (5) hardness of the outer tips, or nails.

"How can a man of any intelligence refer all this to chance as its cause? or, if he deny this to be the effect of foresight and skill, I would ask, What is there that foresight and skill do effect? For surely, where chance and fortune act, we see not this correspondence and regularity of parts.

" What! was it chance that made the skin give way so as to produce a mouth? Or, if this happened by chance, did chance also place teeth and a tongue within that mouth? For, if so, why should there not be teeth and a tongue in the nostrils or in the ear? . . . Did chance dispose the teeth themselves in their present order? Which, if it were any other than it is, what would be the consequence? If, for instance, the incisors and canine teeth had occupied the back part of the mouth, and the molar or grinding teeth had occupied the front, what use could we have made of either? Shall we, then, admire the skill of him who disposes a chorus of thirty-two men in just order? and can we deny the skill of the Creator in disposing the same number of teeth in an order so convenient, so necessary even, for our existence?"

The argument of Galen is wholly teleological. This is the natural result of his studies. Physiology presents the best examples in nature of specific results so wrought out that they seem to indicate an intelligent purpose. These examples made a profound impression upon the mind of Galen; and his reasonings upon them cover the whole ground, and exhaust the evidences in this line, so far as the method is concerned. Whatever has been said since about the perfection of the human body as a machine, is only of the nature of additional examples and illustrations. No new argument in that line was possible.

What was Galen's method? It was the same which holds the foremost place in later teleology, and may justly be characterized as the *mechanical* method. Here are certain machines produced by human art, — a ship, a dial, or a watch; but there are animal machines too. The human body is a most wonderful and elaborate piece of mechanism. It required a skilful workman to construct the former: how much greater must have been the wisdom of that being who produced the latter! Such is the style of this mechanical argument. It is foreshadowed in Cicero; but in the hands of Galen, a very competent anatomist and practical physician, to whom the details of the human form, as well as those of many animals, were as familiar as the alphabet, this method at once bloomed out to its full dimensions.

Something more might be said after Galen on account of the advance in anatomical science; but the method was the same. And what use of piling up new examples and illustrations of it when there was already more than was needed? It was only an embarrassment of riches.

Dr. Coxe thinks that not only have later writers failed to strike out any new paths of argument, but that their handling of the old argument respecting the mechanical perfection of the body is inferior to Galen's : —

"The treatise on the hand by Sir Charles Bell, much as it has been admired, is, in my opinion, infinitely inferior to these books of Galen on the same subject. Indeed, his best parts may be regarded as abstracted from Galen, and clothed in the language of the present age." [1]

That is pretty hard on Sir Charles. "Infinitely inferior" to Galen, even after he had stolen so much from him! But what could the man do? Having the task of writing a whole book on the *human hand*, he was bound to cross Galen's track somewhere. Did not Galen himself repeat the arguments of Socrates and Cicero without acknowledgment. The position and character of the various kinds of teeth was an argument employed by the Greeks several centuries before the Christian era; and yet Galen, in the second century after Christ, employs it as if for the first time. It seems probable that this and similar examples were repeatedly cited by the Greeks and Romans, handed down from generation to generation, until they came to be regarded as a sort of common teleological armory,

[1] The Writings of Hippocrates and Galen. Epitomized by John Redman Coxe, M.D.; note, p. 523.

from which any individual might draw the weapon which pleased him, without any consciousness of plagiarism. Still, these ill-natured charges of borrowing and stealing, such as the one brought against Sir Charles Bell by Dr. Coxe, are very common in teleology, as we shall see hereafter.

Here are three great minds of antiquity whose thoughts upon this stupendous problem, How far can God be known from his works? we have briefly examined. Here is the greatest of the Greek philosophers, the most eloquent of the old Romans, and the most renowned physician of Greece and Rome; for Galen belonged to both, or strictly speaking to neither, but was cosmopolitan, a citizen of the world. What can these men tell us about God? Galen was the only one of the three who had any knowledge of the Christian Scriptures. He quotes from the writings of Moses, but without giving them any greater credence than to any other ancient documents. Still his conceptions of God were manifestly influenced by them: he is the only pronounced monotheist of the three. But in the utterances of Socrates and Cicero we have an exact measure both of the strength and the weakness of natural theology. They had no aid from revelation, and yet they knew a great deal about the divine nature. Still, with all their splendid gifts of intellect, they groped among the shadows, and failed to grasp true conceptions of the one God.

CHAPTER II.

THE NATURAL THEOLOGY OF THE MIDDLE AGES:
THOMAS AQUINAS, SEBONDE.

IT would betoken a levity ill suited to the dignity of my theme if, following a famous precedent, I should begin a chapter with the above heading, and end it by saying, There was no natural theology in the Middle Ages. That would be about as near truth as wit, but not a shining example of either. Natural theology was not wholly ignored; though, as compared with the copious supply of it in the seventeenth and eighteenth centuries, it was a scarce article.

During the early centuries the church Fathers built up their systems of theology almost wholly upon a scriptural basis. Each doubtful point must be settled by a text from the Bible, instead of an appeal to human reason, or to nature's storehouse of facts and laws: hence we may look in vain for design-arguments in their writings. Subsequently a school of theology sprang up which added to the scriptural method of verification, that of appeal to the Fathers themselves. If no sacred text was ready to hand, a quotation from Origen, Ambrose, or Augustine, would serve quite as well. It was not until the later mediæval ages, in the times of the schoolmen, that we find much attention given to the rational proofs of theological doctrines; and even then those proofs which may be drawn from external nature are quite subordinate to those which rest upon first principles. The *à priori* proofs are preferred to the *à posteriori :* it is rational, rather than natural, theology to which they resort to confirm scriptural theology.

Such as it was, however, the new departure was most weighty in its consequences. The revolt against authority once begun, there was no telling where it would end. The notion that an appeal to the Scriptures and the Fathers was not sufficient to stop all controversy being once broached, there was logically no stopping-place until human reason was completely emancipated from that bondage to authority which almost justifies the term sometimes applied to the mediæval period, the Dark Ages. Much contempt has been heaped upon the schoolmen, and a great deal of it is well deserved; but to them belongs the honor of leading men once more to think for themselves. As early as the middle of the ninth century Scotus Erigena taught that an appeal to the Fathers should be kept as a last resort, and then only used to convince those "men, who, unpractised in reasoning, yield rather to authority than to logic." Even this mild form of rationalism drew upon him the thunders of orthodox denunciation.[1]

In the twelfth and thirteenth centuries we find theologians drawing out the rational proofs of the existence of God without any scruple, or any suspicion of heterodoxy. The revival of learning had then made some progress, and reason was getting on its feet. The emancipation of reason, however, is one thing, and the use it shall make of itself when free is quite another thing. It had not yet even become free in any large

---

[1] Lewes: Hist. of Phi., ii. 11.

sense, and it made a poor use of the little liberty it had achieved. The schoolmen exhausted their strength in subtile disputations, logomachies pure and simple; that is, contests in which *words* rather than substantial verities were the things in dispute. They were little inclined to observation or the contemplation of nature, and not much in the direction of natural theology is to be expected of them.

Still, teleology was not wholly neglected. A fair example of the extent to which it was employed, and of its subordination to the causal and ontological arguments, is furnished by the method of Thomas Aquinas [1] for proving the existence of God: "The existence of God may be proved in five ways." I give a condensed summary of the first four, and the fifth in full: (1) From the principles of motion: there must be a *primum movens*, — something which originated all movement. (2) From the law of efficient cause: there must be a *prima causa*, or First Cause. (3) From the principle of possibility and necessity: certain things exist whose non-existence is possible; but something must exist whose non-existence is impossible, and this necessarily existing being is God. (4) From the grades of existence: as there are degrees of various qualities, hot, hotter, hottest, — noble, more noble, most noble, — "there must be some being which is the source of excellence, or of any sort of perfection whatever in all beings." (5) "From the government of things. For we see that certain things without intelligence, as natural bodies for instance, work according to a purpose, which appears from this, because they always, or very often, work in the same way as if they followed that which was best. Whence it is plain, that they reach the re-

---

[1] Born 1227, died 1274.

sult, not by chance, but by intention. But things without thought would not work to a purpose unless they were directed by some conscious and intelligent being, as an arrow by a bowman. Therefore there is some intelligent being by whom all things in nature are directed to an end; and this being, we say, is God." [1]

The first two arguments are one and the same; for, if there is a *prima causa*, it is also a *primum movens*. The First Cause accounts for the existence of motion just as well as any other form of existence. These both fall, therefore, into the category of causal, or cosmological, arguments. The third and fourth, in like manner, fall together under the head of ontological, or *à priori*, arguments; for the conception of some being whose non-existence is impossible, and the conception of a perfect being, the crowning excellence of the several grades of existence, are both of them of the nature of first, or *à priori*, principles. The fifth mode of proving the existence of God is clearly teleological. The statement of it is general, and it is not fortified by any examples. It stands, therefore, as a mere assertion, that "natural bodies without intelligence work to a purpose, as if they followed that which is best." Perhaps the "angelic doctor" was wiser to leave it so than some later teleologists, who affect to fortify their general assertions by examples either ill fitted or positively inimical to their purpose.

Design-arguments were, generally speaking, at a discount with the schoolmen. A subtle dialectic method was more agreeable to their taste. No author during the Middle Ages (regarding, with Hallam, the end of the fifteenth century as the mediæval limit) has made much of teleology. Even Sebonde, whose work we

[1] Quaes. ii. Art. iii.

shall notice next, and who has been called the "father of natural theology," does not employ the teleological method at all; though his argument, being to some extent eutaxiological, is to the same extent a design-argument.

Raymond Sebonde, or Sabieude,[1] was professor of medicine, philosophy, and theology at Toulouse early in the fifteenth century. Dugald Stewart places his residence there "towards the end of the fourteenth century;"[2] but in this he was undoubtedly mistaken, as he was also respecting the object of Sebonde's work, and the language in which it was written. Very little is known about Sebonde, not even the date of his birth; and authorities do not agree as to the year of his death. The Abbot Trithemius says that he died in 1432. But, from one of the manuscripts examined by Dr. Kleiber in the Imperial Library of Paris, it appears that Sebonde's "Natural Theology"[3] was finished in the University of Toulouse "in 1436, in the month of February, the sixth day, which was the sabbath day." Kleiber says, —

" It is certain that the ' Natural Theology ' was written by Raimundus at Toulouse from the year 1434 to the year 1436, and that he was born in Spain. The rest of his life is un-

---

[1] For some curious particulars about his name, see Dr. C. C. L. Kleiber's " De Raimundi quem vocant de Sabunde vita et scriptis," Berlin, 1856. Kleiber found some manuscript copies of the "Theologia Naturalis" in the Imperial Library of Paris, by means of which he was able to correct several errors which had been current respecting Sebonde; for I shall still call him by that name, since it is pretty well fixed by usage. Kleiber thinks the correct spelling is Sabieude. He gives a dozen other variations of the spelling.

[2] Essays, p. 103.

[3] The full title is " Theologia Naturalis, sive Liber Creaturarum," — Natural Theology, or, the Book of Creatures. *Sebonde was the first to use the term " natural theology."*

certain. Raimundus wrote nothing but the 'Natural Theology.' All the other writings which have borne his name
are only abstracts from the 'Natural Theology.' The
'Natural Theology' was written, not in the Spanish, but in
the Latin language.''

Sebonde's book has never been translated into English. Montaigne translated it into the French language
in obedience to a request made by his father a short
time before his death. The book had been presented to
the elder Montaigne by Peter Bunel, a learned man,
who commended it highly as an antidote to the doctrines of Luther, which were just then beginning to
make serious inroads upon the ancient faith.

Montaigne also wrote a long essay entitled, "Apology
for Raymond Sebonde." But the witty Frenchman
gave a loose reign to his fancy, and wandered widely in
the realms of thought, touching up the manners and
morals of ancient and modern nations; comparing man
to other animals, quite to the advantage of the latter;
inquiring whether the elephant has any sentiments of
religion; ridiculing science and philosophy; and, by a
skilful play of words, slyly poking fun at religion also
at the very moment when he seemed to be uttering the
most pious sentiments: so that, all in all, you shall find
a hundred words on other subjects to one for Sebonde.

His translation of the "Natural Theology" was published in 1569.[1] The rendering is free, but substantially
correct. Indeed, the wonder is that Montaigne should
have had the patience to execute so laborious a task as
well as he did. The original is in such bad Latin, and

---

[1] "The original Latin work was first printed at Deventer in 1487, and
was often reprinted in France during the sixteenth and seventeenth
centuries."— Montaigne's Essays, p. 200, note. The copy in the British
Museum is marked *Deventrie*.

so full of abbreviations,[1] that I almost repented having undertaken to translate one chapter of the three hundred and thirty.

Sebonde had a strong conviction of the value of those inferences respecting the being and attributes of God which we may draw from nature. This abundantly appears in the following extract from the preface to his " Natural Theology : " —

" Two books have been given to man by God; namely, the book of the whole universe of created things, or the book of nature; and the other is the book of the Sacred Scriptures. This first book was given to man from the beginning, when the world was made, because any creature you please is nothing else than a certain letter written by the finger of God; and from many creatures, as from many letters, a book is composed.[2] Thus is composed the book of creatures, in which book man also is included, and is the chief letter of it all. And these letters and the words made from them are significant, and contain knowledge and a diversity of meanings and wondrous thoughts. . . . Moreover, the first book, that is the book of nature, cannot be falsified nor destroyed nor wrongly interpreted; for this reason even heretics cannot misunderstand it, nor can any one become a heretic by reason of it.[8] But the second can be falsified, and wrongly interpreted, and misunderstood. Nevertheless, each book is from the same person : the same God both formed all created things, and revealed the Sacred Scriptures. Hence they mutually agree, and do not contradict the one the other; yet the first is to us connatural, the

[1] *Querams e'yo qure res pmi ijds nó hnt pls ǫm eĉ;* for, *Queramus ergo quare res primi gradus non habent plus quam esse* is a moderate example of Sebonde's parsimony in the use of letters.

[2] Hence the sub-title *Liber Creaturarum*, the Book of Creatures. This is the running-title in Montaigne's translation.

[8] This notion may have suggested to Peter Bunel that Sebonde's book would serve as an antidote against the Lutheran heresy.

second supernatural. Furthermore, since man is by nature rational and capable of instruction; and since he had in fact from his creation no knowledge, but was apt to acquire it; and since knowledge cannot be had without a book in which it is written, — it was very appropriate, lest man might in vain be capable of learning, that divine wisdom should have created a book for him, in which, without a master, he might for himself learn what was necessary for salvation."

Sebonde's classification of natural objects, or "creatures," is not only something of a curiosity to a modern naturalist, but it is so important as a basis for his demonstration of the existence of God, that it must not by any means be omitted. In his first chapter he enumerates the following classes of creatures, or grades of existence : —

First, every thing having mere existence, but which neither lives (*vivit*), nor feels (*sentit*), nor knows (*intelligit*), nor has free will (*vult libere*).

Secondly, every thing having existence and life, without sensation or knowledge.

Thirdly, every thing which exists, lives, and feels; "and this sensation includes seeing, hearing, tasting, smelling, and touch." .In this class he gives three subdivisions: (*a*) Animals having the sense of touch without memory or hearing; as shell-fish. (*b*) Animals having the sense of touch and memory, but not hearing; as ants. (*c*) Animals having memory, and hearing, and all that belongs to "*animalia perfecta;*" as dogs and cats.

Fourthly, every creature which exists, lives, feels, knows, discerns, and has free will.

In brief, his four classes are minerals, plants, animals, and man. In the second chapter he enters into an elaborate comparison of man with the three other grades of existence. His third chapter contains his argument for the existence of God, and is worthy of being reproduced entire. Montaigne's headings to the chapters are usually condensed from the original, and that is the case with the heading to this chapter. In the French translation it is, " That there is one invisible master who built the world." Sebonde's heading is, " Here is shown the result of that comparison [i.e., the comparison of man to the inferior grades of existence given in Chap. II.]: It is plainly demonstrated and concluded, that there is some invisible lord above man who has constructed and arranged all these grades of being."

Following is a free rendering of his third chapter:—

" Now, it behooves us to consider what conclusions we ought to draw from this comparison. We ought thence to infer, that, since man has collectively all those things which other creatures have severally, it is the very same one, and none other, who has imparted to each of them his portion, and has combined all in man himself; that is to say, existence, life, sensation, intelligence, and free will. Therefore he who gave to inferior creatures what they have, is the same who gave to man what he has. But, as man did not give to other creatures what they possess, so he did not impart to himself what he has. As he did not give them being, life, and sensation, so he did not give himself being, life, sensation, and intelligence. Therefore the same hand made all things : the same lord and artificer has proportioned and limited and arranged all things.

" Let us inquire why the creatures of the first degree have nothing but existence ; why the elements have neither life nor sensation. Who prescribed to them that they should not have more? [*Who cut their allowance so short? —* Montaigne.] Who prescribed to plants that they should have nothing higher than life, and to animals that they should have nothing more than sensation? Who has caused animals to rise one grade above plants, and caused plants to be of one rank rather than another? Who has measured out their portion thus, and not otherwise? Why has man intelligence and free will, the power to choose or refuse, in addition to the first three qualities? Who was it that joined those three qualities with free will, so that there is no creature higher than man, but he is the end and consummation of things, and nothing is wanting to him? Who exalted man above trees and brute beasts?

" Let us inquire whether man has himself united these things in himself in order that he might want nothing, and whether he has exalted himself above all other creatures, or whether some other being has done this.   Let us inquire whether those other creatures have ordained and measured out their portion to themselves, that each should have so much and no more, or whether some other being has done this ; whether all creatures have bestowed upon themselves their faculties, so much and no more, or whether some other being has done this. Now, it is impossible that all these creatures should have imparted to themselves what they possess ; and yet it has been imparted and measured out. Therefore *some being superior to them all* has arranged, apportioned, and limited all those things, and given its portion to each creature. The same master, the same artificer, the same hand, has arranged all things in order, and given to each its appropriate place ; and it is the same being who caused trees to rise above the elements in rank, and animals above trees, and men above animals. He who ordained that trees should live by taking nutriment immediately from the earth by means of their roots descending into the soil, is the same who ordained that animals should live by taking nutriment through the mouth instead of roots, and that man should live more nobly than either plants or animals. Now, who ordained and contrived these three modes of living? Was it not the same lord and artificer? Moreover, who is it

that preserves all these in such manner that each remains in
its own rank, station, and order? Who made these distinct
grades of existence permanent, so that they remain without
confusion? Who holds the land and the sea in their places?
Is it not the same who made them at first?

" Conclusion : Thou, O man, hast received thy faculties
from the same being from whom other creatures have received theirs! Therefore thou also pertainest to the same
system as other creatures, and makest one series and hierarchy with them. It follows, therefore, that thou belongest to
him who owns all the rest : thou art preserved and ruled by
him who rules all the rest. As other creatures are not their
own, but his who made them, so thou art not thine own, but
his who owns all the others. Thou belongest to him who
owns the earth, the ocean, and the elements where thou
dwellest.

" Conclude further : Thou, O man, hast neither given to
thyself what thou hast, nor have inferior beings given it to
thee, or made thee such as thou art! Therefore *some* ONE
greater than thou, who is above thee, has given thee what
thou hast, because thou hast it not from another creature,
nor from thyself, nor from eternity."

In the fourth, fifth, and sixth chapters he undertakes
to prove the unity of God, and that his nature is truly
infinite. Some confused notion of proving the unity
of God at the same time that he proved his existence
seems to have been running in his head all through the
third chapter also. It got the better of the primary
notion of proving God's existence in several places, for
instance, where he speaks of one and the same hand
having arranged all things, and repeats similar expressions over and over. Then, again, the first half of the
conclusion is partly of the nature of a religious exhor-
tation, but more emphatically a statement of the origin
of all things from one sole fountain of being. It is

only in the second part of it that he gets back to his primary notion of existence pure and simple. The notion of unity is so prominent in the chapter, that it has crept into Montaigne's heading, although it is not in Sebonde's.

Chapter VII. is headed, "How by the comparison of the four grades of existence it is proved that God has being, life, sensation, intelligence, and free will ; " and its conclusion is, " It follows that he exists, lives, feels, understands, and exercises free will." In subsequent chapters Sebonde shows that existence is the foundation and the means of proving all the other divine attributes. From all this it is plain that the third chapter, containing his demonstration of the existence of God, is the basis of all his subsequent arguments.

The first forty-five chapters contain all of the natural theology proper; and his summary of the work up to this point is, " We have infallibly demonstrated that a Maker of the world exists, lives, feels, knows, and has power."

Then he wanders off into " the mystery of the Trinity," transubstantiation, penances, purgatory, and other abstruse matters and insalubrious places, where we need not follow him.

It is obvious at a glance, that Sebonde's argument is unique. He does not follow the well-beaten paths of teleology: He draws his inferences from the open page of nature, the book of creatures, as he calls it; but he reads this book in a way of his own. Fixing his attention upon the complex hierarchy of lifeless and living things, organized in ascending series from senseless elements to rational humanity, he inquires in the first place for the source of those qualities which constitute the ground of distinction between these grades of being.

Especially does he press the query with respect to man, who is "the consummation of things, to whom nothing is lacking." His fundamental and very pertinent question is, "Whence did man derive his faculties?" He has not existed from eternity: therefore, thought Sebonde, his faculties have had a beginning at some point of time. He had not heard of the modern theory, that life, sensation, and intelligence were latent in the primitive cosmic gas. His notion was, that human faculties had their starting-point in time simultaneous with the introduction of man upon the earth. They were not derived from inferior creatures, nor did man confer them upon himself: hence they must have been imparted by a being competent to bestow such gifts, — that is, by a conscious, intelligent, and free agent.

So far his argument is causal. He is seeking for an adequate cause of those forms of existence which he beholds in the universe.

But there is not only the existence of certain faculties to be accounted for; there is also the fact, that these have been so measured out as to constitute definite grades of existence in an ascending scale. This eutaxy, this orderly arrangement, is a mark of intelligence. As a ground of inference, it is just as reliable as, and leads to its conclusion more directly than, the search for a First Cause adequate to the impartation of the faculties and properties which mark off the several ranks, and distinguish them each from the others.

Although Sebonde does not make the mental analysis of his argument in this way, it clearly contains the elements of these two distinct lines of reasoning; namely, the *causal* and the *eutaxiological*. He says that "some being superior to them all has given its portion to each creature;" and that "the same lord and artificer preserves all these in such manner that each remains in its own rank, station, and order."

His argument is somewhat awkwardly stated; and this is due in part to his confused double aim of proving the unity and existence of God at the same time. Then it may be remarked further, that, in subsequent chapters, he presses the argument to unwarrantable conclusions, endeavoring to establish the whole body of systematic theology upon a natural basis. This makes his reasoning appear weaker than it really is. His first point is well taken.

This real strength in one part of his book, while other parts are lame in their logic, and mingle pious reflections, crude metaphysics, and downright absurdities confusedly together, may account for the various and conflicting opinions respecting the merit of the work. Hadrian Turnebus, a learned friend of Montaigne, said it was so admirable that it must have been stolen from Thomas Aquinas.[1] The Jesuit, Theophilus Raynaud, speaks of it with contempt.[2] Comenius commends it highly, as does Montaigne himself also; that is, if we could ever be absolutely sure what a man means who is so skilful a master of that art commended to diplomatists by another famous Frenchman,[3] — the art of using words so as to conceal your meaning. There is a possible *double entendre* in Montaigne's eulogy of Sebonde : " I think nobody can go farther than he upon that subject, and that none did ever equal him."

Dugald Stewart is taken sharply to task by Henry Hallam for saying that "the principal aim of Sebonde's book, according to Montaigne, is to show that Christians are in the wrong to make human reason the basis

[1] Montaigne's Essays, p. 200.
[2] Prolegomena Theologia Naturalis, 86.   [3] Talleyrand.

of their belief, since the object of it is only conceived by faith, and by a special inspiration of the divine grace." "Far from such being the aim of Sebonde," says Hallam, "his book is wholly devoted to the rational proofs of religion."[1] Hallam's own statement, subsequently made, is as follows: "The object of Sebonde's book is to develop those truths as to God and man which are latent in nature, and through which man may learn every thing necessary. . . . He undertakes to prove the Trinity from the analogy of nature."

I rather sympathize with Stewart than blame him. Any man who should undertake to find out from Montaigne's essay what Sebonde was driving at, deserves commiseration. It is more than most men can manage to follow the meteoric flights of Montaigne himself, and know what *he* would be at.

That Stewart really obtained his mistaken notion of Sebonde from Montaigne's "Apology" appears from the fact, that his language is an almost exact copy of a sentence in that essay. Montaigne is stating the objections that have been made against Sebonde by certain over-zealous Christians: "The first thing they reprehend in his work is, 'That Christians are to blame to repose their belief upon human reason, which is only conceived by faith and the particular inspiration of divine grace.'"

If the reader will glance back at Stewart's statement, he will see that it is copied from this ambiguous expression of an objection, — ambiguous because it is so worded that it may easily be taken for the thing objected to instead of the objection. Stewart says, "It is proper to add, that I am acquainted with Sebonde only through the medium of Montaigne's version," leav-

[1] Lit. of Eu., i. 140.

ing us to infer that he gathered his opinion of the work from Sebonde himself in his French dress. Ungracious as it may seem to doubt this, it is more charitable than to accept it; for, if we must take him at his word in this matter, our sympathy for him in his perplexity, seeking amid the mazy whirl of Montaigne's rhetoric to find out what Sebonde meant, turns at once to censure. His reading must have been very superficial indeed not to discover that the object of his author was precisely the opposite of what he understood Montaigne to say it was. He seems to have thought the original was in the Spanish language.[1]

Another modern author has tripped in respect to this very rare book. Professor Baden Powell of Oxford says that Sebonde assumed the *existence* of God. " The argument was solely as to the *perfection* of the Creator." [2] On the contrary, the demonstration of God's existence is the best part of the work, and the foundation of all the rest. It is probable that Powell, like Stewart, took his opinions of this book at second hand.

[1] Essays, p. 103.   [2] Order of Nature, p. 36.

CHAPTER III.

NATURAL THEOLOGY IN THE SEVENTEENTH CENTURY: MORE AND CUDWORTH.

THE sixteenth century was one of the most stirring and revolutionary periods of human history. It was the seed-plot of whatever is most characteristic in modern civilization. It witnessed the birth of Protestantism, and of modern science. It was the age of Luther, Copernicus, and Galileo. The thunders of the Reformation resounded through Europe during its earlier years: its later decades were illumined by the ghastly light of martyr-flames kindled in the vain hope of extinguishing the new faith. The massacre of St. Bartholomew stained it with innocent blood; and its expiring notes were mingled with the dying groans of Giordano Bruno, who was burned at Rome for the double offence of repudiating the authority of the Pope in religion, and of Aristotle in science.

Such commotions and agitations were not favorable to the study of natural theology. The great religious movement of the age, the Reformation, resulted in the restoration of scriptural theology to the place it held in the earliest centuries. The Bible had been hidden from the world. Luther brought it forth from its concealment, and made its interpretation his main business as a theologian. All the Protestant divines followed his example; and, as for the Catholic theologians, they were too busy with the refutation of heresies, and the invention and management of the Inquisition, to give any attention to natural theology.

At the opening of the seventeenth century the movement of human thought assumed two marked phases: it began to flow in two currents, distinct, and in some sort opposed to each other. The struggles of the sixteenth century had compelled men to think, and they now began to assume that boldness of utterance, that daring and unrestrained expression of the results of thought, which struck the death-knell of authority. Human reason was at last fairly on its feet; and the next question was whither it should walk, and by what rule or method its steps should be guided.

It has often been remarked, that, in each great emergency in human affairs, some leader has arisen whose genius was the beacon-light revealing a way of escape or a path of progress. In this emergency of human thought newly emancipated and seeking for a method, Francis Bacon was the first to propose one.[1] To him is justly accorded the honor of pointing out one legitimate path of progress for the human mind seeking truth independently of authority; viz., the inductive method. By observation and experiment men can accumulate a store of facts; and, by reasoning upon these, they can formulate general laws and construct the various sciences. Upon this path of progress men entered with eagerness, pursued it with great success, and are still engaged in the good work, with the prospect of even grander results yet to be attained.

But there are certain truths or principles not to be

. [1] Bacon's work on the Advancement of Learning was first published in the English language in 1605. It was subsequently much enlarged, and published in Latin in 1623.

reached by observation and experiment, because they lie in the mind itself, and can only be drawn out by reflection. From these first principles others may be obtained by deduction, and thus a body of philosophy may be built up. Here is a distinct method, metaphysical and deductive, instead of experimental and inductive. René Descartes is the author of this subjective and deductive method.[1] The justice of according to Bacon and Descartes the honor of inventing these two methods may be called in question; because both had undoubtedly been used before these men were born, but never with that full comprehension of them as distinct methods, and never with that complete and fearless abandonment to their guidance which these two men exhibited.

Thus early in the seventeenth century, under the leadership of two great minds, human thought began to flow in these two distinct channels. Properly considered, the Baconian inductive method and the Cartesian subjective method are complementary, and not antagonistic to each other. Moreover, they had at their origin this in common, and as a bond of sympathy, that both were directly and irrepressibly hostile to the baneful influence of authority. But a common point of antagonism operates as a bond of sympathy and union, only so long as the enemy is in the field. A marked antagonism was soon developed between the adherents of these two schools of thought.

This antagonism in turn split, and separated into cross-currents. There was a purely metaphysical phase of it, dividing philosophy into what might, broadly speaking, be called the English school and the Continental school of metaphysicians; and there was the

---

[1] Descartes' Discourse on Method was published in 1637.

theological phase of it, which is the only one that concerns us at present. This latter antagonism did not arise from the fundamental positions of Bacon and Descartes, as the metaphysical antagonism did, but from certain principles of the Cartesian philosophy which were not at all necessarily or essentially involved in his method. Inasmuch as this antagonism is directly and intimately related to the development of natural theology in the seventeenth century, it is no digression, but lies precisely in the line of my work, to point out its existence, and trace it to its causes.

In the first place, there was the Cartesian theory of "vortices." This was an attempt to explain the origin and movements of the earth and of celestial bodies upon mechanical principles, — a sort of crude evolution hypothesis, less tenable than the nebular hypothesis of La Place, — the cosmic-gas theory, as the Germans call it, — but, like that, welcomed by atheists and deprecated by theists. The following account of it is quoted from Whewell: [1] —

"He asserts it to be also manifest, that a vacuum in any part of the universe is impossible: [2] the whole must be filled with matter; and the matter must be divided into equal angular parts, this being the most simple, and therefore the most natural, supposition. This matter being in motion, the parts are necessarily ground into a spherical form; and the corners thus rubbed off (like filings or sawdust) form a second and more subtile matter. There is, besides, a third kind of matter, of parts more coarse and less fitted for motion. The first matter makes luminous bodies, as the sun and the fixed stars; the second is the transparent substance

[1] Hist. of Ind. Sci., ii. 142.
[2] It is said that Descartes first framed his theory of the cosmos upon the basis of a vacuum ; but, hearing that a vacuum was not then *popular* at Paris, he changed his basis to a *plenum!*

of the skies ; the third is the material of opaque bodies, as
the earth, planets, and comets. We may suppose also, that
the motions of these parts take the form of revolving circular
currents, or *vortices*. By this means the first matter will be
collected to the centre of each vortex, while the second, or
subtile matter, surrounds it, and, by its centrifugal effort,
constitutes light. The planets are carried round the sun by
the motion of his vortex, each planet being at such a distance from the sun as to be in a part of the vortex suitable
to its solidity and mobility."

In the second place, there was the total rejection of
teleology by Descartes : —

"We wholly reject from our philosophy the search for
final causes ; for we ought not to take so much upon ourselves as to believe that God wished us to take part in his
counsels."

We are not thence to infer, however, that he was at
all inclined towards atheism or irreligion. It is well
known, that he made more of the ontological argument
for the existence of God than had been done by any
previous writer. One author uncharitably suggests
that he had an interest in making away with teleology
in order to have a clear field for his favorite ontology.

I have said that these two things — his vortex theory
and his rejection of teleology — were not necessary consequences of his method ; and this I am free to maintain.
At the same time they were, in a sense, natural consequences, though not necessary consequences, of his
subjective method. His fondness for the ontological
proof was a direct consequence of his method, and
needs no other explanation ; and the very fact that his
mind was so filled with the importance of that proof
would be an obstacle to his appreciation of teleology.

But there is another reason why he was inclined to disparage the teleological argument, and this is more · directly related to his method. Teleology thrives upon the observation of nature; and Descartes' method, instead of leading to such observation, was based upon reflection, meditation, and introspection. For the same reason his vortex theory was harmonious with his method, though that particular theory was not necessary to it. It was a construction of the universe out of the depths of his own consciousness, just as his method required all philosophy to be constructed.

It might seem at first glance, that the rejection of teleology was a point of agreement between Bacon and Descartes, since the former stigmatized final causes as "sterile virgins." But, accurately speaking, it was not final causes that he criticised, but the misplacement of them; and it was the *search* for them in the province of physics that he said was *barren*. Moreover, the Baconian philosophy of induction was the immediate occasion of a group of writers on natural theology springing up in the last half of the seventeenth century. The cultivation of the sciences, stimulated and guided by that philosophy, revealed so many new illustrations of God's wisdom in the creation, that a crop of teleology followed just as naturally as harvest follows seeding.

Of the English group of teleologists in the seventeenth century, consisting of More, Cudworth, Boyle, Ray, and Newton, the last three were ardent disciples of the Baconian method. More and Cudworth were more nearly allied to the Cartesian than to the English school of metaphysics; but, in respect to the theological antagonism to Descartes on account of his vortex theory and his rejection of teleology, they were as violently anti-

Cartesian as the other three. Thus we see how the cross-currents and counter-currents of opinion brought the same men into sympathy on some points and into antagonism on other points. More and Cudworth accepted Descartes' ontology with thanks, but antagonized him on other points. They were not strictly Cartesians on any point, but Platonists; and this fact of their attempting to resuscitate Platonic philosophy, while it allied them with Descartes rather than with the English school of metaphysics as represented by Locke, and was thus in one sense a bond of sympathy, still in another sense it was a symbol of antagonism. Plato's opinion that the world was animated, which was the fountain of Cudworth's "plastic-nature" theory, was pointedly opposed to the Cartesian mechanical theory of the universe.

This whole group of English teleologists might justly be called the anti-Cartesian group, but this expression must be strictly construed as referring to a theological antagonism of opinion. They all attack Descartes on account of his vortex theory and his rejection of teleology: but they were friendly enough to his other opinions; and More was on such friendly terms as to carry on a personal correspondence with the French philosopher, the object of which was to relieve the latter of any suspicion of atheism in the minds of the English public on account of the two obnoxious elements of his philosophy.

With this preliminary view of the tendencies of speculative thought during the seventeenth century, we are prepared to enter more intelligently upon the detailed study of the writings of the anti-Cartesian group.

Henry More, D.D., the first of this group, was a man of considerable learning, and a prominent figure among the English divines of his day, as might be inferred from the fact of his correspondence with Descartes. Besides his "Antidote to Atheism," which contains his natural theology, he was the author of several other theological treatises. The "Antidote" was published in 1662. In his preface the author claims, that, if it be granted as a postulate, "*That our faculties are true,*" then he has "*demonstrated that there is a God.*"

In some cases, as we shall see in the sequel, it is difficult to ascertain whether a given writer makes it his aim to prove the existence of God by means of teleology, or only to illustrate the divine attributes of wisdom, power, and goodness. But in this case we are not left in doubt as regards More's intentions at the outset, nor as regards his own opinion of his success in his undertaking. He distinctly assumed the task of demonstrating God's existence, and supposed that he had succeeded in the attempt.

His work is divided into three books. Book I. is devoted to the ontological and moral or anthropological arguments. Book II. is devoted to physico-theology, and mainly to teleology; but, without conscious analysis of it as a distinct argument, he introduces in several places clear examples of eutaxiological reasoning. Still more frequently does he, through the failure to make that analysis and to draw that distinction, affect to extract a teleological conclusion from the facts of order in the cosmos; thus making a lame attempt where he might have made a strong argument. As a clear case of eutaxiology, take the following: —

"That the rising and setting of the lights of heaven, the vicissitude of day and night, winter and summer, being so ordered and guided as if they had been settled by exquisite consultation and by clearest knowledge : therefore that which did thus ordain them is a *knowing principle*, able to *move*, *alter*, and *guide* the *matter* according to his own will and pleasure; that is to say, *that there is a God*. . . . And it is observable, that, if nature shape any thing near this *geometrical* accuracy, we take notice of it with much content and pleasure. For *symmetry*, *equality*, and *correspondence of parts* is the discernment of *reason*, and not the object of *sense*, as I have heretofore proved."

Cosmical harmonies in the heavens, and geometrical accuracy in the formation of crystals, are widely different topics; but they both illustrate the principle of eutaxy, good order, and both serve well as a basis for the eutaxiological argument.

For an example of spoiling a good case of eutaxiology in order to make a poor piece of teleology, this will serve : —

" But I will rather insist upon such things as are easy and intelligible even to idiots, who if they can but tell the joints of their hands, or know the use of their teeth, they may easily discover it was *counsel*, not *chance*, that created them. For why have we *three* joints in our legs and arms, as also in our fingers, but that it was much better than having *two* or *four*? "

The doctor is convinced that three joints are better than two or four; but, if there had been but two, as is actually the case in the thumb, he would probably have thought that was best. There is a notable disposition manifest, not only in his writings, but in those of the old teleologists generally, to see divine wisdom in every petty detail; though, if the arrangement so interpreted were something other than it actually is, they would find it an equally conclusive proof of wisdom. In this case, it is true, he touched a very interesting topic, but unfortunately he did not know how to handle it.

His radical error consists in misplacing the argument. By claiming that this number of joints is better than any other, he makes it teleological. The *utility* of the arrangement — its reference to an *end* — is the uppermost thought in his mind. His attempt to turn it to a teleological account shows how fully he was possessed and dominated by the Aristotelian maxim, that nature does nothing in vain, which he quotes in several places. But, curiously enough, this very fact of a definite number of joints in limbs and digits is one of the greatest obstacles to the acceptance of that maxim. The three-jointed limb terminating in five three-jointed digits is not limited to man alone. It is not an isolated fact, but takes hold of wide homologies, and has a deep significance in the animal kingdom. It is a morphological type of very wide range, especially as regards the first element of it; namely, the three-jointed limb. The mode of its termination in five three-jointed digits, or, at all events, in five digits with a variable number of joints, is also a pronounced typical form, but not so widely prevalent as the three-jointed limb.

But now this fact of the existence of typical forms results in the existence of useless rudiments. A joint is lopped off here, another there, a whole digit gone with all its joints, even several of them missing if any special end of utility is to be served by it. In this wholesale and seemingly reckless process of clipping and pruning, there are certain fragments of the digits left behind. These remnants are not destitute of significance, but their meaning is very wide of the teleological mark. It is not the constancy of the type, but the departures from it, which constitute good material for teleological argument. So far from utility causing or maintaining the typical form, it is constantly violat-

ing it; and, in the course of these modifications for
special ends, useless rudiments are left, such as the
splint-bones representing the second and fourth digits
in the leg of a horse, — tag-ends, so to speak, of the typical form. These give the lie to the Aristotelian dictum,
unless you take it in a new sense, not as regards utility
to the animal, or utility in any form whatever; for, if
utility is the standard, nature does do some things in
vain. But there are other standards than that of utility.
Nature does nothing in vain in the sense that all she
does has a rational meaning. The meaning of useless
rudiments is that there is a typical form. But all such
forms are examples of the orderly methods of nature.
Morphology, the doctrine of typical forms, is a branch
of eutaxiology. The relative constancy of the type, in
spite of the numerous inroads made upon it by the
pressure of special utilities, is so remarkable, that we
are justified in the inference that this type is an *arche-
type*, that it existed as a divine thought before it was
embodied in living forms. Thus the three-jointed pattern of the limbs of vertebrate animals furnishes the
basis of a good design-argument when rightly used.
But it must be considered simply as a fact of eutaxy,
of orderly arrangement, without raising the question of
the end, or purpose, or whether it is better or worse
than some other arrangement. The moment you make
it teleological you spoil it altogether.

This may seem a harsh and sweeping judgment, but
a little consideration will amply justify it. In the first
place, this is a weak piece of teleology, because it
would put Dr. More, or any other man, to his wits'
end to tell *why* three joints are better than any other
number. Insects seem to be quite happy with more
than three joints in their legs, and mollusks are entirely

contented with none at all. But, in the second place, if he should succeed in that desperate undertaking, he would only be steering the argument into deeper water than ever. If the three-jointed type is the best possible type, then the utility of it may have operated to produce it by natural selection. It is an extremely interesting question whether it has not done so, — a question, too, of such difficulty that it is not to be disposed of out of hand by any *ex cathedra* judgment. But there is one weighty consideration opposed to it; viz., that this type was first developed in fishes, where the limb is so buried in the body that the three joints are of little use. It is true that the homology of the bones supporting the pectoral fins of fishes to the humerus, radius, and ulna in higher animals, is not very clear, and that the typical number of five digits with three joints is ignored in that class of vertebrates. But the case is little better for natural selection if we shift our ground, bringing the origin of the type in question to a later period, and into a higher class ; for, in the case of many amphibians and reptiles having three distinct segments to their limbs, some of the joints are still buried in the flesh.

"Hitherto we have only considered the more rude and careless strokes and delineaments of divine providence in the world, set out in those larger phenomena of day and night, winter and summer, land and sea, rivers, mountains, metals, and the like. We now come to a closer view of God and nature in vegetables, animals, and man."

This is the opening sentence of Chapter V., Book II. It is evident that More considered his teleology the strongest part of his work. The most charitable supposition for us to make is, that he was mistaken in this view of the relative excellence of the several parts; for, if the rest is not so good as the teleology, silence respecting it would be the greatest kindness.

" And first of vegetables, where I shall touch only these four heads, their *form* and *beauty*, their *seed*, their *signatures*, and their great *use*, as well for medicine as sustenance."

Having argued that the seeds of plants indicate a providence, he proceeds : —

" Nor is it material to object that stinking weeds and poisonous plants bear seed too, as well as the most pleasant and useful ; for even those have their use. For, first, the industry of man is exercised by them to weed them out where they are hurtful."

Great danger that men might become lazy if it were not for the weeds ! The very lack of usefulness becomes a use. In the second place, the doctor thinks they suck up the poisonous matter of the soil, and make it purer, as " toads, and other poisonous serpents, lick the venom from off the earth." And, lastly, they may have medicinal virtues of which we are ignorant.

It is plain that in all this discussion the doctor's notion of utility has reference to *human* uses. The usefulness of seeds to plants themselves in the struggle for existence did not occur to him, but not so when he comes to animals. Here he shows that he is quite capable of entertaining the idea of usefulness without any reference to man ; for it is not to be imagined that in what he says about cock's spurs he had an eye to the brutal sports of his day : —

" I demand, therefore, concerning the cock, why he has spurs at all ; or, having them, how they came to be so fittingly placed. For he might have had none, or so misplaced that they had been utterly useless, and so his courage and pleasure in fighting had been to no purpose."

He makes a novel suggestion as to the use of the turkey's wattles: —

"Nor are we to cavil at the red-puggered attire of the turkey, and the long excrescency that hangs down over his bill, when he swells with pride and anger; for it may be a receptacle for his heated blood, that has such free recourse to his head."

Might save him from a fit of apoplexy, I suppose.

"We come now to the *signatures* of plants. . . . The decoction of *quinces*, which are a *downy* and *hairy* fruit, is accounted good for the fetching again *hair* that has fallen off.

"Scorpion-grass is like the crooked tail of a scorpion, and adder's-tongue has a very plain and perfect resemblance of the tongue of a serpent, as also *ophioscorodon* of the entire head and upper parts of the body; and these are all held very good against poison, and the biting of serpents. And generally all such plants as are speckled with spots like the skins of vipers or other venomous creatures are known to be good against the stings or bitings of them, and are powerful antidotes against poison. Thus did Divine Providence, by natural hieroglyphics, read short physic-lectures to the rude wit of man."

That is very flimsy teleology; and of course there are much better specimens in the book. He cites the usefulness of domestic animals; he describes the eye at great length, and as well as the anatomical science of his age permitted; and the same may be said of his arguments from the structure of the lungs, heart, and teeth. In his preface he says, —

" Only I may say thus much, that I did on purpose abstain from reading any treatises concerning this subject, that I might the more undisturbedly write the easy emanations of my own mind."

Thus he forestalls any charges of plagiarism, though, of course, he repeats arguments which had been used by previous writers.

Next to his teleology, Dr. More thought his ghost-argument was the best. What! did he not only believe in ghosts and witchcraft, but thought to make capital of them against atheism? Certainly, that is all true; and he was not at all peculiar in that. Clergymen of that day, and indeed for a long time afterwards, made constant use of the belief in apparitions to convince men that there were spirits. The utility of ghosts in this respect was a prime cause of the tardiness with which they yielded to the force of rational views respecting their unreality. Some good people have imagined that the phenomena of modern spiritualism might be utilized in the same way. Very likely it might be done in the same way in one respect; that is, the attempt would be just as silly and contemptible in one case as the other. But in another respect the result would be very different. Men are not so easily caught by shams and delusions as they were in the seventeenth century. But let us see how it was done in that age : —

" Thus we have gone through the manifold effects represented to our senses on this wide theatre of the world ; the faintest and obscurest whereof are arguments full enough to prove the existence of a Deity. . . . And such are especially these last two I insisted upon, — *the curious frame of man's body* and *apparitions.*

" Bodinus relates how himself and several others at Paris saw a young man with a *charm* in French move a sieve up and down. And that ordinary way of divination which they call *coskinomancy,* or finding who stole or spoiled this or that thing by the *sieve* and *shears,* Pictorius Vigillanus professeth he made use of thrice, and it was with success.''

In regard to the ceremonies which witches perform in order to raise tempests, he says, —

"But whether there be any causal connection between those ceremonies and the ensuing tempests, I will not curiously decide. [He is thinking of physical causation evidently, and he will not deny that there may be some hidden bond of that sort; and yet he goes on to show that it cannot be any ordinary action of natural law.] But that the connection of them is *supernatural,* is plain at first sight. For what is the casting of flint-stones behind their backs toward the west, or flinging a little sand in the air, or striking a river with a broom, and so flinging the wet of it towards heaven, or the stirring of urine or water with their finger in a hole in the ground, or the boiling of hog's bristles in a pot? what are these fooleries available of themselves to gather clouds, and cover the air with darkness, and then to make the ground smoke with peals of hail and rain, and to make the air terrible with frequent lightnings and thunder? Certainly nothing at all. Therefore the ensuing of these tempests after such like ceremonies must be either from the prevision of the Devil (as Wierus would have it) who set the witches on work, or else from the power of the Devil which he hath in his kingdom of the air.''

As regards the power of witches to fill the bodies of their victims with a whole arsenal of heterogeneous missiles, he says, —

" I will begin with that memorable story that Langius tells of one Ulricus Neusesser, who, being grievously tormented with a pain in his side, suddenly felt under his skin, which was yet whole, an iron nail as he thought; and so it proved when the chirurgeon had cut it out. But, nevertheless, his great torments continued, which enraged him so that he cut his own throat. The third day, when he was carried out to be buried, Eucharius Rosenbader and Johannes ab Ettenstet, a great company of people standing about them, dissected the corpse, and, ripping up the ventricle, found a *round piece of wood* of a good length, *four knives*, some even and sharp, others indented like a saw, with other *two rough pieces of iron* a span long. There was also *a ball of hair*. This happened at Fugenstall, 1539.

"Wierus tells also of one that was possessed, of which himself was an eye-witness, that vomited up *pieces of cloth with pins stuck in them, nails, needles*, and such like stuff. . . . Cardan relates the like of a good simple country-fellow, and a friend of his, that had been a long time troubled with vomiting up *glass, iron, nails*, and *hair*, and that, at the time he told Cardan of it, he was not so perfectly restored, but that something yet crashed in his belly as if there were a bag of glass in it."

He tells of a witch raising a tempest, and being herself "discharged by that last thunder-clap upon the top of the oak, and there hung amongst the boughs;" and several other stories of the same sort: —

"We might abound in instances of this kind (I mean supernatural effects unattended with miraculous apparitions) if I would bring in all that that I have myself been informed of [it does not appear that Dr. More ever saw any thing of this nature himself] by either eye-witnesses themselves or by such as have had the narrations immediately from them [he takes his information at first or second hand, but there he draws the line], — as, for example, bricks being carried round about a room without any visible hand; multitudes of stones flung down at a certain time of the day from the roof of a house for many months together, to the amazement of the whole country; pots carried off from the fire, and set on again, no hand touching them; the violent flapping of a chest-cover, nobody meddling with it; the carrying-up linens that have been a-bleaching so high that table-cloths and sheets looked like napkins, and this when there was no wind, but all calm and clear; . . . boxes carefully locked unlocking themselves, and flinging the flax out of them; . . . women's pattens rising up from the floor, and whirling against people [he should have mentioned that the women's feet were not in them] ; the breaking of a comb in two pieces of itself in the window, the pieces also flying in men's faces [no wonder it broke if they propped the window up with it] ; the rising-up of a knife also from the same place, being carried with its haft forwards [the witches or spirits were more thoughtful than some people, who will hand you a knife blade foremost] ; with several other things which would be too voluminous to repeat with their due circumstances.

"But, if the objector will yet persist in his opinion. let him read the circumstances of the second conjuration of this witch. For the same maid being sent again to her from the same party to inquire in what part of the house the poison was that should be given to her mistress, hereupon she took her stick as before, and. making therewith a circle, *the wind rose forthwith.* Then, taking a besom. she swept out the circle, and made another ; and, looking in her book and glass as formerly, and using some words softly to herself, she stood in the circle, and said, *Beelzebub, Tormentor, Lucifer,* and *Satan,* appear ! There appeared first a spirit in the shape of a little boy, as she (the maid) conceived, which then turned into another shape something like a snake, and then into the shape of a shagged dog *with great eyes,* which went about in the circle. And in the circle she set an earthen [it must not be iron or tin] pan of coals, wherein she threw something which burned and stank. and then the spirit vanished. After which the witch took her book and glass [it must be a *green* glass] again, and showed the maid in the glass Sarah Goddard's chamber [Sarah and Anna Goddard were step-daughters, and their amiable step-mother, aided by the witch and the maid, was trying to convict them of an attempt to poison her] the color of the curtains and the bed turned up the wrong way, and under that part of the bed where the bolster lay she *showed the poison in a white paper.*

"The transformation of a boy into a snake, and of that snake into a shagged dog with staring eyes, is a feat far above all human art or wit whatsoever." [Quite so, doctor.]

To finish up this uncanny business while we are about it, let us note that the next writer of this group, Ralph Cudworth, D.D., also employs the ghost-argument: —

"For, if there be once any invisible ghosts or spirits acknowledged as things permanent, it will not be easy for any one to give a reason why there might not be one supreme ghost also presiding over them all and the whole world. . . . To these phenomena of apparitions may be added those two others of witches and demoniacs, both of these proving that spirits are not fancies, nor inhabitants of men's brains only, but of the world; as also that there are some impure spirits (is) a confirmation of the truth of Christianity. The confident exploders of witchcraft (are) suspicable of atheism."[1]

Cudworth's "Intellectual System of the Universe" was published in 1678. It was declared to be "the vastest magazine of reasoning and learning that ever singly appeared against atheism." Its author was undoubtedly quite familiar with the literature of Greece and Rome. He illustrates almost every point by copious quotations from the old philosophers, especially from Plato and Aristotle for confirmation, and from Democritus, Epicurus, and Lucretius for refutation. He was a decided Platonist, and his peculiar theory of

[1] From the heading to Chapter V. of the Int. Sys. of the Universe.

"plastic natures" was an adumbration of the Platonic notion of a world-soul. With all his learning it must be confessed, that, upon a candid examination of his "Intellectual System," we are compelled to pronounce it an ill-digested mass of erudition, and to concur in the judgment of some critics of his own time, that he raised more objections than he was able to answer.

One of the most remarkable things in Cudworth is that alluded to above; viz., his plastic-nature theory: —

"For, unless there be such a thing admitted as a plastic nature that acts, ἕνεκά του, for the sake of something, and in order to ends, regularly, artificially, and methodically, it seems that one or other of these two things must be concluded; that, either in the efformation and organization of the bodies of animals, as well as the other phenomena, every thing comes to pass fortuitously, and happens to be as it is, without the guidance and direction of any mind or understanding; or else that God himself doth all immediately, and, as it were, with his own hand, form every gnat and fly, insect and mite." (I. 218.)

He seems to be of the opinion that there is a species of thought in nature itself: —

"For, if clear and express consciousness be supposed to be included in cogitation, then it must needs be granted that cogitation doth not belong to the plastic life of nature; but, if the notion of that word (cogitation) be enlarged so as to comprehend all action distinct from local motion, and to be of equal extent with life, then the energy of nature is cogitation." (I. 246.)

Unconscious cogitation co-extensive with life — that is, existing in plants as well as animals — would be a very low form of thought; but to that extent, in so far as that can be called thinking, Cudworth believed that

nature itself thinks.   His plastic-nature theory would
knock the bottom out of teleology.

But he even gives a sort of personality to the plastic
nature : —

" From what hath been hitherto declared concerning the
plastic nature, it may appear, that though it be a thing that
acts for ends artificially, and which may also be called the
divine art, and the *fate* of the corporeal world ; yet, for all
that, it is neither god nor goddess, but a low and imperfect
creature." (I. 250.)

Having proved that the plastic nature is not corporeal, he goes on : —

" Now, if the plastic nature be incorporeal, then it must
of necessity be either an inferior power or faculty of some
soul which is also conscious, sensitive, or rational ; or else
a lower substantial life by itself, devoid of animal consciousness." (I. 255.)

Of these alternatives he shows that Plato and Aristotle took the latter ; that is, they held that the world-
soul was not an inferior faculty of the Deity, but a life
by itself.   And Cudworth agrees with them so far, but
differs only in that he makes it depend "immediately
upon the Deity itself," though it is not an inferior
power or faculty of the Deity; while Plato and Aristotle made it a distinct and independent being.

" Though there were no such mundane soul as both Plato
and Aristotle supposed, distinct from a supreme Deity, yet
there might, notwithstanding, be a plastic nature of the universe depending immediately upon the Deity itself." (I.
271.)

" Besides this general plastic nature of the universe, and
those particular plastic powers in the souls of animals, it is

not impossible but that there may be other plastic natures also, as certain lower lives or vegetative souls.

"And now we have finished our first task, which was to give an account of the plastic nature, the sum whereof briefly amounts to this: that it is a certain lower life than the animal, which acts regularly and artificially, according to the direction of mind and understanding, reason and wisdom, for ends, or in order to good, though itself do not know the reason of what it does, nor is master of that wisdom according to which it acts but only a servant to it, and a drudging executioner of the same; it operating fatally and sympathetically, according to laws and commands prescribed to it by a perfect intellect, and impressed upon it; and which is either a lower faculty of some conscious soul, or else an inferior kind of life or soul by itself, but essentially depending upon a higher intellect."

The several parts of this summary are not entirely consistent. A thing which "acts fatally according to laws prescribed to it and impressed upon it by a perfect intellect," would be simply the ordinary conception of matter. And in that aspect of it, the ends in nature being wrought out by natural laws impressed upon matter by an intelligent being, there would be some chance for teleology, as there is also upon the supposition that evolution is a true theory. But in other parts of his description he gives a sort of life, and even a low form of thought, to his plastic nature, as if it were a person, acting under God's control it is true, but yet "a lower substantial life by itself." Now, the moment you admit the intervention between God and the products of nature, of a creature having any degree of intelligence, even the lowest sort of "cogitation" conceivable, you cut off completely and utterly the possibility of any inferences respecting God from those products. How are you to know what things are due to that imperfect intelligence of the plastic nature, and what to the perfect intelligence of the Deity? It is true, that Cudworth strove to guard this point by saying that his plastic nature was wholly dependent upon God; but that was inconsistent with the radical feature of the theory, which consists in making the plastic nature capable by itself, by virtue of its own low degree of intelligence, of acting "for the sake of something, and in order to ends, regularly, artificially, and methodically." Plato and Aristotle were more consistent than Cudworth. They made the world-soul independent of God. Cudworth took the theory from their hands, and, in order to adapt it to a Christian theism, made the world-soul a blind instrument "acting fatally according to laws impressed upon it." His theistic annex is in a totally different style of architecture, and does not harmonize well with the main body of the old pagan theory : —

"We proceed to our second undertaking, which was to show how grossly these two sorts of atheists before mentioned, — the Stoical or Cosmo-plastic, and the Stratonical or Hylozoic, — both of them acknowledging this plastic life of nature, do mistake the notion of it, or pervert it, and abuse it, to make a certain spurious and counterfeit God-Almighty of it."

It must in all soberness be admitted, that his plastic nature was very likely material to be moulded into "a certain spurious and counterfeit God-Almighty." He accepted it from Plato and Aristotle, in order to confute the mechanical theory of the Epicurean atomists, and more especially that of Descartes, whose theory of vortices Cudworth thought was more improbable than, and quite as atheistic as, the fortuitous-concourse-of-atoms theory of Democritus. But, instead of braining his adversaries, he unwittingly put a club in their hands. The atheists had been especially puzzled to account for the exquisite perfection displayed in organic structures. They immediately seized upon Cudworth's theory of a plastic nature to supply that defect in their system. With the mechanical theory for the heavens and the plastic-nature theory for animals and plants, they were armed and equipped at all points, and ready to account for every thing without any divine intervention.

Cudworth's theory was attacked by Pierre Bayle, and defended by Le Clerc. A long controversy followed, in which the champion of a plastic nature was worsted; and that theory has long been buried in oblivion. This controversy occurred in the early part of the eighteenth century; but in Cudworth's own day he was himself assailed as an atheist in disguise, partly on account of his pet theory, but still more because he had given such fair and ample statement of atheistic objections and arguments.

Perhaps the plastic-nature theory might as well have been left in that limbo of exploded and forgotten things to which it was consigned nearly two centuries ago. But, besides the fact that it is a piece of obsolete natural theology which it falls in my way to investigate, it has curious relations with evolution by natural selection, which are food for thought. In fact, a greater amount of thinking might be generated and nourished upon the pabulum of these relations than could well be set down in this place. The summing-up and conclusion of such thoughts would, however, in my opinion, reveal a greater number of relations of difference than of likeness between the two theories. One apparent similarity is, that both were welcomed by atheists as enabling them to explain organic structures without invoking the *deus ex machina*. But however much aid and comfort they might extract from the plastic nature, they were hasty in supposing that evolution was harnessed to their cart. It has simply reduced the phenomena of biology under the reign of natural law, where vastly the greater part of the universe was already; thus making the problem of the relation of the cosmos to the Creator the same uniform problem for all sorts of phenomena. That is a very different thing from interposing a quasi-intelligent being between God and organic phenomena.

It would hardly be expected that Cudworth could make much of teleology; yet he does devote considerable space to it in the second volume. And this he does, notwithstanding his plastic-nature theory, which fills up so much of the first volume, had sapped the foundations of teleology. A great many of these old authors seem to enjoy a happy exemption from all sense of obligation to be consistent with themselves; or perhaps it would be more accurate to say, that they enjoy a happy obliviousness to the fact that they are not self-consistent. His teleology appears in the form of a doctrine of *final causes;* but he takes a singular view of *final cause*, making it synonymous with *mental* cause. This is, of course, correct to this extent, that final cause, or purpose, is mental; but incorrect when pushed to the extreme of exclusiveness, that is, when it is asserted that all mental causality is final. This is not indeed asserted, but it is plainly implied; although in the very same passage it is also implied that *efficient* cause may also be *mental*, thus furnishing a new illustration of the doctor's happy exemption from the bonds of self-consistency. Still more forcibly does it illustrate the power of working mischief and confusion, which is latent in the doctrine of final causes. But, although the passage in question is a long one, the reader shall see it for himself, and then judge whether Cudworth was not all at sea in regard to final and efficient cause : —

" It is no idol of the cave or den (to use that affected language) [1] — that is, no prejudice or fallacy imposed upon . ourselves, from the attributing our own animalish properties to the things about us — to think that the frame and system of this whole world was contrived by a perfect understanding Being or Mind (now also presiding over the same) which hath everywhere printed the signatures of its own wisdom upon the matter. . . . For it is altogether inconceivable how we ourselves should have mind and intention in us were there none in the universe, or in that highest principle from whence all proceeds. Moreover, it was truly affirmed by Aristotle, that there is much more of art in some of the things of nature, than there is in any thing artificially made by man ; and therefore intention, or final and mental causality, can no more be secluded from the consideration of natural, than it can from that of artificial, things. Now, it is plain that things artificial, as a house or clock, can neither be understood, nor any true cause of them assigned, without design, or intention for ends and good. For to say that a house is stones, timber, mortar, iron, glass, lead, etc., all put together, is not to give a definition thereof, or to tell what indeed it is, it being such an apt disposition of all these materials as will make the whole fit for habitation, and the uses of men. Wherefore this is not sufficiently to assign the cause of a house neither, to declare out of what quarry the stones were dug, nor in what woods or forests the timber was felled, and the like. [Here follows, in accordance with Cudworth's custom of fortifying each point by a classical quotation, a pas-

[1] He refers to Bacon's classification of fallacies.

sage from Aristotle, which I omit. It is Cudworth's opinion, not that of the Stagirite, that I am after.] Nor, lastly, if, as the same Aristotle elsewhere also suggesteth, one should further pretend that a house was therefore made such merely because the hands of the laborers, and the axes and hammers and trowels and other instruments, chanced all to be moved so and so, we say that none of all these would be to assign the true cause of a house, without declaring that the architect first framed in his mind a model or platform of such a thing to be made out of those materials, so aptly disposed into a foundation, walls, roof, doors, rooms, stairs, chimneys, windows, etc., as might render the whole fit for habitation, and other human uses. And no more certainly can the things of nature (in whose very essence final causality is as much included) be either rightly understood, or the causes of them assigned, merely from matter and mechanism, or the necessary and unguided motion thereof, without design and intention for ends and good. Wherefore to say that the bodies of animals became such, merely because the fluid seed, by motion, happened to make such traces, and beget such stamina and lineaments, as out of which that *compages* of the whole resulted, is not to assign a cause of them, but to dissemble, smother, and conceal their true efficient cause, which is the wisdom and contrivance of that divine Architect and Geometer, making them every way fit for the inhabitation and uses of their respective souls. Neither, indeed, can we banish all final — that is, all mental — causality from philosophy or the consideration of nature, without banishing at the same time reason and understanding from ourselves, and looking upon the things of nature with no other eyes than brutes do." (II. 608, *seq.*)

The whole passage is an argument against the exclusion of final causes from natural philosophy, in which Lord Bacon regarded them as intruders. You cannot account for a house, says Cudworth, without considering the plan of the architect, — that mental conception of the house which existed before the house itself. This is true enough, but not pertinent: the plan of the architect is neither the final nor the efficient cause, speaking in the language of a believer in final causes. Then he goes on to say, that the things of nature cannot be understood, or the causes of them assigned, "merely from matter and mechanism;" implying that the exclusion of final causes would leave only matter and mechanism; that is, that all mental causality is final. But in the next sentence he calls the "wisdom and contrivance of the divine Architect" an *efficient* cause; and again in the last sentence goes back to the notion that final causality includes "all mental causality." In short, he is completely tangled up and confused in regard to final and efficient causes.

The greater part of his teleology is brought in by way of replies to the objections raised by Lucretius, Epicurus, and the other old atomists. Thus he quotes from the Roman poet-philosopher: —

"You are by all means to take heed of entertaining that so dangerous opinion (to atheism) that eyes were made for the sake of seeing, and ears for the sake of hearing. But to think [says Cudworth] that not only eyes happened to be so made, and the use of seeing unintended followed, but also that in all the same animals ears happened to be so made too, and the use of hearing followed them; and a mouth and tongue happened to be so made likewise, and the use of eating and (in men) of speaking was also accidentally consequent thereupon; and feet were in the same animals made by chance too, and the use of walking followed; and hands made in them by chance also, upon which so many necessary uses depend; besides innumerable other parts of the body, both singular and organical, none of which could have been wanting without rendering the whole inept or useless. I say, to think that all these things should happen by chance to be thus made in every one and the same animal, and not designed by mind or counsel, that they might jointly concur and contribute to the good of the whole : this (supposition) argues the greatest insensibility of mind imaginable.''

As an argument against the hypothesis that chance, or a fortuitous concourse of atoms, produced, not only each organ, but all of them in their proper places and relations in the same animal, this is perfectly sound. But the Epicurean poet casts the objection in another form ; viz., —

" ' That eyes could not be first of all made intentionally for the use of seeing, nor ears intentionally for the use of hearing, and so for the rest ; because, forsooth, these things were all of them, in order of time and nature, before their several uses. There was no such thing as seeing before eyes were made, nor hearing before ears, nor speaking before the tongue. But the origin of the tongue much precedeth speech ; so likewise eyes and ears were made before there was any seeing of colors, or hearing of sounds. In like manner, all the other members of the body were produced before their respective uses.' The force of which argument consisteth in this proposition : that whatsoever is made for the sake of another thing must exist in time after that other thing, for whose sake it was made ; or that for which any thing is made must not only be in order of nature, but also of time, before that which is made for it. And this that Epicurean poet endeavors to prove by sundry instances : ' Darts were made for the sake of fighting, but fighting was before darts, or else they had never been invented. Bucklers were excogitated and devised for the keeping-off of blows, but the declining of strokes was before bucklers. So were beds contrived for the sake of resting and sleeping ;

but resting and sleeping were older than beds, and gave occasion for the invention of them. Cups were intended and designed for the sake of drinking, which they would not have been had there not been drinking before.' According to the force of which instances, the poet would infer that whosoever affirms eyes to have been made for the sake of seeing must suppose, in like manner, there was some kind of seeing or other before eyes. But, since there was no seeing at all before eyes, therefore could not eyes be made for the sake of seeing. . . . But it is evident that this logic of the atheists differs from that of all other mortals, according to which [that is, according to the logic of ordinary mortals] the end, or that for which any thing is made, is only *in intention* before the means, or that which is made for it, but in time and execution after it. And thus was the more effectual way of fighting and doing execution, for whose sake darts were invented, in time after darts, and only in intention before them. It is true, indeed, that fighting in general was before darts, sleeping before beds, and drinking before cups; and thereby did they give occasion for men to think of means for the more effectual fighting, and more commodious sleeping and drinking, men being commonly excited from the experience of things, and the sense of their needs and wants, to excogitate and provide fit means and remedies. But it doth not follow that the Maker of the world could not have at once beforehand a preventive knowledge of whatsoever would be useful and for the good of animals, and so make them intentionally for those uses.''

This is a satisfactory rejoinder. Because the function arises in time after the organ, — seeing after eyes were made, and so for the other organs and functions, — it does not from this fact necessarily follow that seeing might not have been thought of and intended before any eye existed. Both the objection and the response,

however, labor under some difficulty and obscurity
of expression, on account of the lack of a clear analysis of teleological reasoning.   Cudworth might have
made his answer much more clear and brief if he had
grasped the distinction between function and purpose,
as it is laid down in the introduction to this volume.
The *function* follows, but the *purpose* precedes, the
organ in the order of time.

He justly ridicules some of the consequences of the
fortuitous-concourse-of-atoms theory: —

"But our atomic atheists still further allege, that, though
it might well seem strange that matter fortuitously moved
should, at the very first jump, fall into such a regular frame
as this is, having so many aptitudes for uses, so many cor-
respondences between several things, and such an agreeing
harmony in the whole; yet it ought not to seem a jot strange
if atoms, by motion, making all possible combinations and
contextures, and trying all manner of conclusions and experiments, should, after innumerable other freaks and discon-
gruous forms produced, in length of time fall into such a
system as this is.   Wherefore they affirm that this earth of
ours, at first, brought forth divers monstrous and irregular
shapes of animals, 'some without feet, some without hands,
some without a mouth and face, some wanting fit muscles
and nerves for the motion of their members.'   And the old
philosophic atheists were so lavish herein, that they stuck
not to affirm, that, amongst those monstrous shapes of animals, there were once produced centaurs and scyllas and
chimæras, 'mixtly boviform and hominiform,' biform and
triform animals.   But Epicurus, a little ashamed of this, as
that which must needs look oddly and ridiculously, and
seeming more cautious and castigate, pretends to correct the
extravagancy of this fancy: 'Nevertheless, there were not
then any centaurs, nor biform and triform animals;' he add-
ing, that they who feigned such things as these might as

well fancy 'rivers flowing with golden streams, and trees budding with sparking diamonds, and such vastly gigantean men as could stride over seas, and take up mountains in their clutches, and turn the heavens about with the strength of their arms.' [Epicurus is squirming a little under the consequences of his theory ; and not having the boldness to face it out, and say with the founders of his school that Nature made an infinite number of vain and silly attempts before she produced a perfect animal, he is hedging, and building bridges in his rear to make good his retreat. But Dr. Cudworth is not going to let him off so easily. He has caught the old pagan in a ridiculous posture, and he proposes to pin him there.] Against all which, notwithstanding, he gravely gives such a reason as plainly overthrows his own principles : 'Because things, by a certain covenant of nature, always keep up their specific differences without being confounded together.' For what covenant of nature can there be in infinite chance? or what law can there be set to the absolutely fortuitious motions of atoms to circumscribe them by? [Very well said, doctor. If there is any "covenant of nature" about it, then it is no longer a fortuitous-concourse-of-atoms theory, but an evolution theory, proceeding by fixed laws.] Wherefore it must be acknowledged, that, according to the genuine hypothesis of the atomic atheism [away with your weak Epicurean dilutions of the genuine old theory !] all imaginable forms of inanimate bodies, plants, and animals, as centaurs, scyllas, and chimæras, are producible by the fortuitous motions of matter, there being nothing to hinder it [no "covenant of nature," or natural law], whilst it doth 'put itself into all kinds of combinations, play all manner of freaks, and try all possible conclusions and experiments.' "

Why, then, are not some of these monstrous shapes still in existence? Here comes in a theory of natural selection much more ancient than that of Charles Darwin : —

" But they pretend that these monstrous, irregular shapes of animals were not therefore now to be found, because, by reason of their inept fabric, they could not propagate their kind by generation, as neither indeed preserve their own individual existence. And that this atheistic doctrine was older than Epicurus appeareth from these words of Aristotle : ' When animals happened at first to be made in all manner of forms, those of them only were preserved, and continued to the present time, which chanced to be fitly made [survival of the fittest !] ; but all the others perished, as Empedocles affirmeth of the partly ox and partly man animals.' "

Replying to the objection of Descartes that it is presumptuous in man to affect a knowledge of the purposes of God, he says, —

" But the question is not whether we can always reach to the ends of God Almighty, and know what is absolutely best in every case, and accordingly make conclusions, that therefore the thing is or ought to be so ; but whether any thing at all were made by God for ends and good, otherwise than would have resulted of itself from the fortuitous motion of matter."

A very different question, truly, from the first. It would be presumption and folly for man to affect a knowledge of all the reasons why God has done this or that ; but when one or more of his reasons seems to be thrust in our very faces, as, in the case of the eye, its function of sight seems to be so obvious a reason for its existence, then Dr. Cudworth thinks very justly that it is no presumption at all to open our eyes, and see this purpose of the Creator : on the contrary, it would be the height of folly, and a piece of affected humility, to close our eyes to it, and say meekly that we decline the honor of knowing God's intentions. But this misunderstanding of the real question at issue, this notion that the teleologist was prying into the remotest corners and most ultimate grounds of God's purposes, all this trouble grew out of the phrase *final cause.*

" We see no reason at all why it should be thought presumption, or intrusion into the secrets of God Almighty, to affirm that eyes were made by him for the end of seeing (and accordingly so contrived as might best conduce thereunto), and ears for the end of hearing, and the like. This being so plain that nothing but sottish stupidity or atheistic incredulity (masked, perhaps, under an hypocritical veil of humility) can make any doubt thereof."

The learned doctor is rather handy with his epithets. " Insensibility of mind," " stupidity," " sottishness," are some of the pet names which he lavishes upon those mental states which do not absorb his opinions readily enough. He even becomes so much worried and wrought up as to speak of " these confounded atheists." [1] A worthy minister of the gospel once expressed his sense of the desirableness, in certain exasperating circumstances, of some form of words that would afford relief to pent-up feelings without committing the sin of profanity. If Cudworth did not completely solve this problem, he, at all events, reached a proximate solution, which seemed to afford him great contentment, judging from the frequency with which he applied it to practice.

---

[1] " That these confounded atheists themselves, who deny that there is any idea of God at all, must, notwithstanding, of necessity suppose the contrary; because otherwise, denying his existence, they should deny the existence of nothing." There is a curious sort of " double-back-action " in that argument. The heading to the fifth chapter, from which it is taken, is, by the way, " fearfully and wonderfully " gotten up. It occupies twenty closely printed pages; and in it the doctor laid out so much work that the chapter itself occupies more than seven hundred pages.

Dr. Cudworth gives a learned and very interesting disquisition upon the question, How far is it true that the ancients reached a conception of one only God? His conclusion is, that many of them believed in a Supreme Deity, but never wholly rid themselves of the notion of numerous inferior gods; and this is true even of Socrates, of whom "it hath been frequently affirmed, that he died a martyr for one only God." "And how conformable Socrates was to the pagan religion and worship may appear from those last dying words of his (when he should be most serious), after he had drunk the poison, wherein he required his friends to offer a votive cock for him to Æsculapius." A pagan he was, no doubt, every inch of him, and to the last gasp; but what a pagan!

CHAPTER IV.

SPINOZA'S CRITICISM OF FINAL CAUSES.

THE human mind is so constituted, that, upon every issue which takes any deep hold of the intellect and the emotions, enemies as well as advocates will be found. Whenever any large body of literature is produced in favor of a doctrine, some criticism is sure to follow. We have given the advocates of teleology a hearing: it is now in order to listen to the other side.

The "Ethics" of Benedictus de Spinoza, published in 1677 (the author having previously died in the same year), contains an appendix on "Final Causes:"—

"It is sufficient for the present to lay down this principle which everybody ought to admit, that all men are born in ignorance of causes, and that a universal tendency of which they are conscious leads them to search for that which is useful to themselves. The first consequence of this principle is, that men believe themselves to be free because they are conscious of volitions and desires, and do not at all consider the causes which influence them to will and to wish. It results, in the second place, that, as men act always for the sake of an end, — namely, the good or advantage which is the natural object of their desire, — so they come to demand always to know only the final causes of all possible actions ; and when they have heard these they are satisfied, not having within themselves any ground for further doubt. But, if they are unable to learn these final causes from some one else, nothing remains to them but to turn in upon themselves,

and to reflect upon the ends by which they are themselves
wont to be determined to similar actions; and thus they
necessarily judge of the mind of another by their own.

" Further, as within themselves and out of themselves they
discover many means which are highly conducive to the pursuit of their own advantage, — for example, eyes to see with,
teeth to masticate with, vegetables and animals for food, the
sun to give them light, the sea to nourish fish, etc.. — so they
come to consider all natural things as means for their benefit; and because they are aware that these things have been
found, and not prepared by them, they have been led to believe that some one else has adapted these means to their
use, for, after considering things in the light of *means*, they
could not believe these things to have made themselves, but
they must conclude that there is some ruler or rulers of nature endowed with freedom like men who have provided all
these things for them, and have made them all for the use of
men.   Moreover, since they have never heard any thing of
the mind of those rulers, they must necessarily judge of this
mind also by their own; and hence they have argued that
the gods direct all things for the advantage of man, in order
that they may subdue him to themselves, and be held in the
highest honor by him.   Hence each has devised, according
to his character, a different mode of worshipping God, in
order that God might love him more than others, and might
direct all nature to the advantage of his blind cupidity and
insatiable avarice.   Thus this prejudice has converted itself
into superstition, and has struck deep root into men's minds;
and this has been the cause of the universal tendency to
frame a conception of final causes, and to search for them.
But, while they have sought to show that nature does nothing in vain, — that is to say, nothing which is not useful to
men, — they seem to me to have shown nothing else than that
nature and the gods are as foolish as men.   And observe. I
pray you, to what a point this opinion has brought them.
Together with the many useful things in nature, they neces-

sarily found not a few injurious things ; namely, tempests, earthquakes, diseases, etc. How to explain these? They thought these happened because the gods were angry on account of offences committed against them by men, or because of faults incurred in their worship ; and although experience every day protests, and shows by infinite examples that benefits and injuries happen indifferently to pious and to ungodly persons, they do not therefore renounce their inveterate prejudice. For it was easier for them to class these phenomena among other things, the cause of which was unknown to them, and thus retain their present and innate condition of ignorance, than to destroy all the fabric of their belief, and excogitate a new one. Men have therefore maintained that the thoughts of God far exceed the limits of their understanding, and that opinion has kept the truth hidden from mankind until the science of mathematics taught another means of discovering it ; for everybody knows that this science does not proceed upon the principle of final causes, but regards solely the essence and the properties of figures. Add to this that, besides mathematics, we can assign other causes (of which it is needless to make an enumeration here) which have helped to open men's eyes to their prejudices, and to lead them to a true knowledge of things.

" These considerations will serve for the first point which I promised to explain. It remains to be shown that nature does not propose to itself any end in its operations, and that *all final causes are nothing but pure fictions of human imagination*. I shall have little trouble to demonstrate this ; for it has already been solidly established, as well by the explanation just given of the origin of the contrary prejudice, as by Prop. XVI. and the corollary to Prop. XXXII., without mentioning all the other demonstrations by which I have proved that all things produce themselves, and link themselves together by the eternal necessity and supreme perfection of nature. I will, however, add a few words in order to accomplish the total ruin of final causes. [Hear! hear!]

"The first fallacy is that of regarding as a cause that which is an effect, and *vice versa;* in the second place. that which is by nature anterior, it makes posterior; and, finally, it debases to the last degree of imperfection that which is most elevated and most perfect. To say nothing of the first two points, which are self-evident, it results from Props. XXI., XXII., and XXIII., that the most perfect effect is that which is produced immediately by God, and that an effect becomes more and more imperfect in proportion as the intermediate causes are more numerous. But, if those things which God produces immediately were made for the sake of an end which God proposes to himself, it will follow that those which God produces last will be the most perfect of all, the others having been made for the sake of these."

Which would be contrary to Props. XXI., XXII., and XXIII.: therefore final causes are nothing but pure fictions of human imagination, *quod erat demonstrandum!*

Lewes, in his "History of Philosophy" (ii. 207), quotes the first part of this passage, in which Spinoza vents his spleen at final causes in general terms and wordy declamation about "inveterate prejudices;" but he prudently omits the last part, containing the puerile mathematical demonstration of the fallacies of teleology, and the arrogant boast of Spinoza that he is now about to "destroy that whole doctrine of final causes."

His sixteenth proposition to which he refers, and which I give in order to do the fullest justice to his mathematical demonstration, is as follows: —

"Of necessity there must flow from the divine nature an infinity of things infinitely modified; that is to say, every thing which can fall under his infinite intelligence."

The thirty-second proposition is, "The will cannot be called a free, but only a necessary cause;" and the corollary to which he refers is, "It follows from this that God does not act by virtue of a free will."[1]

Granting that he had made good these propositions, it was certainly an easy task to make a complete wreck of final causes. If all natural objects flowed from God by virtue of a fatal necessity, and if he exercised no free will in creating any thing, of course it would be folly to look for any traces of a special purpose in his work. The substance of the other three propositions referred to by Spinoza is stated by himself in the above extract; viz., "that the most perfect effect is that which is produced immediately by God."

This refutation of final causes is a good example of the famous mathematical method of Spinoza. He seeks to give the effect of mathematical certainty to his conclusions; but, when we look closer to see how he does it, we perceive that the mathematics of it is in the *form*, rather than the internal principle, of his method. It is very easy to frame arbitrary assertions, label them *propositions* and *corollaries*, number them after the fashion of a text-book of geometry, and go through the motions of demonstrating them, and referring to them by number, in order to establish something else; but, when all is done, there is no more mathematical certainty about it than if it were not cast in a mathematical form. Bad logic is not good mathematics.

There is another point in respect to the garbling of this passage by Lewes. In his "Prolegomena" to the "History of Philosophy" he makes an elaborate metaphysical attack upon design-arguments. The gist of it is, that design-advocates are guilty of the fallacy of ὕστερον πρότερον, or "putting the cart before the horse."

[1] I have quoted from "Œuvres de Spinoza, traduites par Emile Saisset:" Paris, 1861, Vol. III. Ethics, Book I., and Appendix.

The notion of a *plan*, says he, arises in the mind by the contemplation of orderly phenomena. For instance, the notion of the vertebrated type among animals: the animals simply grew in that way, and the notion of a plan is superinduced upon the contemplation of such structures. The notion is posterior to the objects in the order of time, since it is aroused in the mind by the sight of these objects. But men invert this natural order of things, and say that the plan was conceived first, and the objects were made to conform to it; and this is "putting the cart before the horse."

Now, Spinoza said the very same thing: "That which is by nature anterior, it [the doctrine of final causes] makes posterior." Taken in connection with all that he had said about the origin of the prejudice in favor of final causes, it is very plain that Spinoza meant, that while the objects are naturally anterior to that human conception of their final cause, which he maintains arises simply from inveterate prejudice, and is a "pure fiction of human imagination," men invert this order, and make this "fiction" anterior to the object, and the cause of it. His "first fallacy, that of regarding as a cause that which is an effect, and *vice versa*," is the same notion under the aspect of cause and effect instead of chronological sequence; so that, if Lewes had gone a little farther in his quotation from Spinoza, the source of his inspiration in his labored attack upon design-arguments would have been too conspicuous. Not that any particular injustice was done to Spinoza in this matter. It was not his property that Lewes appropriated. He got the notion from the old atheistic atomists. It is essentially the same question to which Cudworth gave a tolerable answer.

Let us, however, examine the specific form in which

Spinoza and Lewes cast this old objection. Design-advocates, say they, are guilty of a fallacy of inversion, in that they project their own conception arising from the contemplation of an object beyond the object, and previous to it, as its cause, or as the plan according to which it was shaped. The accusation is perfectly valid upon one condition; viz., that there are no plans or purposes in nature back of the object, and according to which it was shaped. But suppose there are such plans and purposes? Then design-advocates have *not* been guilty of the fallacy of inversion. The plan did exist before the object; and it is not the human conception which is projected back into eternity as the Creator's thought, but that thought itself, which man *perceives* upon the contemplation of the object, instead of conceiving it as a "fiction of his imagination."

But, whether there are any such plans or not, one thing is plain: Spinoza and Lewes *assume* that there are none. The charge of a fallacy of inversion is valid only on that condition: hence, in making that charge, these men begged the question. There is a bald fallacy of *petitio principii* on their part, at any rate, no matter whether design-advocates are guilty or innocent of a fallacy. And, as regards the latter point, the accusation of a fallacy of inversion is not pertinent. It is not a legitimate attack. Design-advocates assert that there are plans and purposes in nature. That is their main position. The fact that these are prior in time is involved in this fundamental proposition. Now, Spinoza's attack resolves itself into this: Upon the assumption that your fundamental proposition is *false*, you are guilty of a fallacy of inversion.

As regards the tendency to look upon the whole universe with reference to its utility to man, Spinoza was attacking a real fallacy; and his exposure of it probably helped to banish it from teleology. We shall see evidence of greater care on this point in the next writer, whose work appeared after the publication of Spinoza's "Ethics." Considering how some men have in all ages made religion a cloak for "blind cupidity and insatiable avarice," we can have some charity for Spinoza's remarks on that head also.

CHAPTER V.

NATURAL THEOLOGY IN THE SEVENTEENTH CENTURY (*CONTINUED*): BOYLE AND RAY.

TEN years after the publication of Cudworth's "Intellectual System of the Universe"—namely, in 1688—appeared, in small octavo, a less pretentious, but more solid and sensible, treatise by Robert Boyle, a contemporary of Sir Isaac Newton, and himself holding a high and honorable place as a scientist. It is entitled "A Disquisition about the Final Causes of Natural Things." His friend, Mr. Henry Oldenburgh, secretary of the Royal Society, had propounded to Mr. Boyle these four questions:—

1. Whether, generally or indefinitely speaking, there be any final causes of things corporeal, knowable by naturalists.

2. Whether, if the first question be resolved in the affirmative, we may consider final causes in all sorts of bodies, or only in some peculiarly qualified ones.

3. Whether, or in what sense, the acting for ends may be ascribed to an unintelligent and even inanimate body.

4. How far, and with what cautions, arguments may be framed upon the supposition of final causes.

He opens fire at once upon the Epicureans and the Cartesians,—upon the former because they "think the world was the production of atoms and chance, without any intervention of a Deity;" upon the latter because "they judge, with Descartes, that God, being an omniscient agent, 'tis rash and presumptuous for men to think that they know, or can investigate, what ends he proposed to himself in his actings about his creatures." Inasmuch as the Epicureans have, in his opinion, been amply refuted already, he points his heaviest artillery at the Cartesians. At the same time he speaks very deferentially of Descartes himself, and lays the blame of his rejection of teleology upon the extravagances of the schoolmen : —

" Perhaps one thing that alienated that excellent philosopher from allowing the consideration of final causes in physics, was that the school-philosophers, and many other learned men, are wont to propose it too unwarily, as if there were no creature in the world that was not solely, or at least chiefly, designed for the service or benefit of *man:* insomuch that I remember I have seen a body of divinity published by a famous writer, wherein, to prove that the world would be annihilated after the day of judgment. he urgeth this argument: That, since the world was made for the sake of man in his travelling condition (*hominis viatoris causa*), when once man is possessed of his everlasting state of happiness or misery, there will be no further use for the world."

But twenty years earlier, in his work on "The Usefulness of Experimental Natural Philosophy," Boyle had himself stated the purposes of creation to be, (1) The glory of God; (2) The service of man.

In view of these abuses of the doctrine of final causes, Boyle proceeds to an analysis and classification of the ends in nature: (1) Universal ends, such as the displaying of the wisdom and power of the Creator; (2) Cosmical ends, such as may be involved in the distribution and motions of celestial bodies; (3) Animal ends, "which are those that the particular parts of animals are destinated to, and for the welfare of the animal itself;" (4) Human ends, which are further divided into *mental* and *corporeal*. As a means of guarding against the abuse referred to above, this classification of ends was a capital idea. It enables him to say to the Cartesians, We teleologists don't pretend to know *all* of God's purposes, but only *some* of them; nor do we pretend that the purpose we allege in any instance is the *only* one. Thus, in respect to the eye, " 'Tis not to be denied that he may have more uses for it than one, and perhaps such uses as we cannot divine; but this hinders not, but that among its several uses, *this*, to which we see it so admirably adapted, should be one."

But still more obviously does it meet the objection raised by Spinoza. Here is one teleologist, who, so far from regarding the whole universe with reference to human ends, makes these to constitute but one class out of four. We shall find from this time onward, that, notwithstanding occasional relapses upon the part of individuals, teleologists generally maintained a cautious and prudent reserve in respect to the extent to which nature was destined for human uses.

Boyle answers the first question in the affirmative. There are, he thinks, " final causes of things corporeal, knowable by naturalists."

Proceeding to the second question, Whether we may consider final causes in all sorts of bodies, or only in some peculiarly qualified ones, he, in the first place, very wisely rejects the celestial bodies from the list of things whose final cause we may, without presumption, affect to understand : —

"I am apt to fear that men are wont, with greater *confidence* than *evidence*, to assign the systematical ends and uses of the celestial bodies, and to conclude them to be made and moved only for the service of the earth and its inhabitants."

Very naturally he pitches upon the province of biology as containing the "peculiarly qualified" bodies whose final causes may be legitimately inquired after. And in this province he selects the *eye* as the best instance of all. He was well qualified to talk about the eye, having given much study to it; and there was bound up within the same covers containing his "Disquisition about Final Causes," a treatise with the title, "Some Uncommon Observations about Vitiated Sight." After a full description of the human eye, he proceeds to notice some peculiarities in the eyes of other animals, tracing each departure from the human type to some wise purpose in respect to the habitat or wants of the animal. Thus, in regard to the third eyelid of the frog's eye, he says, —

"In furnishing frogs with this strong membrane, the providence of nature seems to be conspicuous; for, they being amphibious animals, designed to pass their lives in watery places, which abound with sedges and other plants with sharp edges or points, and the progressive motion of this animal being to be made, not by *walking*, but by *leaping*, if his eyes were not provided with such a sheath as I have been mentioning. he must either shut his eyes, and so leap *blindly*, and by consequence *dangerously*, or, by leaving them open, must run a venture to have the *cornea* cut, pricked, or otherwise offended, by the edges or points of the plants. or what may fall from them upon the animal's eye : whereas this membrane, as was said, is like a kind of spectacle that covers the eye without taking away the sight, and. as soon as the need of employing it is past, the animal at pleasure withdraws it into a little cell, where it rests out of the way till there be occasion to use it again."

Harvey said of Lord Bacon, that he wrote about science like a lord chancellor : that is not Boyle's style. Even in this book on final causes, wherein he has turned theologian for the time being, he writes like a practical naturalist on familiar ground. Thus he goes on to tell the reader how to verify what he has said about the nictitating membrane of the frog : —

"This you may see if you apply the point of a pin or a pen, or any such sharp thing, to the eye of a frog whilst you hold his head steady ; for to screen his eye he will presently cover it (at least the greater part) with this membrane, which, when the danger is over, he will again withdraw."

With all his admirable caution, so sharply contrasted with the recklessness of many other teleologists, he gives some very dubious examples. For instance, he quotes with approval the opinion of "an ingenious cultivator of optics," that the reason why the pupil in the eyes of horses and oxen is a transverse slit, but in cats a vertical slit, "may be that horses and oxen being usually to find their food growing on the ground, they can more conveniently receive the images of the laterally neighboring grass, etc., by having their pupils transversely placed; whereas cats, being to live chiefly upon rats and mice, which are animals that usually climb up or run down walls and other steep places, the commodiousest situation of their pupil for readily discovering and following these objects was to be perpendicular."

To be able to accomplish the same end by a diversity of means, shows a high degree of skill. Thus, argues Boyle, it is a proof of man's wisdom that he can cause

the hours to be measured off and designated by means
of weights as the motive-power in clocks; but still
more skill is required to reach the same end in several
ways, as by using a spring for the motive-power instead
of a weight. So the Creator's wisdom is demonstrated
in that he has reached the end of the flight of animals
in the air by means of the feathered wings of birds,
the skinny membrane of bats, and even by means of
fins, as in the flying fishes.

Again the great variety of exquisite mechanical contrivances in nature carries the same inference, though
they be not all for the same end : —

"To be able to frame both clocks and watches and ships
and rockets and granadoes and pumps and mills, etc.,
argues and manifests a far greater skill in an artificer than
he could display in making but one of those sorts of engines, how artificially soever he contrived it."

This question of *degree* of skill manifested in the
productions of nature is quite another affair from that
with which teleology usually busies itself; viz., the
proofs of God's existence. Boyle seems to assume the
latter, or to regard it as certain enough upon other
grounds; and he employs teleology, as Cicero did,
solely to prove the wisdom and providence of God.
It does not appear distinctly from any thing he has
written, whether he supposed he was proving the existence of God, when, in fact, he was only giving instances of creative skill, and of the providential care
of his creatures exercised by a being whose existence
was quietly assumed instead of being demonstrated;
or whether he clearly perceived that he was only illustrating the wisdom and providence of God, and delib-
erately chose to cast his teleology in that form instead

of making it an argument for the existence of God.
Upon the first supposition he was guilty of a *petitio
principii*. If he set out to prove God's existence, he
begged the question. It would be too harsh to so
judge him without ample grounds for it; and, so far
from such grounds existing, all the probabilities are
against the first alternative. He was answering the
question whether there are any final causes at all; and
he did not concern himself with the further question,
What use can be made of teleology, supposing there is
such a thing? He did not attempt to prove God's existence by means of it.

Such, I say, seems to be the probable *status* of his
mind in respect to what he was attempting to do; and
hence there is no sufficient reason for accusing him of a
fallacy of the sort mentioned above. But yet we can
hardly go so far as to take the second alternative, and
say that he had a clear notion of simply illustrating
God's wisdom as displayed in nature. It is probable,.
rather, that he was in some measure involved in a
fallacy of confusion respecting the use of teleology.
This is the more likely, because, as we shall find in the
sequel, many other teleologists did set out with a confused notion of what they were going to accomplish by
means of teleological reasoning. Teleology is generally
regarded as an argument for the existence of God, and
so these writers view it in the abstract. But in the
practical development of it they treat it as a means of
illustrating the perfections of a being whose existence
is assumed; and just that is certainly what Boyle has
actually done, whatever it may have been that he intended to do. It is really a curious problem to study
this tendency of teleology. It was manifested so early
as the time of Socrates, and has cropped out all along

the line of its historical development. Men suppose they are going to prove the proposition, There is a God; but, when all is done, it turns out that they have assumed his existence, and argued for his wisdom or providence.

But if that argument is sound, if they have made good their propositions, God is wise, or God exercises a providence over his creation : does not that *include* the proof of his existence? Certainly it does, if providence and wisdom had been demonstrated independently; but they have not. The argument runs in this fashion : These structures (being God's work) are so exquisitely perfect, and so exactly adapted to the needs of animals, that God must be both wise to contrive them, and kind to provide his creatures with them. The words in parentheses are not expressed in the teleological reasonings of these writers, but they are understood. There would be no pertinence in what they say about providence and wisdom, except upon the assumption that the structures they are describing are the work of God. Now, it is perfectly legitimate to make that assumption, if their aim is simply to prove providence and wisdom, and nothing more. It amounts to something like this : Grant, for the sake of argument, that there is a God, and I will prove that he is wise, and cares for the wants of his creatures. But, having thus proved his providence and wisdom upon the assumption of his existence, it would be arguing in a circle to turn about, and claim that such a method of proving his providence proves also his existence.

Boyle's summary of his answer to the second question is as follows : —

" (1) I think, that, from the ends and uses of the parts of *living* bodies, the naturalist may draw arguments, provided he do it with due cautions, of which I shall speak under the fourth question. (2) That the *inanimate* bodies here below that proceed not from seminal principles have a more parable texture (if I may so speak), as earths, liquors, flints, pebbles, and will not easily warrant ratiocinations drawn from their supposed ends."

His third point, in respect to celestial bodies, has been given already. Biology is, in his opinion, the only legitimate field for teleology.

To the third question, "Whether, or in what sense, the acting for ends may be ascribed to an unintelligent and even inanimate body," he delivers a very thoughtful and prudent answer. It is to the effect, that such bodies do appear to act for ends, but without themselves having any knowledge whatever of what they do : they are mere instruments of the divine will. This is quite a different doctrine from the "plastic nature" of Cudworth.

In respect to the relation of matter and force to the divine will, modern theologians have drawn some fine distinctions. The different theories vary all the way from ascribing all natural phenomena to second causes, up to the opposite extreme of ascribing them all to the immediate agency of the divine will. One must walk a narrow plank among all these sharp distinctions : he must go far enough, and not too far. If he grants too much to second causes, his system becomes *mechanical;* if too little, it squints towards pantheism. Now, in what I said about the prudence of Boyle's answer to the third question, I had no reference, of course, to these fine distinctions. Judged by them he would probably be set down as too mechanical. He accounts for the action of bodies destitute of intelligence in such manner that they seem to work out

rational results, just as if they knew and intended what
they do, by the supposition that matter was so constituted in the beginning as that such actions should
follow, the results being foreseen and intended by the
Creator when he originally imparted to matter those
properties by virtue of which such results are from
time to time wrought out. He states his opinion very
briefly, apologizing for its brevity, and proposing to fill
out the section to a bulk proportionate to the others
by inserting some thoughts not properly coming under
the head of a response to the third question.

One is tempted to wish that he had felt strictly
bound by "the laws of method," which he admits
would have required him to stop when he was done;
For, upon examining the matter thus irrelevantly thrown
in as a sort of stuffing, or padding, we find that it is a
retraction or apology for excluding the celestial bodies
from teleology, as he had done in delivering his response to the second question. Here we see the unhappy consequences of leaving the arguments of physico-theology so long without proper analysis. Boyle
seemed to feel, that in excluding celestial phenomena
from teleology he had shut them out altogether, — a
thing which he knew would give offence, besides seeming in opposition to the Bible. "The heavens declare
the glory of God" keeps ringing in his ears, and he
must find some use for the stars in his system. Now, if
he had realized that the bare fact of celestial harmony,
irrespective of any end to be served by it, is a good
ground for argument, then he might have quieted his
conscience without committing the blunder of bringing
back into teleology a class of phenomena which he had
before excluded on good grounds. The heavens do
indeed declare the wisdom and power of the Creator;

but it is simply by virtue of their harmony and beauty, not because we know what all the stars are good for; that is to say, the argument from them belongs to eutaxiology instead of teleology. Boyle's first thoughts were better than his second thoughts. If he had made the analysis of physico-theological reasoning, and drawn the line between the argument from order and the argument from ends, he might have spared himself the labor and mortification of an apology for excluding teleology from astronomy.

But some one will say, If the heavens furnish a good argument for the existence of God, that in itself is an excellent end which they serve; and thus we bring celestial phenomena under teleology after all! That is, in fact, the very device to which Boyle resorted. And the other teleologists, if they were at a loss in assigning the purpose of any thing, were always ready to fall back upon the notion, that, if it wasn't good for any thing else so far as they knew, at all events it furnished good material for them to argue from. In that way they brought every thing in heaven and earth under teleology. Teleology was synonymous with *design*, and design was nearly synonymous with natural theology. It was all "adaptation," "contrivance for a purpose," "adjustment of means to ends," from the opening sentence to the last page of their books.

This misplacing of arguments was something more mischievous in its consequences than simply wasting good material by putting it in the wrong place. It robbed Peter without paying Paul. Eutaxiology was despoiled without enriching teleology: on the contrary, teleology was visibly and disastrously weakened by the mass of examples thrust bodily in where they did not belong. Reasoning from the adaptation of means to ends upon the strength of instances in which the end was quite out of sight and out of reach, was a barren occupation. The temptation to assign hypothetical and fanciful uses was constant and pressing. Thus, in respect to the stars, it was customary to argue that they must be inhabited (unless the teleologist took the view which Boyle deprecates, that the whole universe was made for the service and benefit of man); for otherwise they would be in vain, and nature does nothing in vain. It would have been a fine example of *circulus in probando* if they had then argued the wisdom of God from the provision thus made for so many more rational and happy creatures. Those creatures must be there, because God's wisdom would be impeached by the supposition of any useless thing in nature; and God must be wise because he has provided habitations for them. They did, in fact, go through the first half of that circle, and by plain implication traversed the other half also.

Proceeding to the fourth question, " With what cautions final causes are to be considered by the naturalists," Boyle at once draws a useful distinction as to the kinds of arguments which may be drawn " from the supposed ends of things." These may be *physical*, or physico-theological, — the former when we infer the nature of bodies from their supposed ends, " because by *this* and not by *that*, or by *this* more than by *that*, the end designed by nature may be best and most conveniently attained;" the latter when "from the uses of things men draw arguments that relate to the Author of nature." He regards the fourth question as having to do chiefly with the first, or the physical considerations and inferences from supposed ends; and he frames his first two propositions with especial reference to that interpretation of the question. The first proposition is, in substance, that we cannot infer the *nature* of celestial bodies from their final causes. That is sound and indisputable. In the second proposition he affirms, that, in respect to the bodies of animals, final causes are useful as a guide for investigation; and here occurs the original citation, so often repeated in later teleology, of Harvey's discovery of the circulation of the blood: —

" And I remember, that when I asked our famous Harvey, in the only discourse I had with him (which was but a while before he died), what were the things that induced him to think of a circulation of the blood, he answered me, that, when he took notice that the valves in the veins of so many several parts of the body were so placed that they gave free passage to the blood towards the heart, but opposed the passage of the venal blood the contrary way, he was invited to imagine that so provident a cause as nature had not placed so many valves without design; and no design seemed more probable than that, since the blood could not well, because of the interposing valves, be sent by the veins to the limbs, it should be sent through the arteries, and return through the veins, whose valves did not oppose its course that way."

We have shown in the Introduction, that this claim of a physiological value for teleology is based upon a confusion of ideas respecting *function* and *purpose*. If the reader will glance back at the several quotations I have given from Boyle, he will see that this author glides from *uses* to *ends*, and from *functions* to *purposes*, without appreciating their proper distinctness of meaning. Hence it was not to be expected that he would detect the fallacy in question.

The supposition of a certain end having been designed, is based upon the structure of the organ. For instance, the purpose of the venal valves to guide the blood towards the heart is inferred from the fact that they open in that direction. That is one inference. Now, says Boyle, we go on and infer the use or function from the end. But the fact is, that we make only one inference instead of two. We go directly from the structure to the function, instead of going about the circuit of inferring the end from the structure, and then the use from the end. There is no need of bringing in teleology at all, so far as the mere physiological investigation is concerned. And, if it ever comes in, it will be *subsequent* instead of *antecedent* to the determination of the function. After we have found out the actual use of a thing, we may then go on to argue that it was *intended* to be so used because of its eminent fitness for that function. What sort of a teleology could have been built up from the venal valves *before their function was discovered?*

In the third proposition he comes back to physico-theology : —

" It is rational, from the manifest fitness of some things to cosmical or animal ends or uses [ends and uses again spoken of as if they were synonymous], to infer that they were framed or ordained in reference thereunto by an intelligent and designing agent."

Under this proposition he brings in the great body of his teleology. As in the question, whether there are any final causes, he aimed more especially at the Cartesians; so in this part of his treatise he has the Epicureans more in view : —

" But because I observe, not without grief, that of late years too many otherwise perhaps ingenious men have, with the innocent opinions of Epicurus, embraced those irreligious

ones wherein the Deity and Divine Providence are quite excluded from having any influence upon the motions of matter, all whose productions are referred to the casual concourse of atoms: for this reason, I say, I thought it a part
of my duty, as well to the most wise Author of things, as
to their excellent contrivance and mutual subserviency, to
say something, though briefly yet distinctly and expressly, to
show that at least in the structure of animals there are
things that argue a far higher and nobler principle than is
blind *chance.*"

So he goes on to construct teleology from " *supera-
bundant provision for casualties,*"—*two* eyes, for instance,
where one might have served,—"in short, nature has
furnished men with double parts of the same kind;"
from *temporary expedients,* as the *foramen ovale* in the
fœtus, giving direct passage to the blood from the right
to the left ventricle of the heart, without passing through
the lungs, as it does after the child is born; from *the instincts of animals,* especially of bees, spiders, birds, and
beavers; from *the teeth,* an old topic, but more largely
and skilfully treated by him than by any previous
writer; and from the wings of bats, the mouths of various animals, the eyes of fishes, etc.

The fourth proposition is judiciously framed as a
caution both to the theologian and the naturalist:—

" That we be not over-hasty in concluding, nor too positive
in asserting, that this or that must be, or is, the particular
destinated use of such a thing, or the *motive* that induced
the Author of nature to frame it thus."

In the fifth proposition he comes again upon purely
physical grounds, and speaks as a naturalist:—

" That the naturalist should not suffer the search or the
discovery of a *final cause* of nature's works to make him

undervalue or neglect the studious indagation[1] of their *efficient causes.*"

Boyle's treatise did much to rescue teleology from the reproach to which it had been subjected by the incautious zeal of its advocates. This result was due, in the first place, to the judicious handling of his theme; but that would not have availed much in an obscure author. Boyle, however, was a prominent figure among the scientists of his day; and the adhesion of such a man to their cause was a strong point for the teleologists, — not that they were particularly in need, however, of such support. Teleology was the fashion among English scientists. The very next writer, and the last of the anti-Cartesian group of the seventeenth century, was no less a person than the celebrated botanist, John Ray. His little book on " The Wisdom of God manifested in the Works of the Creation" was published in 1691. Like Boyle, he was involved in some degree of confusion as to the function of teleology. Was it to be used to prove God's existence, or to prove his wisdom and providence? Shall teleology be our premise, and God's existence our conclusion, or *vice versa?* In the following passage he takes the latter alternative. Granting that God exists, then he must have intended certain results. A special direction has been purposely given to matter and force: there is such a thing as teleology.

" Since we find materials so fit to serve all the necessities and conveniences, and to exercise and employ the wit and industry of an intelligent and active being, and since there is such an one created that is endued with skill and ability to use them, and who by their help is enabled to rule over and subdue all inferior creatures, but without them had been left necessitous, helpless, and obnoxious to injuries above all

---

[1] Latin *indago*, to search out: "indagation" is obsolete.

others; and since the omniscient Creator could not but know all the uses to which they might and would be employed by man, *to them that acknowledge the being of a Deity*, it is little less than a demonstration that they were created intentionally, I do not say only for those uses."

The Italics are mine, introduced for the purpose of drawing attention to the words which define his standpoint. He is arguing for teleology rather than for the existence of God, just as Boyle did in the greater part of his work. But in the following passage he is using teleology in the customary way to prove the existence God : —

"For if in the works of art, as for example, a curious edifice or machine, counsel, design, and direction to an end appearing in the whole frame and in all the several pieces of it, do necessarily infer the *being* and operation of some intelligent architect or engineer, why shall not also in the works of nature, that grandeur and magnificence, that excellent contrivance for beauty, order, and use which is observable in them, wherein they do as much transcend the effects of human art as infinite power and wisdom exceed finite, infer the *existence* and efficiency of an omnipotent and all-wise Creator?"

It is my purpose to let each author speak for himself as much as possible. It may be that I am inclined to err in the direction of quoting too much; but I hope I may be pardoned for that, in consideration of the fact that my readers thus get some notion of the style of these old writers, which they would not do from a bare abstract of their arguments, however accurate that might be. Though the following passage is long for a quotation, there is a piquancy about it which will repay its perusal : —

"Methinks, by all this provision for the use and service of man, the Almighty interpretatively speaks to him in this

manner : I have placed thee in a spacious and well-furnished
world ; I have endued thee with an ability of understanding
what is beautiful and proportionable, and have made that
which is so agreeable and delightful to thee ; I have provided
thee with materials whereon to exercise and employ thy art
and strength ; I have given thee an excellent instrument, the
hand, accommodated to make use of them all ; I have distinguished the earth into hills and valleys and plains and
meadows and woods, all these parts capable of culture and
improvement by thy industry ; I have committed to thee, for
thy assistance in thy labors of ploughing and carrying and
drawing and travel, the laborious ox, the patient ass, and the
strong and serviceable horse ; I have created a multitude of
seeds for thee to make choice out of them of what is most
pleasant to thy taste, and of most wholesome and pleasant
nourishment ; I have also made great variety of trees, bearing
fruit both for food and physic, those, too, capable of being
meliorated and improved by transplantation, stercoration, in-
sition, pruning, watering, and other arts and devices.   Till
and manure thy fields, sow them with thy seeds, extirpate
noxious and unprofitable herbs, guard them from the invasions
and spoil of beasts ; clear and fence thy meadows and pas-
tures ; dress and prune thy vines, and so dispose them as is
most suitable to the climate ; plant the orchards with all sorts
of fruit-trees in such order as may be most beautiful to the eye,
and most comprehensive of plants [it is fortunate, when Providence sets out to speak "interpretatively," that she speaks
through the mouth of a systematic botanist] ; gardens for culinary herbs, and all kinds of salletting ; for delectable flowers
to gratify the eye with their agreeable colors and figures, and
thy scent with their fragrant odors ; for odoriferous and ever-
green shrubs and *suffrutices;* for exotic and medicinal plants
of all sorts, and dispose them in that comely order as may
be both pleasant to behold, and commodious for access.   I
have furnished thee with all materials for building, as stone
and timber and slate and lime and clay, and earth whereof

to make bricks and tiles. Deck and bespangle the country with houses and villages convenient for thy habitation, provided with out-houses and stables for the harboring and sheltering of thy cattle, with barns and granaries for the reception and custody and storing up of thy corn and fruits. I have made thee a sociable creature, ζῶον πολιτικὸν,[1] for the improvement of thy understanding by conference and communication of observations and experiments. For mutual help, assistance, and defence, build thee large towns and cities, with straight and well-paved streets, and elegant rows of houses, adorned with magnificent temples for my honor and worship, with beautiful palaces for thy princes and grandees [a truly loyal and royal sort of a Providence this], with stately halls for public meetings of the citizens and their several companies, and the sessions of the courts of judicature, besides public porticos and aqueducts. I have implanted in thy nature a desire of seeing strange and foreign, and finding out unknown, countries for the improvement and advancement of thy knowledge in geography by observing the bays and creeks and havens and promontories, the outlets of rivers, the situations of the maritime towns and cities, the longitude and latitude, etc., of those places; in politics, by noting their government, their manners, laws, and customs, their diet and medicine, their trades and manufactures, their houses and buildings, their exercises and sports, etc.; in physiology or natural history, by searching out their natural rarities, the productions both of land and water, what *species* of animals, plants, and minerals, of fruits and drougues, are to be found there, what commodities for bartering and permutation,[2] whereby thou mayest be enabled to make large additions to natural history, to benefit

[1] Of course Providence understands the classical languages. No wonder she *can* speak Greek; but *would* she, in addressing mankind in general, learned and ignorant all in a mass?

[2] "Permutation," exchange of specimens. Ray was a great traveller and collector; and, when Providence speaks through him, the message is slightly tinged with his personal experiences and idiosyncrasies.

those other sciences, and to benefit and enrich thy country by
increase of its trade and merchandise. I have given thee
timber and iron to build thee hulls of ships, tall trees for
masts, flax and hemp for sails, cables and cordage for rig-
ging; I have armed thee with courage and hardiness to
attempt the seas, and traverse the spacious plains of that
liquid element; I have assisted thee with a compass to
direct thy course when thou shalt be out of all ken of land,
and have nothing in view but sky and water. Go thither for
the purposes before mentioned, and bring home what may be
useful and beneficial to thy country in general, or thyself in
particular.''

Ray's Providence is evidently a stout, English,
church-and-king affair. I say this in no spirit of levity,
nor have I introduced this quotation simply for its
quaintness. The purpose of it is to point a moral,
rather than to adorn and lighten the dry pages of this
review of obsolete teleology. The moral is this: Here
is a man telling what God would say to mankind, rehearsing the divine message inscribed upon the open
page of nature; and he makes the Almighty talk, not
only like a man, but like an Englishman; not only like
an Englishman, but like an English scientist of the
seventeenth century; not only like an English scientist
of the seventeenth century, but verily like a sort of
sublimated *John Ray!* This is anthropomorphism with
a vengeance! No wonder that Hume charged teleologists with fashioning their God entirely upon the human
model when he had such examples as this before him!

He opens his argument by an attempt to show that
the number of God's creatures is infinite; this being "a
demonstrative proof of the unlimited extent of the
Creator's skill, and the fecundity of his wisdom and
power." To get at this point, he begins with the

acknowledged fact that the number of fixed stars is "next to infinite;" secondly, each star is a sun "with a *chorus* of planets circling about it;" thirdly, "each of these planets is in all likelihood furnished with as great a variety of corporeal creatures, animate and inanimate, as the earth is." That would give us a " prodigiously great " number of creatures, without question.

Still running upon the idea of numbers as an evidence of divine Wisdom, he next gives an estimate of terrestrial species. This is worth quoting, if for no other reason, simply because it is the work of the foremost naturalist of his day, and thus exhibits the *status* of natural history two centuries ago as compared with what it is to-day.

Premising that "how much the more imperfect any genus or order of beings is, so much the more numerous are the *species* contained under it. If this rule, I say, holds good, then there should be more species of *fossils*,[1] or generally of inanimate bodies, than of vegetables; of which there is some reason to doubt, unless we will admit all sorts of formed stones to be distinct species."

" *Animate bodies* are divided into four great *genera*, or *orders*, — *beasts, birds, fishes,* and *insects.*

" The species of beasts, including also serpents, are not very numerous; of such as are certainly known and described, I dare say, not above a hundred and fifty.

" The number of birds known and described may be near five hundred; and the number of fishes, secluding shell-fish, as many; but, if shell-fish be taken in, more than double the number. How many of each genus remain yet undiscovered one cannot certainly nor very nearly conjecture, but we may suppose the whole sum of beasts and birds to exceed by a third part, and fishes by one-half, those known.

---

[1] He takes " fossils " in a more generic sense than is customary now.

" The insects, if we take in the exsanguious, both terrestrial and aquatic, may, in derogation to the precedent rule, for number, vie even with plants themselves. For the exsanguious alone, by what that learned and critical naturalist, my honored friend Dr. Martin Lister, hath already observed and delineated, I conjecture, cannot be fewer than eighteen hundred or two thousand species, perhaps many more."

This being the number of " the exsanguious alone," he reaches, by conjecture and estimate, the conclusion that " the species of insects in the whole earth (land and water) will amount to ten thousand; and I do believe they rather exceed than fall short of that sum."

" The number of plants contained in C. Bauhin's ' Pinax' is about six thousand, which are all that had been described by the authors that wrote before him, or observed by himself."

Ray thinks that many of Bauhin's species were not good ones; they being erected upon the supposition "that different color or multiplicity of *leaves in the flower*, and the like accidents, were sufficient to constitute a specific difference. But, supposing there had been six thousand then known and described, I cannot but think that there are in the world more than double that number."

Only about thirty thousand species of animals and plants altogether! Certainly a very modest estimate, considering that the interests of his argument would be served best by making the number as large as possible.

" What can we infer from all this? If the number of creatures be so exceeding great, how great, nay immense, must needs be the power and wisdom of him who formed them all ! "

In opposition to Descartes' exclusion of final causes from natural philosophy, Ray says, —

"For first, seeing, for instance, that the eye is employed by man and all animals for the use of vision, which, as they are framed, is so necessary for them that they could not live without it, and God Almighty knew that it would be so; and seeing it is so admirably fitted and adapted to this use that all the wit and art of men and angels could not have contrived it better, if so well, — it must needs be highly absurd and unreasonable to affirm either that it was not designed at all for this use, or that it is impossible for man to know whether it was or not."

Here, again, he is arguing for the existence of teleology, which is all very well in itself. Teleology had been attacked, and it was entirely proper to defend it. But mark how it is done. "God Almighty knew that it would be so," that eyes would be used for seeing: therefore he intended them for this end; that is to say, there is a teleology. Even that is all legitimate enough, unless he proposes to use teleology to prove God's existence. Then it will be reasoning in a circle. But that is precisely what he does next. His first argument against Descartes being that just quoted, the second is, "How can man give thanks and praise to God for the use of his limbs and senses" unless he knows they were intended for their respective functions? And the third is that Descartes' opinion "supersedes and castrates the best *medium* we have to demonstrate the being of a Deity." It is plain that he still regards teleology as a means of proving God's existence, although *he is compelled to assume the latter in order to show that there is any such thing as teleology.*

Ray quotes largely from Boyle and Cudworth, and generally with approval. But he attacks Boyle's hypothesis of an original endowment of matter with such properties as to work out the regular, and, so to speak, artful, productions of nature. He thinks that these properties and motions of matter need to be constantly maintained as well as originally imparted, and for this service he brings in Cudworth's "plastic nature" to supplement Boyle's doctrine. He thinks that the "vegetative soul" of plants cannot account for their growth and nutrition, because "the segments and cuttings of some plants — nay, the very chips and smallest fragments of their body, branches, or roots — will grow, and become perfect plants themselves; and so the vegetative soul, if that were the architect, would be divisible, and consequently no spiritual or intelligent being, which the *plastic principle* must be as we have shown. For that must preside over the whole economy of the plant, and be one single agent, which takes care of the bulk and figure of the whole, and the situation, figure, and texture of all the parts, root, stalk, branches, leaves, flowers, fruit, and all their vessels and juices. I therefore incline to Dr. Cudworth's opinion, that God uses for these effects the subordinate ministry of some inferior *plastic nature*, as in his works of providence he doth of angels."

He thinks it still more incredible "that the *bodies of animals* can be formed by matter divided and moved by what laws you will or can imagine, without the immediate presidency, direction, and regulation of some intelligent being. . . . You will ask me who or what is the operator in the formation of bodies of man and other animals? I answer, The sensitive soul itself, if it be a spiritual and immaterial substance, as I am inclinable to believe; but, if it be material, as I can hardly admit, then we must have recourse to a *plastic nature*."

He is even more positive than Cudworth that the "plastic nature" is intelligent; and he is sure it must be invoked to account for the symmetrical growth of plants, and in one contingency of animals also. It is strange that he did not perceive how fatal this would be to teleology. While he thus leans to Cudworth in respect to the plastic nature, he differs from that learned divine in respect to the composition of matter: he "rather inclines to the *atomic hypothesis.*" He "can hardly admit" that the *soul* is *material!* He was accused of being a materialist, and such doubtful language as that almost justifies the charge.

He makes use of cutaxiology as well as teleology: "For the celestial or heavenly bodies, the equability and constancy of their motions, the certainty of their periods and revolutions, the conveniency of their order and situations, argue them to be ordained and governed by wisdom and understanding; yea, so much wisdom as man cannot easily fathom or comprehend." It is evident, however, that he was unconscious of any distinction between the two kinds of reasoning. Practically it was all teleology to him. If he argued from the order of nature, it was with some mental reference to an end after all. And the greater part of his work is clearly teleological. Thus he goes over the list of the elements, — fire, water, earth, and air, — giving detailed statements of the usefulness of each.

"The uses of fire (I do not here speak of the Peripatetics' elementary fire in the concave of the moon, which is but a mere figment, but our ordinary culinary) are in a manner infinite for dressing and preparing of victuals baked, boiled, and roast," etc. "The air serves us all and all animals to breathe in, containing the fuel of that vital flame we spake of, without which it would speedily languish and go out. . . . Water is one part, and that not the least, of our sustenance, to say nothing of those inferior uses of washing and bathing, dressing and preparing of victuals. But if we shall consider the great *conceptacula* and *congregations* of water, and the distribution of it all over the dry land in springs and rivers, there will occur abundant arguments of wisdom and understanding. The sea, what infinite variety of fishes doth it nourish! . . . Another meteor is the wind, which how many uses it doth serve to is not easy to enumerate, but many it doth: viz., to ventilate and break the air, and dissipate noisome and contagious vapors, which otherwise, stagnating, might occasion many diseases in animals; and therefore it is an observation concerning our native country, *Anglia ventosa, si non ventosa venenosa.*"

Speaking of the symmetrical forms of minerals, —

"Many of them shoot into regular figures, as crystal and bastard diamonds into hexagonal; others into those that are more elegant and compounded, as those formed in imitation of the shells of testaceous fishes of all sorts, shark's teeth, and vertebræ. etc., — if these be originally stones, or primary productions of nature in imitation of shells and fishes' bones, and not the shells and bones themselves petrified, as I have sometimes thought."

He had a faint suspicion of the true nature of fossils. Tournefort thought they grew from seeds like plants.

Having thus gone through with the elements — fire, water, earth, and air — in his systematic review of nature, he comes to plants. Here he is on familiar ground, and speaks with authority. It is impossible to do justice to this part of his teleology by means of quotations. To make them long enough to exhibit his views completely would be tedious; and to begin to quote without giving enough would be unjust. He quotes from Dr. More frequently, but his own views are much sounder than those of that pioneer in the teleological work of the seventeenth century. Especially is he to be commended for the total rejection of More's doctrine of the *signatures* of plants.

Passing on to the animal kingdom, it is evident at a glance that he is less guarded in his selection of examples just in proportion to the inferior degree of his mastery of the principles of zoölogy as compared with botany. He dwells at great length upon those animal actions which may be referred to instinct, though he does not so refer them in many cases. One of the elements of popularity in teleological works is developed in this part of his book. The teleologist has a splendid opportunity to select the curious and striking things in natural history, and describe them in popular language, thus making his book attractive to readers whose very lack of scientific training is the best qualification for the enjoyment of such descriptions, because they read them with a vague wonder at the erudition of the author, the dexterity of nature, and the wisdom of the Creator; and also with a complacent feeling that they are themselves becoming naturalists by virtue of the possession of a heterogeneous mass of the curious secrets of nature. And as the lack of thorough scientific knowledge is the best qualification for the readers of a teleology based upon such examples, so it is of the author also. The amateur in science whose information is bookish, rather than observational, is the very man to do such work with zeal and complacency. Thus we see that Ray is much more cautious on botanical ground where his knowledge was extensive, than upon zoölogical ground where it was much less complete. He describes at length the tongues of ant-eaters, and of the

chameleon, and of the woodpecker. These and the disposition of the toes of the woodpecker, two behind and
two in front, so favorable to the climbing habits of that
species, he regards as very striking examples of the
wisdom of the Author of nature. Besides the incongruity of inferring infinite wisdom from isolated and
trivial examples, there are one or two other objections to
such a line of reasoning. The example of the woodpecker's tongue cuts both ways; being so nicely adapted for
dragging grub-worms out of their holes, the provision
of it was certainly kind to the bird, but hard on the
worm. And, with respect to the tongues of toothless
animals, the same double-edged quality appears: the
ants deserve some consideration as well as the ant-eaters. But beyond that objection emerges once more the
singular paradox which we have already observed, that
the old teleologists are equally happy no matter whether
the event turns out thus and so, or just the very opposite. If teeth are present, it was wise to provide them;
if they are absent, it was wise to do without them.

Having thus taken a cursory survey of the whole
universe, he proceeds to "select some particular pieces
of the creation, and to consider them more distinctly.
They shall be only two, (1) The whole body of the
earth; (2) The body of man." His teleological bias
leads him to maintain that no part of the earth is useless. The polar regions support great multitudes of
fishes; and "we know that the chief whale-fishing is in
Greenland [in the waters adjacent, I suppose he meant],
and on land, bears and foxes and deer, in the most
northerly country that was ever yet touched; and,
doubtless, if we shall discover farther to the very North
Pole, we shall find all that tract not to be vain, useless,
or unoccupied." The same extreme claim of utility

in every part is maintained with respect to the human body: " There is nothing in it deficient, nothing super- fluous, nothing but hath its end and use."

In a multitude of his examples he is grinding over the same grist which had already been through the mills of previous teleologists. This is true of his ex- tended discussion of the eye and the hand, — those two favorite examples, which cut such a prominent figure in teleology from the earliest times to the latest. What- ever original contributions he. added to the science we find in like manner caught up by his successors, and served anew with some tempting adjuncts in the form of modern phrases, as cooks trick out their warmed- up dishes with fresh and attractive trimmings. Here is a piece of teleology which appears in Paley's work a century later : —

" The great wisdom of the Divine Creator appears in that there is pleasure annexed to those actions that are necessary for the support and preservation of the *individuum*, and the continuation and propagation of the *species;* and not only so, but pain to the neglect or forbearance of them. For the support of the person it hath annexed pleasure to eating and drinking, which else, out of laziness or multiplicity of busi- ness, a man would be apt to neglect, or sometime forget."

Ray's example justifies the criticism of Brougham, that the earlier writers made no distinction between natural theology and natural religion. He passes ab- ruptly from the one to the other; and the last pages of his book are entirely hortatory, in the style of the "im- provements" which commentators used to append to their exegeses.

CHAPTER VI.

NEWTON, GREW, AND DERHAM.

THE eighteenth century abounds in teleological productions. Some of the greatest minds of that century lent their brilliant powers and the prestige of their names to the construction of teleology, and its propagation among the masses. On the other hand, some of the most acute reasoners and profoundest thinkers of the age subjected teleology to a searching criticism. Foremost of the former class stands Sir Isaac Newton; among the latter, Immanuel Kant and David Hume.

The service which Newton rendered was more that of a silent than an active partner. He wrote very little about teleology; but his position in its favor was so frankly and distinctly avowed, that it carried over to that side all the weighty influence which his great name was capable of exerting. The following passage, quoted from his "Optics" (Book III., Query 81), published in 1721, is a specimen of the style in which he handled design-arguments:—

"For, while comets move in very eccentric orbs in all manner of positions, blind fate could never make all the planets move one and the same way in orbs concentric. . . . Such a wonderful uniformity in the planetary system must be allowed the effect of choice. And so must the uniformity in the bodies of animals, they having generally a right and left side shaped alike, and on either side of their bodies two legs behind, and either two arms, or two legs or two wings, before upon their shoulders ; and between their shoulders a neck running down into a backbone, and a head upon it; and in the head two ears, two eyes, a nose, a mouth, and a tongue alike situated."

That is, situated in the same relative positions in different animals. He is getting at the notion of general morphology, a common type for all vertebrates. This, of course, is eutaxiology rather than teleology, as is the argument drawn by him from celestial phenomena. It is interesting to note how prominent eutaxiology becomes in his treatment of design-arguments. The remainder of this passage is more teleological; for he no doubt uses " contrivance " in the conventional sense of teleologists, — that of adaptation of means to an end. At all events, he framed clear examples of teleological reasoning in other cases.

" Also the first contrivance of those very artificial parts of animals — the eyes, ears, brain, muscles, heart, lungs, midriff, glands, larynx, hands, wings, swimming-bladders, natural spectacles [probably he has reference to the nictitating membranes of birds and other animals, so fully discussed by Boyle], and other organs of sense and motion, and the instinct of brutes and insects — can be the effect of nothing else than the wisdom and skill of a powerful, ever-living Agent."

Newton belongs as much to the seventeenth century as the eighteenth, — more, indeed, as regards his general work and influence. He was lecturing on Optics at Cambridge in 1669, 1670, and 1671, when Cudworth was writing his " Intellectual System ; " and his greatest work, the " Principia," came out two years before Boyle's " Disquisition on Final Causes." But his theological work was of later date, and falls within the next century.

It is a great descent from Sir Isaac Newton to Nehemiah Grew, M.D. The "Cosmologia Sacra" of the latter appeared in 1701. Book I. contains his arguments for the existence of God. He begins with the ontological and causal arguments in the first chapter. In the second chapter he recites the leading facts of astronomy and meteorology. At first one would suppose that he was constructing a eutaxiology; but, instead of arguing simply from the order of the heavens, he turns it all into a teleology by claiming that the moon and all the planets have a distribution of land and water similar to the earth, and have an atmosphere with rains, dews, and snow, "and herewithal a suitable, though perhaps a different, furniture of animals, plants, and mines." He even extends his inference to the fixed stars with all their planets. For "there can be no manner of symmetry in furnishing so small a part of the universal expansion with so noble an apparatus as aforesaid, and letting innumerable and far greater intervals lie waste and void. If, then, there are many thousands of visible and invisible fixed stars, or suns, there are also as many planetary systems belonging to them, and many more planetary worlds. For we can have no sight nor conception of the utmost bounds of the universe, no more than of the omnipotent wisdom by which it was made." He goes through both halves of the *circulus in probando* referred to in the last chapter.[1] He infers the inhabitation of the planets from divine wisdom, and the boundless extent of that wisdom from the contemplation of the countless hosts of heaven being all the abodes of happy creatures.

[1] See p. 144 of this vol.

However, in the third chapter he does construct a eutaxiological argument, and lets it stand as such, without spoiling it by referring the objects which he describes to the principle of utility. He takes up the phenomena of crystallization, describing some very beautiful forms, and referring to a paper of his on the subject in the proceedings of the Royal Society.

" Wherefore, by the regularity of compounded bodies which we see, we are sure of it [that is, sure of regularity] in their principles, which we see not. Now regularity, which is certain, cannot depend upon chance, which is uncertain; for that were to make uncertainty the cause of certainty. Suppose we then that any figures can be made by motion upon matter, yet regular figures can never come but from motion regulated, and therefore not casually made; for then it would be casually regular, or by rule of chance, which is nonsense. [The phrase '' rule of chance '' is nonsense, he thinks, because self-contradictory : rule and chance are antagonistic, and mutually destructive.] It is therefore evident, that, as matter and motion, so the sizes and figures of the parts of matter, have their original from a divine Regulator, — the curious and manifold varieties of which [that is, of the sizes and figures of the parts of matter, if we could penetrate to its most intricate recesses] could we see, they would doubtless make as fine a show as all the beauties of nature which lie before us."

In the fourth and fifth chapters his reasoning is entirely teleological : —

. " What can be more admirable than for the *principles* [this word means atoms, or molecules, with Dr. Grew] of the fibres of a tendon to be so mixed as to make it a soft body, fit to receive and to communicate the species of sense [that is, nervous impressions], and to be easily nourished and moved, and yet with this softness to have the strength of iron! — as appears it hath by the weight which the tendon lying on a horse's gambrel doth then command, when he rears up with a man upon his back. [A truly remarkable case!]

"What more wonderful than to see two humors of equal use to true vision, bred so near together as to be contained within one common coat, yet one of them clear as crystal, the other black as ink?"

He refers to the crystalline lens and the black pigment of the choroid coat of the eye.

"How great a comprehension of the nature of things did it require to make a menstruum that should corrode all sorts of flesh coming into the stomach, and yet not the stomach itself, which is also flesh!"

And so the doctor goes on with an abstract of human anatomy, dwelling especially upon the ear and eye: —

"Among the many varieties [variations?] both in the inner and the outer ear, those which appear in the passage into the *rock-bone* are remarkable. For in an owl, that perches on a tree or beam, and harkens after the prey beneath her, it is produced further out *above* than it is below, for the better reception of the least sound. But in a fox, that scouts underneath the prey at roost, it is for the same reason produced further out *below*. In a polecat, which harkens straight forward, it is produced behind for the taking-in of a forward sound; whereas in a hare, which is very quick of hearing and thinks of nothing but being pursued, it is supplied with a bony tube, which, as a natural *otocoustic*, is so directed backward as to receive the smallest and most distant sound that comes behind her. And in a horse, which is also quick of hearing, and receives the sound of the driver's voice or whip behind, the passage into his ear is not unlike to that in a hare.

"Among the varieties of teeth in the rabbit and hare this

is singular : that within, or behind the fore-teeth of the upper jaw, there stand two other teeth, which may be called *incudes*. These, by receiving the appulse of the two incisors or chisels in the nether jaw, do thereby secure both the gums of the upper from being contused, and the muscles of the nether from being strained, by over-shooting."

One thing at least may be said to the credit of Dr. Grew, — namely, that he is quite original in his illustrations ; and, considering how thoroughly the field of teleology had already been ransacked in his day, this is a considerable merit. Another noteworthy thing is, that he does not, strictly speaking, construct any argument whatever from his examples. He is content to say, " This is very singular ; " " How admirable is this contrivance ! " " What a stupendous machine is the eye, if we survey the muscles, membranes, and humors, whereof it is composed ! " (p. 25.) That, by the way, is *not* an original example of teleology ! Thus he goes on dealing out exclamations and notes of admiration, but does not inform us either what conclusion we shall draw from these examples, or by what logical steps he expects us to reach whatever conclusion he desires. It is impossible to say whether he means to use teleology to prove God's existence, or, assuming that, to prove the greatness of his wisdom and the minuteness of his providential oversight of his creatures.

" What a catalogue of uses hath one small part, the tongue ! Sundry whereof anatomists take no notice of. It is so necessary unto speech as to assist in the making at least *eighteen* of the *twenty-four* letters, and in all vocal music helpeth the windpipe to modulate the sounds. 'Tis the tasting test of all kinds of meats, drinks, and medicines. No sort of teeth would serve us to eat without a tongue, which rolls the meat from one side of the mouth to the other, and puts it between the grinders as it needs them. Children and others could not suck without it; for, in drawing any liquid into the mouth, it doth the same as the sucker of a syringe or pump. Nor therefore could we sup or swallow without it, while [i.e.. since] it helps us with the tip end to take what we eat and drink into our mouths, and by the middle or vertical part, and the root, to convey it down the throat; as also it doth to cleanse our lips and teeth when we have done. No man could spit from him without it, but would be forced to drivel like some paralytics or a fool; the tongue being a stop-cock to the air, till, upon its sudden removal, the spittle is thereby driven away before it. Nor would any one be able to snite[1] his nose, or to sneeze; in both which actions the passage of the breath through the mouth being intercepted by the tongue, 'tis forced, as it then ought to do, to go through the nose. Besides the uses it hath in other creatures, as in the woodpecker to catch the prey, as is before described; in dogs to lick and lap, which is their drinking; and in cats for scratching and combing their hair, the tongue of a cat being furnished with crooked prickles, like the wires of a card, for that purpose.

"Nor is the manifold use of one part more admirable than to see how many parts conspire and serve together unto one use. We cannot so much as talk without the concurrence of twelve or thirteen different parts, — viz., the nose, lips, teeth, palate, jaw, tongue, weasand, lungs, muscles of the chest, diaphragm, and abdomen, — which are likewise so many systems of other organical parts [that is, each of the dozen parts is a system of subordinate parts, making the whole business still more complicated], all serving to make or to modulate the sound; besides the ears, which, by commission from the chamber of audience in the brain, set all the rest on work."

---

[1] "To snite his nose;" that is, to blow his nose. The preterite's *not* entirely obsolete.

It is uncertain just what he means by the ears setting all the rest at work. Does he refer to the fact that the deaf are also mute, or to the reflex action of speech in response to a voice? In either case his language is inaccurate. The ears do not, by commission from the brain, set the vocal organs in motion; although it is true that the trained movement of those organs in articulate speech depends upon hearing.

"No less than forty or fifty muscles, besides all other subservient parts, go to execute that one act of laughter; divers of those in the nose, lips, cheeks, and chin for figuring the face; of those in the weasand, chest, diaphragm, and abdomen for making the noise by the explosion of the air."

He makes out a curious mathematical proportion in respect to the correlation of structures: —

"In the use of things is seen that relation which answers in some sort unto geometric proportion. So those creatures whose motion is slow are blind, but those which have a quick motion have eyes to govern or determine it; that is, as blindness is to a slow motion, so is sight to a quick. So those animals which have ears have also lungs; and, *vice versa*, those which have no ears have no lungs: for as eyes are to motion, so are ears to speech.

"This relation is likewise seen in the agreeableness between man and other parts of the universe, and that in sundry respects. With respect to his figure; for he might as easily have been made a reasonable beast or a reasonable bird. But, had he been a quadruped, his figure would have wanted that majesty which is suitable to his dominion over all other creatures. His fore-feet would also have hindered his amicable and his conjugal embraces. Had he been a bird, he would have been less sociable; for, upon every true or false ground of fear or discontent, and other occasions [occasions enough in all conscience], he would have been fluttering away to some other place; and mankind, instead of cohabiting in cities, would, like the eagle, have built their nests upon rocks. And in both cases [beast or bird] he must have wanted hands. As also with respect to his bulk; for, had he been a dwarf, he had scarce been a reasonable creature. For he must then have either had a jolt-head, and so there would not have been body or blood enough to supply his brain with spirits; or he must have had a small head, answerable to his body, and so there would not have been brain enough for his business. Certain it is that no man, monstrously great or little, was ever known to be very wise. Or, had the species of mankind been gigantic, he could not have been so commodiously supplied with food; for there would not have been flesh enough of the best edible beasts to serve his turn. And, if beasts had been made answerably bigger, there would not have been grass enough. Boats and shipping, likewise, must have been answerably bigger, and so too big for most rivers and sea-coasts. Nor would there have been the same use and discovery of his reason, in that he would have done many things by mere strength for which he is now put to invent innumerable engines, and so far he had been reasonable in vain. Neither could he so conveniently have used a horse, the noblest of all beasts, nor divers other creatures, had he been much less or much bigger than he is. But, being of a middle bulk between the largest and the least, he is the better fitted to manage and use them all. For no other cause can be assigned why a man was not made five or ten times bigger than he is, as well as ten times bigger than a fox or a monkey, but his relation to the rest of the universe."

This is sound enough on the whole. The bulk of man's body is accommodated to his environment; but, when the doctor argues that he could not use his reason so well if his own strength sufficed for that which now requires the invention of machinery, he enters doubtful territory. If man were really much stronger, some teleologist would make *that* the basis of a design-argument. Let it be thus, or let it be the reverse: either way the event turns, teleological ingenuity will make it the basis of an argument.

The remark previously made, that Grew merely pours out a flood of illustrations and examples accentuated with exclamation-points, while it is true for the most part, must not be taken in the most sweeping sense. He gets down to actual argumentation — but it is a queer kind of argument, after all — in respect to the correlation of animal structures : —

"Should any man, then, that knows not the admirable structure of an eye or an ear [if he did know its structure, the doctor thinks it would be impossible for him to think it was made by chance] be so weak as to think it possible for matter fortuitously moved or mixed to hit upon the making of an eye or an ear, yet [suppose some man is foolish enough for that] did wings design the making of an eye [swift motion and sight being correlative as he had before stated]? Or did lungs design the making of an ear [speech and hearing being also correlative]? Did no teeth — that is, *nothing* — design the making of three stomachs [birds, for example, being toothless, have a compensating apparatus in the crop and gizzard]? Did the eye take care there should be light for it to see by? or the light forecast to match itself with an eye? or man to be furnished with the world about him? Nothing can be more vain than so to speak or think. We must therefore conclude that there is a most perfect Reason or Mind, infinitely above the operation of matter and chance, which is apparent both in the make or structure, and in the use and relation, of things."

He does not stop with the inference of God's existence, but goes on to prove his benevolence : —

" The nature of this action and use, in not being any way destructive or troublesome, but tending in each thing apart and conspiring in many together, to conserve and gratify, is an evidence of their proceeding from the greatest goodness. For there be many who are very cunning and subtile in the invention of evil ; and engines have been fitted with a great deal of art and contrivance for the tormenting of men. In like manner it had been altogether as easy for the Maker of the world to have stocked it with all sorts of creatures, had he so pleased, which should never have moved so much as one limb without pain ; which should never have seen, heard, smelt, tasted, or felt any one thing but together with the greatest torment, nor have conceived any one fancy but with melancholy and horror. And the greatness of his understanding would have been demonstrated in the contrivance, though of such creatures as these. But in that he hath made so many kinds of creatures, and bestowed among them so many sorts of motion, and of sense and cogitation, all of them, so far as natural [that is, normal, not diseased], agreeable, and delightful ; he hath herein given a most noble instance that his goodness is equal to his understanding ; that he hath employed his transcendent wisdom and power in order that by these he might make way for his benignity as the end wherein they ultimately acquiesce."

In Book II. Dr. Grew announces his theory of a " vital principle" permeating matter in general, both organic and inorganic. This is very similar to the "plastic nature" of Cudworth ; and the two theories were coupled together in the lively discussions of the early part of the eighteenth century, — one party claiming that these theories promoted atheism, because they furnished a mode of accounting for the regular and artful structure of organized bodies without a creator ; the other claiming that they were entirely theistic, because Grew made his vital principle, and Cudworth made his plastic nature, subordinate to the Deity, as a mere instrument in his hands. The following account of the " vital principle " is a little obscure, but it is the best I can select for a single quotation : —

" The lowest species of life of which we can have cognizance, is such a sort of life as is without sense, the being whereof is not impossible ; for intellection, which is one species of life, is absolutely distinct from life, as shall be proved. But a distinction, on any one hand, supposeth a possibility on either ; and it seems as easy to conceive the being of some sort of life without sense, as the being of any one sense without another. [That can hardly be granted.] Yet neither by this life, nor the subject of it, do I mean a principle of motion ; the universal stock of motion, as that of matter, being neither increased nor diminished, but only transferred. But I mean a certain power to determine the manner of its being transferred, or of returning an impression upon bodies suitable unto that which it receives ; and more especially upon the principles [molecules?] of bodies, wherewith it seemeth chiefly to correspond.

" By virtue of this power, I suppose it is, that all bodies have their sphere of activity, whereby they operate one upon another more or less ; that there are dark rays as well as light ones ; that the odors, and other like *effluvia* of bodies, which waft and tend to dissolve them, depend upon an external force, viz., the air ; but that the radiations by which bodies are united depend upon a force internal. And therefore, that, as the congruity between life and motion maketh the union between the soul and the body, so the congruity between motion and motion maketh or promoteth the union or inclination of one body to another. This aforesaid power, from whence ariseth the sphere of activity, is more conspicuous in all the sorts of magnetic inclination, and in the gravitation of all bodies, but is that also wherewith every corporeal principle [molecule] may probably be endowed, or, to speak properly, may be *animated*. For since the most simple bodies, having a certain regular and immutable size and figure, are hereby made organs or instruments, truly and properly so called, it is as congruous to assign such a *vital principle* to each of these as is suitable to its simple organism, as another suitable one to any organ more compounded; that is to say. to allow like to like, as well to an atom as to a man.

" Neither can we ascribe unto atoms any innate motion, as some do, so reasonably as a *certain principle of life*. For although it be true that all bodies are some way or other in motion, or that there is no state of absolute rest, yet a relative rest there is and must be, without which there could be no union of bodies. So that any one atom having lost its proper motion by its union with another, whatever motion it receives afterwards from without is *adventitious*, and cannot be called *innate*. Much less can it be supposed to be suitable and regular without such a *vital principle* as aforesaid to direct it. Of which principles we must then allow a stock, answerable to the corporeal as one moiety of the universe. [That is, the vital principles in the aggregate constitute one phase, or one aspect, or one-half, of the universe; and the corporeal principles in the aggregate constitute the other half. The universe is formed of life and matter.] On the directive power of the former, and the regularity of the latter, whereby it is capable of direction, depends the generation of all bodies; the said power being one and the same vegetable life infused into all parts of corporeal nature, but more remarkably into animals and plants.

" Book III. showeth that God governs the universe he hath made, and in what manner.

" Book IV. showeth that the Bible, and first the Hebrew code or Old Testament, is God's positive law.

" Book V. showeth that the New Testament is also God's positive law."

The next writer is the Rev. William Derham, whose physico-theology appeared in 1713. This was one of

the most popular books on natural theology ever published, running rapidly through several editions, and
being translated into the Continental languages. He
takes his stand clearly for that view of design-arguments
which regards them as a means of proving the existence
of God, as well as illustrating his power, wisdom, and
providence. This appears in his full title, which also
brings out another point of interest in connection with
this book: "Physico-Theology; or, A Demonstration
of the Being and Attributes of God from his Works of
Creation. Being the Substance of Sixteen Sermons
preached in St. Mary-le-Bow Church, London, at the
Hon. Mr. Boyle's Lectures in the Years 1711 and 1712."

In a foot-note to the dedication he gives a short
history of the Boyle lectures: —

"It may not only gratify the reader's curiosity, but also
be of use, to give the following account of Mr. Boyle's
lectures: —

"Mr. Boyle [the same Robert Boyle who wrote the "Disquisition about Final Causes "], by a codicil dated July 28,
1691, and annexed to his will, charged his messuage or dwell-
ing-house in St. Michael's Crooked Lane, London, with the
payment of the clear yearly rents and profits thereof to some
learned divine in London, or within the bills of mortality, to
be elected for a term not exceeding three years, by his Grace
the present Lord Archbishop of Canterbury (then Dr. Teni-
son), Sir Henry Ashurst, Sir John Rotherham, and John
Evelyn, Esq. The business he appointed those lecturers
was, among others, *to be ready to satisfy real scruples, and to
answer such new objections and difficulties as might be started,
to which good answers had not been made;* and also *to preach
eight sermons in the year,* the first Monday of January, February, March, April, and May, and of September, October,
and November."

He alludes to the object of this lecture foundation in the preface also : —

"And forasmuch as his lectures were appointed by him for the proof of the Christian religion against atheists and other notorious infidels, I thought, when I had the honor to be made his lecturer, that I could not better come up to his intent than to attempt a demonstration of the being and attributes of God in what I may call Mr. Boyle's own (that is, a *physico-theological*) way. And, besides that it was for this very service that I was called to this honor, I was the more induced to follow this method by reason none of my learned and ingenious predecessors in these lectures have done it otherwise than in a transient, piecemeal manner."

Derham, therefore, aims to give a completeness to physico-theology which it never possessed before. The problem, as he seems to have set it before himself, was to review the circle of the sciences, and digest them all into a system of theology. That was practically the same thing which Ray attempted, and the same which all the teleologists of the eighteenth century, and of the earlier part of the nineteenth century also, regarded as their proper function and the mission to which they were called. Of course they were traversing the same ground over and over. Derham says that he "industriously endeavored to avoid doing over what they [Ray and others] had before done, and for that reason did not for many years read their books until I had finished my own. If, then, the reader should meet with any thing mentioned before by others, and not accordingly acknowledged by me, I hope he will candidly think me no plagiary, because I can assure him I have all along (where I was aware of it) cited my authors with their due praise; and it is scarce possible, when men write on the same or on a subject near akin, and the observations are obvious, but that they must often hit upon the same thing."

Dr. More took the same method to avoid plagiarism and repetition. One would suppose it would have been better to read all the previous authors diligently, instead of avoiding the perusal. Did they fear that course would leave them nothing to say? If so, it would have been as well not to say any thing. If they had any truly original contribution to make, it would have been done all the more intelligently with a fresh and thorough knowledge of what had already been accomplished. The course which they adopted, of avoiding the perusal of works previously written upon the subject they intended to handle, reveals two facts respecting the mental attitude in which they stood as they contemplated the task they were about to undertake. In the first place they regarded it as an easy task. Derham speaks of the "observations" being "obvious." Let us see how far it was easy, or the reverse. The problem was to digest all the science of the period into a system of natural theology. That is what the admirers of Ray, Derham, and Nieuwentyt claimed that these writers had done. It looks difficult, rather than easy; but, when we observe how it was done, the matter assumes a different aspect.

For the second fact regarding the mental status of these writers is, that they had very loose, vague, and general notions, both of what had been already accomplished in teleology, and of what they themselves expected to accomplish, and how they expected to do it. Most of them set out with the expectation of demonstrating God's existence: but, in the practical handling of their theme, they assume that fundamental fact, and argue for the greatness of his wisdom and power, and

the benignity of his providence; that is, if they argue
at all. More frequently they merely grind over the
huge mass of stereotyped examples; and if they add
any new ones, as they are very likely to do by reason
of new discoveries in science, these are of the same
kind as the old, — a few kernels more to the heap. So
that their work, starting with such conceptions as they
do, cannot be other than a repetition; and to shut their
eyes to what others had done, think out the same series
of facts, and link them together by means of the same
"obvious observations," — such a method of procedure
as this, stupid as it seems, was about the only one which
would correspond to their initial conception. The scientific knowledge requisite for this work need not be profound. The very statement of the problem, as they
viewed it, — namely, to digest all the science of their
generation into a system of theology, — is sufficiently
suggestive of the sort of science it would be, and of
the sort of theology too.

There are tolerably recent editions of Derham's book;
and it is upon the whole so much better known than
those which I have previously reviewed, that it is scarcely necessary to quote from him at any great length for
the purpose of showing how well or how ill he did his
work, as judged from his own standpoint. Suffice it to
say, that in the general survey of terrestrial phenomena
he regards them all — winds, rains, oceans, mountains,
even volcanoes — with reference to their utility. He
turns them all in to the account of teleology. The way
he manages this in respect to such a fiery and intracta-
ble thing as a volcano is sufficiently striking and characteristic to justify a quotation: —

"To instance the very worst of all the things named, viz.,
the volcanoes and ignivomous mountains: although they

are some of the most terrible shocks of the globe and dreadful scourges of the sinful inhabitants thereof, and may
serve them as emblems and presages of hell itself, yet even
these have their great uses too; being as spiracles or tunnels
to the countries where they are, to vent the fire and vapors
that would make dismal havoc, and oftentimes actually do so,
by dreadful succussions and convulsions of the earth.   Nay,
if the hypothesis of a central fire and waters be true, these
outlets seem to be of the greatest use to the peace and quiet
of the terraqueous globe in venting the subterraneous heat
and vapors, which, if pent up, would make dreadful and dangerous commotions of the earth and waters.

"It may be then accounted as a special favor of the
Divine Providence, as is observed by the author before
praised, 'That there are scarcely any countries that are much
annoyed with earthquakes, that have not one of these fiery
vents.   And these (saith he) are constantly all in flames
whenever any earthquake happens; they disgorging that
fire, which, whilst underneath, was the cause of the disas-
ter.'"

The *naïve* simplicity of this style of argument is
something admirable and touching.   A very bad thing,
volcanoes, wards off a worse thing, earthquakes: therefore the first is "a special favor of Divine Providence."
If the earthquakes were the work of demons, the reasoning might hold; but, considering that they, too, are
God's work, the argument is seen to be of the flimsiest
texture.   What he suggests respecting the emblematic
use of volcanoes to serve as "presages of hell" is quite
as sound as any other part of the reasoning.   But he
had still another arrow in his quiver: —

"Should we pretend to censure what God doth?   Should
we pretend to amend his work, or to advise infinite Wisdom, or to know the ends and purposes of his infinite will,
as if we were of his council?   No: let us bear in mind that

these objections are the products, not of reason, but of pee-
vishness.   They have been incommoded by storms and tempests ; they have been terrified with burning mountains and
earthquakes ; they have been annoyed by the noxious animals,
and fatigued by the hills ; and therefore they are angry, and
will pretend to amend these works of the Almighty.   But,
in the words of St. Paul, we may say, ' Nay, but, O man !
who art thou that repliest against God ? ' "

There spoke the preacher rather than the physico-
theologist.   If he could not silence the objector's guns
by all the missiles which nature and reason furnished
to his hand, he would quote Scripture at him.

The first four books contain a general view of the
earth with its inhabitants; and here is the conclusion of
this part of his task : —

"And now let us pause a little, and reflect.   And upon
the whole matter, what less can be concluded than that there
is a Being infinitely wise, potent, and kind, able to contrive
and make this glorious scene of things, which I have given
only a glance of ?   For what less than Infinite could stock so
vast a globe with such a noble set of animals, all so contrived as to minister to one another's help in some way or
other, and most of them serviceable to man peculiarly, the
top of this lower world, made as 'twere on purpose to observe, and survey, and set forth the glory of the infinite
Creator manifested in his works?   Who?   What but the
great GOD could so admirably provide for the whole animal
world, every thing serviceable to it, or that can be wished
for either to conserve its species, or to minister to the being
or well-being of individuals?   Particularly, who could *feed*
so spacious a world, who could please so large a number of
palates, or suit so many palates to so great a variety of food,
but the infinite Conservator of the world?   And who but the
same great HE could provide such commodious clothing for
every animal, such proper houses, nests, and habitations,

such suitable armature and weapons, such subtilty, artifice, and sagacity, as every creature is more or less armed and furnished with, to fence off the injuries of the weather, to rescue itself from dangers, to preserve itself from the annoyances of its enemies, and, in a word, to conserve itself and its species? What but an infinite superintending Power could so equally *balance* the several species of animals, and conserve the numbers of the individuals of every species so even, as not to over or under people the terraqueous globe? Who but the infinitely wise Lord of the world could allot every creature its most suitable *place* to live in, the most suitable element to *breathe* and *move* and *act* in? And who but He could make so admirable a set of organs as those of respiration are both in land and water animals? Who could contrive so curious a set of limbs, joints, bones, muscles, and nerves, to give to every animal the most commodious motion to its state and occasions? And, to name no more, what anatomist, mathematician, workman, yea, angel, could contrive and make so curious, so commodious, and every way so exquisite a set of senses as the *five senses* of animals are, whose organs are so dexterously contrived. so conveniently placed in the body, so neatly adjusted, so firmly guarded, and so completely suited to every occasion, that they plainly set forth the agency of the infinite Creator and Conservator of the world?

" So that here, upon a transient view of the animal world in general only, we have such a throng of glories, such an enravishing scene of things, as may excite us to admire, praise, and adore the infinitely wise, powerful, and kind CREATOR ; to condemn all atheistical principles ; and with holy David to conclude that he is in good earnest a *fool* that dares to say, *There is no God,* when we are everywhere surrounded with such manifest characters and plain demonstrations of that infinite Being."

Having completed his general survey of the world and its inhabitants, he proceeds to a more particular

account of " the tribes of animals," beginning with man.
I quote from the last two chapters of Book V.: —

" Here I would have put an end to my observations relating to man, but that there are three things so expressly
declaring the divine management and concurrence, that I
shall just mention them, although taken notice of more
amply by others; and that is, the great variety throughout
the world of men's faces (1), voices (2), and handwriting
(3). Had man's body been made according to any of the
atheistical schemes, or any other method than that of the
infinite Lord of the world, this wise variety would never have
been: but men's faces would have been cast in the same, or
not a very different, mould; their organs of speech would have
sounded the same, or not so great a variety of, notes; and
the same structure of muscles and nerves would have given
the hand the same direction in writing. And, in this case,
what confusion, what disturbance, what mischiefs, would the
world eternally have lain under! No security could have
been to our persons; no certainty. no enjoyment of our
possessions; no justice between man and man; no distinction between good and bad, between friends and foes. between father and child, husband and wife, male and female:
but all would have been turned topsy-turvy by being ex-
posed to the malice of the envious and ill-natured, to the
fraud and violence of knaves and robbers, to the forgeries of
the crafty cheat, to the lusts of the effeminate and debauched, and what not! Our courts of justice can abundantly testify the dire effects of mistaking men's faces, of
counterfeiting their hands, and forging writings. But now,
as the infinitely wise Creator and Ruler hath ordered the
matter, every man's face can distinguish him in the light,
and his voice in the dark; his handwriting can speak for
him though absent, and be his witness, and secure his con-
tracts in future generations, — a manifest, as well as admirable, indication of the divine superintendence and management.

" And now having taken a view of man, and finding every part of him contrived and made in the very best manner, — his body fitted up with utmost foresight, art, and care ; and this body (to the great honor, privilege, and benefit of man) possessed by a divine part, the *soul*, a substance made as 'twere on purpose to contemplate the works of God and glorify the great Creator ; and since this soul can discern, think, reason, and speak, — what can we conclude upon the whole matter, but that we lie under all the obligations of duty and gratitude to be thankful and obedient to, and to set forth the glories of, our great Creator and noble Benefactor ? And what ungrateful wretches are we, how much worse than the poor irrationals, if we do not employ the utmost power of our tongue, and all our members, and all the faculties of our souls, in the praises of God ! But, above all, should we, who have the benefit of these glorious acts and contrivances of the Creator, be such wicked, such base, such worse than brutal fools, to deny the Creator in some of his noblest works ? Should we so abuse our reason, yea, our very senses ; should we be so besotted by the Devil, and blinded by our lusts, as to attribute one of the best contrived pieces of workmanship to blind chance, or unguided matter and motion, or any other such sottish, wretched, atheistical stuff, which we never saw nor ever heard made any one being in any age since the creation ? No, no ! But, like wise and unprejudiced men, let us with David say, ' I will praise thee, for I am fearfully and wonderfully made.' "

Derham reminds us of Cudworth in his free use of slashing expletives. In the passage last quoted he has wandered from the "demonstration of the being and attributes of God," and adopted a hortatory and homiletical style. It is religion, rather than theology, that he is teaching ; and, having once struck this note, he sounds it out louder and more frequently to the end of this book.

In his "Astro-Theology," published in 1715, he has the good sense to reject "the old vulgar opinion *that all things were made for man;*" and, being thus freed from one temptation to bring every thing under teleology, he goes on to construct a very respectable eutaxiological argument : —

"And now who can reflect upon these things, and not perceive and admire the hand that acteth in them, the contrivance and power of an infinite Workman? For where we have such manifest strokes of wise *order* and management, of the observance of *mathematical proportions*, can we conclude there was any thing less than reason, judgment, and mathematical skill in the case? or that this could be effected by any other power but that of an intelligent Being?"

Still he does not steer entirely clear of teleological hypotheses. If these celestial bodies are not to be regarded in the light of their utility to man, they are probably useful to each other, and possibly to their hypothetical inhabitants, which is all well enough as a speculation, but of no substantial value as an argument for the existence of God. We will dismiss the Rev. William Derham with the two additional quotations following : —

"When, therefore, we actually see and feel those indulgent provisions, those amazing acts of the great Creator; when we have views of their extent into myriads of other the most distant globes; when (to go no farther) we see in our own system of the sun such a prodigious mass of fire placed in the centre to scatter away the darkness, and to warm and cherish us by day, and such a noble retinue of moons and stars attending us and assisting us by night; when we see this indulgence, this care, of the Creator extended to all the other planets, and that, according to their several distances, they have a proportionate provision of a greater number of moons, and Saturn a stupendous ring besides, to supply the decrease of light and heat, — who can be otherwise than amazed at such providential, such useful, such well-contrived, such stately works of God? Who can view their glories and partake of their beneficial influences, and at the same time not adore the wisdom and praise the kindness of their Contriver and Maker? But, above all, should there be any found among rational beings so stupid, so vile, so infatuated with their vices, as to deny these works to God, and ascribe them to a necessity of nature, or indeed a mere nothing, namely, chance? But such there are to be met with among ourselves, and some such the prophet tells us of, — men that had so debauched themselves with drink, and enervated their minds by pleasures, that 'they regarded not the work of the Lord, neither considered the operation of his hands.' Such persons, having led their lives in such a manner as to wish that there was no God to call them to account, would then persuade themselves there is none, and therefore stupidly ascribe those manifest demonstrations of the infinite power and wisdom of God to a mere nothing, rather than to their great Author. But may we not with as good reason imagine a lighted candle. a well-made culinary fire, a flaming beacon or lighthouse, to be the work of chance, and not of man, as those glories of the heavens not to be the works of God? For it is very certain, that as much wisdom, art, and power worthy of God is shown in the lights of the heavens as there is in those upon earth, which no man can doubt were contrived and made by man. And if, from these mean contrivances and works of man, we conclude them to be the works of man, why not the grand, the amazing works of the heavens, surpassing all the wit and power of man, — why not these, I say, — the works of some Being as much superior to man?

" As God's works have been shown to be a manifest demonstration of his existence, so they are no less of his perfections, particularly of his infinite power, wisdom, and goodness, inasmuch as every workman is known by his work. A palace that should have nothing defective in situation, beauty, or convenience, would argue the architect to have been a man of sagacity, and skilful in geometry, arithmetic, optics, and all other mathematical sciences serving to make a man a complete architect. — yea, to have some judgment in physic and natural philosophy too. And so this glorious scene of God's works, the heavens, plainly demonstrates the Workman's infinite wisdom to contrive, his omnipotency to make, and his infinite goodness in being so indulgent to all the creatures as to contrive and order all his works for their good. For what less than *Infinite* could effect all these grand things which I have in this discourse shown to be manifest in the heavens? What architect could build such vast masses, and such an innumerable company of them, too, as I have shown the heavens do contain? What mathematician could so exactly adjust their distances? what mechanic so nicely adopt their motions, so well contrive their figures, as in the very best manner may serve to their own conservation and benefit, and the convenience of the other globes also? What naturalist, what philosopher, could impregnate every globe with a thing of that absolute necessity to its conservation, as that of gravity is? What optician, what chemist, could have ever hit upon such a noble apparatus for light and heat as the sun and moon and the stars are? could amass together such a pile of fire as the sun is? could appoint such lights as the moon and other secondaries are? None certainly could do these things but God?"

CHAPTER VII.

NIEUWENTYT, WOLLASTON, AND MAUPERTUIS.

In 1716 appeared, in the Low Dutch language, a treatise on Natural Theology by Dr. Bernard Nieuwentyt, a
mathematician who had previously made himself somewhat notorious by attacking the accepted principles
of the calculus. This was very soon translated into
English by John Chamberlayne, Esq., F.R.S., with the
full title as follows: "The Religious Philosopher; or,
The Right Use of contemplating the Works of the
Creator. I. In the Wonderful Structure of Animal
Bodies, and, in particular, Man. II. In the no less
Wonderful and Wise Formation of the Elements, and
their Various Effects upon Animal and Vegetable
Bodies. And III. In the most Amazing Structure of
the Heavens, with all its Furniture. Designed for the
Conviction of Atheists and Infidels; throughout which
all the Late Discoveries in Anatomy, Philosophy, and
Astronomy, together with the Various Experiments
made Use of to illustrate the Same, are most copiously
handled by that Learned Mathematician, Dr. Nieuwentyt."

This titlepage shows plainly enough that the book
is in the conventional style of the period; that is, a
compendium of the sciences, with a running commentary of pious reflections, and notes of admiration. The
perusal confirms the expectations aroused by the title:

the doctor has not only happily hit the prevailing mode
of physico-theological discussion, but he has fairly out-
done his contemporaries. He is not only in the fashion,
but somewhat utterly and ultra stylish.

One thing we have to thank him for. Some of the
English teleologists leave us in doubt about two things,
—their *aim* and their *method*. Are they trying to prove
God's existence, or assuming that, and arguing for his
providence? Is it their purpose to use teleology as a
means of proving something else, or to use something
else to prove that teleology is a real thing in nature?
Nieuwentyt relieves us at once on these points. He is
going to prove God's existence by means of teleology:
at least that is *one* thing he proposes to do. In the
twenty-ninth section of his preface he says, —

"After having fully comprehended all the foregoing,
we might now have proceeded to the contemplations of the
world, and the perfections of God, in the composition. parts,
and motions thereof, were it not that we should previously
show after what manner. from the visible world. and that
which we see pass therein, a proof may be formed upon
which we may rely and be assured. — first, that there is a God,
that is to say, a wise, powerful. and gracious Maker and
Director of all things ; and, secondly. that the Bible (his
revealed word) is of a supernatural and divine origin. As
to the manner of demonstrating the first (i.e., God's existence), I shall, without entering into deep speculations, like
some philosophers, seriously entreat every one that with a
composed mind, and divesting himself of his passions and
prejudices, he would silently sit down, and seriously consider : *First*, In case he should see that, (1) not one but a
great many, (2) and various or different (3) things, entirely
ignorant, or unknowing of all, and even of themselves too ;
(4) each of them frequently after a particular manner, (5)
however, always unchangeably and observing the same rule ;

(6) do act and move, not once, but upon many occasions and times ; (7) and not one of them all able to impart such motion unto itself ; (8) nor, unless they thus come together, of themselves can produce one single effect without their own knowledge ; (9) in the production of which effect or thing, if some few circumstances only, or oftentimes but one single one were wanting, it could not either be produced at all, or at least not in its due perfection ; (10) and although that same effect should in itself be of great use and service, and sometimes of the utmost importance. Could he imagine otherwise than that all these things are formed to that end, and brought together with that design, to work such an effect as we observe to be produced by them?

" And, *secondly*, Supposing this first to be true, since these things are in themselves ignorant and unknowing of all that passes, whether everybody must not agree that they are all produced, and made to concur by a wise and understanding Agent, who had such an end and design in his view ; and whether any one can persuade himself that mere chance, or unknowing laws of nature, or other causes ignorantly co-operating, could have place herein, and could have directed and governed these things in all their circumstances and motions for such a purpose.

" That this may be shown after a more plain and not less certain manner, let us apply to some particular thing what has been just now advanced in general, and as it were in an abstracted manner ; and let us suppose that in the middle of a sandy down, or in a desert and solitary place, where few people are used to pass, any one should find a watch, showing the hours, minutes, and days of the months, and, having examined the same, should perceive so many different wheels, nicely adapted by their teeth to each other, and that one of them could not move without moving the rest of the whole machine ; and should further observe that those wheels are made of brass in order to keep them from rust ; that the spring is of steel, no other metal being so proper for that purpose ; that over the hand there is placed a clear glass, in the space of which, if there were any other but a transparent matter, he must be at the pains of opening it every time to look upon the hand.   Besides all which, he might discover in it a hole, and exactly opposite thereto a little square pin. He would likewise see hanging to this same watch a little key composed of two pieces, making a right angle together ; at the end of each of which there was a square hole so ordered that one of them was exactly adapted to the little pin in the said hole, which being applied thereto, a chain would be wound up, and a spring bent, by which means the machine would be continued in motion, which otherwise would be in an entire rest.   He might also find that the other square cavity at the end of the little key was adapted to another pin or instrument, which, turned this way or that, makes the hand move faster or slower.   At the other end of this little key there would be a flat handle, which, being movable therein, might give him the conveniency that in winding it up he should not be obliged to take hold of it at every turn of his fingers.   Lastly, he would perceive that if there were any defect in the wheels, spring, or any other parts of the watch, or if they had been put together after any other manner, the whole watch would have been entirely useless.

" Now, the question is, in order to form a kind of demonstration from hence, *First*, Whether anybody can imagine that such a watch, among other purposes to which it might perhaps be serviceable, was not likewise made for this end, that it should show the hours, minutes, and day of the month. *Secondly*, Whether he should make the least scruple to admit it for a truth, that such a machine was made and put together by an understanding artificer for this very purpose, who, when he made it, himself knew that and to what end he had made it.   And, *thirdly*, Whether it be possible that he can persuade himself that this watch, with all belonging to it, the niceness of its make, figure of so many parts, and other contrivances for showing the time, could have acquired its being and form by mere chance only, which operated indifferently, one way or another, without any certain rule or direction.

" Or, otherwise, whether he could expect to pass for a man of sense and understanding, if, having found this watch in a solitary place, he should pretend to believe that it was not made by a skilful workman, nor that its parts were put together with judgment; but that there was a certain ignorant and yet necessary law of nature prevailing in the world that had brought into a regular method all the parts of which this watch consisted, and had adapted each of them to the use of showing the time of day ; and especially that such a law of nature was not only ignorant and unsensible of all that it did or brought to pass, but likewise that no being endued with any wisdom or understanding had established and produced this law at the beginning, or in the least contributed to the making of the several parts that composed a machine proper to show the hours.

" What has been said above concerning a watch is not less applicable to all other artificial works. It will, therefore, be unnecessary to allege any further examples of mills, ships, sluices, houses, paintings, etc, — in all which the wisdom and understanding of the maker does equally appear.

" *Finally,* We may apply all that has been said above to demonstrate that there is such a wise, mighty, and merciful Being as God, in case we can make appear, with as great (not to say a much greater) certainty and conviction from the construction of the visible world and all that passes therein, that there is a God and great Creator who in wisdom has made them all ; as we can show from the structure of a watch, and the uses that result from the same, that it has been made and put together by a judicious and skilful workman ; and this we doubt not of doing in the following contemplations with all necessary clearness."

The "abstract and general" propositions at the beginning of this quotation present as fine an example of teleological reasoning as can be found in any of the old writers. As for the watch business, the length of the quotation is justified by the fact, that this is *the* illustration, the classical one, the familiar, ever-present, old, reliable illustration of teleology. And this quotation contains the pure, unadulterated, *original* presentation of it. All who used that watch after Dr. Nieuwentyt found it "in the middle of a sandy down" in 1716 were thieves and robbers. Paley, in particular, who pretends that he found it in 1803 "in crossing a heath," and who devotes his first two chapters to it, was unquestionably guilty of plagiarism. In fact, he is accused of stealing his whole book from the "solid Dutchman."

"Not only has the English archdeacon, it is alleged, borrowed the general argument of the Dutch thinker, he has likewise followed his arrangement, appropriated his thoughts, made use of his form, and copied his details, and that without any thing like honorable acknowledgment."[1] ,

Lord Brougham, however, says that Paley stole his matter from Derham, instead of Nieuwentyt.[2] Now, while I cannot deny that he appropriated the watch illustration, I must defend my old friend, whose book I read with so much delight in my youth, from such sweeping charges of plagiarism. Our historical review of natural theology enables us to weigh and estimate such charges more accurately than could be done by those who made them. By this light we see that they were substantially all in the same boat. If Paley was guilty of plagiarism, so were Nieuwentyt and Derham, from whom it is claimed that he filched his matter and

[1] Encyc. Brit., Art. Nieuwentyt.
[2] Discourse of Natural Theology, p. 53.

method. A stock of teleological materials and illustrations had been accumulating from the earliest ages, and they all drew from the common storehouse.

Nieuwentyt divides his book into "contemplations" instead of chapters. Contemplation I. is "Of the Vanity of all Worldly Things;" the second contains ontological and causal arguments for the existence of God; and the third is teleological. Here, *apropos* of the question of plagiarism, the very first thing we strike is the old, old argument about the position and character of the various kinds of teeth. It must be admitted, however, that the doctor injects some originality even into such a threadbare topic; but, unfortunately for him, the additions he makes are the weakest part of the argument: —

"A means was requisite to turn solid bodies into a liquid matter, and even such as should be proper to support and nourish us. For this purpose there are teeth planted in our mouths, of which those that stand foremost are sharp and cutting in order to bite off a part of that food which is taken in, whose semicircular figure is wisely adapted to a just measure of the piece to be bitten, and so to be afterwards chewed with the most conveniency, as every one may experience who makes his biting larger or smaller."

This notion that the teeth are so disposed in a semicircle as to enable us to bite off just enough to satisfy us without overstraining the muscles of the jaw, is original. We can picture the learned doctor patiently experimenting on "making his biting greater or smaller," bravely running the risk of choking himself in the cause of natural theology!

"But herein appear yet more sensibly the design and wisdom of the great Artificer in ordering the food to pass over the orifice of the windpipe as it goes to the throat; for, if any thing falls into the windpipe (which people commonly call *going the wrong way*), every one knows what disorder it occasions in them, so great sometimes as to put them in danger of choking; wherefore it is absolutely necessary, if we would eat with ease, and preserve our life at the same time, that the windpipe, or the mouth of it, should be closed when we swallow, and then immediately opened again in order to draw our breath. Now, can anybody be so dull as not to observe this determinate end and design of our wise and merciful Creator? Let him only take the trouble of viewing the upper part of the windpipe of a sheep or a calf, where he will see more plainly than can be shown him here by a figure, that there lies a cartilage, called the *epiglottis*, which, being pressed down by the food when 'tis swallowed, covers the orifice of the windpipe lying under it, by which means the food passing over it, as if it were a bridge made for that purpose, in its way to the throat is prevented from falling into the windpipe, which would often occasion coughing, straining, and other greater inconveniences. Now, if this cartilage should remain lying thus upon the orifice of the windpipe, the breath would be stopped, and the living creature immediately suffocated. Do we not here again discover a wise design, — that this epiglottis is so contrived as to rise up like a spring that has been pressed down, or, as some say, drawn up by muscular fibres after the food has passed over it? By which means the passage of the breath is immediately opened after swallowing, in case the elastical force of the said epiglottis should be weakened by too much use.''

The argument here runs a somewhat devious course. First, Mr. Atheist, you will please to note " the design and wisdom " of " ordering the food to pass over the orifice of the windpipe." Secondly, admire the skill with which *the mischief incident to the first contrivance* is avoided by providing the epiglottis. Thirdly, surrender, you miscreant, to the overwhelming fact that *the mischief incident to the second contrivance* is prevented by the springing back of the epiglottis! Surely he must have been a "most obdurate and deplorable atheist" who could stand all that. The consideration that God was the Author of the difficulties overcome, as well as of the contrivances by which they were surmounted, seems never to have occurred to the worthy Dutchman. The whole argument is as old as Cicero, at least; and the Stoic presented it in better shape than Nieuwentyt did, since he makes only one "design" out of it instead of three, each for the purpose of escaping the evil consequences of the previous one.

After a similar fashion he goes through the whole human anatomy, and subsequently through the whole circle of the sciences as then known. To a modern scientist his discussions, experiments, speculations, and guesses possess a curious interest throughout, though a very unequal value. His astronomy, for instance, is much sounder than his chemistry. How could it be otherwise, considering that he wrote three-quarters of a century before Priestly discovered oxygen, and that he reckoned fire as an element?

"The Religion of Nature Delineated," by William Wollaston, London, 1725, is a thin folio volume full of pleasant and valuable matter. The author adheres very closely to his chosen theme ·of natural religion as distinguished from natural theology, and yet not exclusively. Section V., on "Truths relating to the Deity," is theological. The rest of the book is a treatise on natural ethics, or the principles of just and right action which may be discovered without the aid of revelation. But, since he takes a broad view of human relations,.the application of these principles leads him to construct the elements of political science and sociology. In those early days, before human knowledge was mapped out into so many distinct provinces, it was natural and almost inevitable for an author, in treating any subject of fundamental importance, to impinge upon the territory of a number of the modern sciences in a single treatise.

The ground principles of his political science are so sound and well put, that, in spite of the incongruity with the general purpose of this historical review, I cannot forbear transcribing two of his propositions: " In a state of nature men are equal in respect of dominion." " No man can have a right to begin to interrupt the happiness of another."

Those sentences sound remarkably like the words of a certain document which astonished the world half a century later, — " free and equal," " inalienable rights," and " life, liberty, and the pursuit of happiness."

Before passing to consider his teleology, which is the main thing aimed at in this notice of his book, let us note his conclusion, which seems to me an admirable summary of natural religion : —

" For a conclusion of the whole matter: let our conversation in this world, so far as we are concerned and able, be such as acknowledges every thing to be what it is (what it is in itself, and what with regard to us, to other beings, to causes, circumstances, and consequences) ; that is. let us by no act deny any thing to be true which is true ; that is, let us act according to reason ; that is, let us act according to the law of our nature. By honestly endeavoring to do this we shall express our duty to him who is the Author of it and of that law, and at the same time prosecute our own proper happiness (the happiness of *rational* beings) ; we shall do what tends to make us easy here, and be qualifying ourselves, and preparing for our removal hence to our long home, — that great revolution, which, at the farthest, cannot be very far off."

In his proof of the existence of God, Wollaston begins with the causal argument; and he puts that in the weakest form, namely, as a *series.* Z is moved by Y, Y by X, X by W, and so on ; but the series must stop with some term whose movement is self-motion, uncaused motion.

He handles the anthropological argument with greater skill.

The general proposition with which he introduces his teleological argument is the following : —

" The frame and constitution of the world, the astonishing magnificence of it, the various phenomena and kinds of beings, the uniformity observed in the productions of things, the uses and ends for which they serve, etc., do all show that there is some Almighty Designer, an infinite wisdom and power at the top of all these things : such marks there are of both."

Two leading ideas run through this statement : the one is that of grandeur, which includes subordinate elements, as that of beauty, harmony, unity in the midst of diversity ; and the other is that of contrivance for a purpose. In other words, his statement includes elements which belong to eutaxiology as well as to teleology. The same thing is true of the detailed statements by which he seeks to establish his general proposition, of which I give characteristic paragraphs : —

" In order to prove to any one the grandness of this fabric of the world, one needs only to bid him consider the sun with that insupportable glory and lustre that surrounds it ; to demonstrate the vast distance, magnitude, and heat of it; to represent to him the chorus of planets moving periodically by uniform laws in their several orbits about it, affording a regular variety of aspects, — guarded some of them by secondary planets, and as it were emulating the state of the sun, and probably all possessed by proper inhabitants; to remind him of those surprising visits the comets make us, the large trains of uncommon splendor which attend them, the far country they come from, and the curiosity and horror they excite, not only among us, but in the inhabitants of other planets, who also may be up to see the entry and progress of these ministers of fate [unless the said inhabitants of other planets were less superstitious than mankind in early ages, which is to be sincerely hoped. Why not suppose that they are accomplished astronomers viewing these comets with telescopes and spectroscopes of the most approved pattern, instead of regarding them with " curiosity and horror " as " ministers of fate " ?] ; to direct his eye and contemplation, through those azure fields and vast regions above him, up to the fixed stars, that radiant, numberless host of heaven ; and to make him understand how unlikely a thing it is that they should be placed there only to adorn and bespangle a canopy over our heads (though that would be a piece of great magnificence too), and much less to supply the places of so many glow-worms by affording a feeble light to our earth, or even to all our fellow-planets ; to convince him that they are rather so many other suns, with their several regions and sets of planets about them ; to show him by the help of glasses still more and more of these fixed lights ; and to beget in him an apprehension of their unaccountable numbers and of those immense spaces that lie retired beyond the utmost reach and even imagination. I say one needs but to do this, and explain to him such things as are now known almost to everybody ; and by it to show, that, if the world be not infinite, it is *infinito similis*, and therefore sure a magnificent structure, and the work of an *infinite* Architect.

But if we could take a view of all the particulars contained within that astonishing compass, which we have thus hastily run over, how would wonders multiply upon us? Every corner, every part of the world, is as it were made up of *other* worlds. If we look upon this our seat (I mean this earth), what scope is here for admiration! the great variety of mountains, hills, valleys, plains, rivers, seas, trees, plants! the many tribes of different animals with which it is stocked! the multifarious inventions and works of one of these; that is, of us men, etc. And yet, when all these (heaven and earth) are surveyed as nicely as they can be by the help of our unassisted senses, and even of telescopical glasses, by the assistance of good microscopes in very small parts of matter, as many new wonders may perhaps be discovered as those already observed, — new kingdoms of animals, new architecture and curiosity of work. So that, as before, our senses and even conception fainted in those vast journeys we were obliged to take in considering the expanse of the universe; so here again they fail us in our researches into the principles and constituent parts of it. Both the beginnings and the ends of things, the least and the greatest, all conspire to baffle us; and which way ever we prosecute our inquiries, we still fall in with fresh subjects of amazement, and fresh reasons to believe that there are indefinitely still more and more behind, that will forever escape our eagerest pursuits and deepest penetration.

"Lastly, it appears, I think, plainly enough in the parts and model of the world, that there is a contrivance and a respect to certain reasons and *ends*. How the sun is posited near the middle of our system for the more convenient dispensing of his benign influences to the planets moving about him; how the plane of the earth's equator intersects that of her orbit, and makes a proper angle with it, in order to diversify the year, and create a useful variety of seasons, and many other things of this kind, though a thousand times repeated, will always be pleasing meditations to good men and true scholars. Who can observe the vapors to ascend, especially from the sea, meet above in clouds, and fall again after condensation, and not understand this to be a kind of distillation in order to clear the water of its grosser salts, and then by rains and dews to supply the fountains and rivers with fresh and wholesome liquor ; to nourish the vegetables below by showers, which descend in drops as from a watering-pot upon a garden, etc. ? Who can view the structure of a plant or animal ; the indefinite number of their fibres and fine vessels, the formation of larger vessels and the several members out of them, and the apt disposition of all these ; the way laid out for the reception and distribution of nutriment ; the effect this nutriment has in extending the vessels, bringing the vegetable or animal to its full growth or expansion, continuing the motion of the several fluids, repairing the decay of the body, and preserving life? Who can take notice of the several faculties of animals, their arts of saving and providing for themselves, or the ways in which they are provided for ; the uses of plants to animals, and of some animals to others, particularly to mankind ; the care taken that the several species should be propagated out of their proper seeds without confusion [Foot-note. — " If any one sitting upon Mount Ida had seen the Greek army coming on in proper order, he ought most certainly to have concluded there was some commander under whose conduct they moved "] ; the strong inclinations implanted in animals for that purpose, their love of their young. and the like? I say, who can do this, and not see a design in such regular pieces, so nicely wrought and so preserved? If there was but one animal, in that case it could not be doubted but that his *eyes* were made that he might *see* with them, his *ears* that he might *hear* with them, and so on, through at least the most considerable parts of him. If it can be much less doubted, when the same things are repeated in the individuals of all the tribes of animals ; if the like observations may be made with respect to vegetables, and other things ; and if all these kinds of things, and therefore much more their particulars, upon and in the earth, waters, air, are unconceivably numerous (as most evidently they are), one cannot but be convinced from that, which is so very obvious to every understanding, and plainly runs through the nobler parts of the visible world, that not only they, but other things, even those that seem to be less noble, have their ends too, though not so well understood. And now, since we cannot suppose the parts of matter to have contrived this wonderful form of a world among themselves, and then by agreement to have taken their respective posts, and pursued constant ends by certain methods and measures concerted (because these are acts of which they are not capable), there must be some other being whose wisdom and power are equal to such a mighty work as is the structure and preservation of the world. There must be some almighty Mind who models and adorns it, lays the causes of things so deep, prescribes them such uniform and steady laws, destines and adapts them to certain purposes, and makes one thing to fit and answer to another."

The inference of "an infinite Architect" from the structure of a universe which is almost infinite, "*infinito similis*," is something of a leap, but no greater than design-advocates frequently make or attempt. Wollaston evidently has outgrown the "inveterate prejudice" attributed to teleologists by Spinoza; namely, regarding the whole universe as contrived for the benefit of man. If the stars were so designed, they are no better than so many "glow-worms." The strong current of eutaxiology which runs through these quotations is noteworthy. He was strongly impressed with the regularity and constancy of nature. The illustration in the foot-note of an army in battle-array, thrown in at the point where he is speaking of the preservation of the several distinct species without confusion, shows how fully he appreciated the goodly and orderly array of the animal kingdom.

Joseph Butler, Bishop of Durham, published his famous "Analogy of Natural and Revealed Religion" in 1736. Excellent as this work is, it requires no more than a mere mention here. It is not an argument for the existence of God, but is addressed to theists. Its aim is simply to show that whatever difficulties and objections arise in the rational criticism of revealed religion, the same difficulties arise also in the contemplation of nature.

The "Discourses on all the Principal Branches of Natural Religion and Social Virtue," by James Foster, D.D., London, 1749, also contains little that needs any comment in this place, except his opinion respecting the importance of natural religion and its relation to Christianity. He relies wholly upon the causal argument to prove the existence of God, stating it in very much the same terms as Wollaston; so that we have here no design-arguments to subject to analysis.

In order to vindicate for natural religion the high place which he thinks it ought to occupy, he urges several considerations, of which I quote the first: —

" First, that all the essential principles of the *religion of nature*, and the moral duties connected with and obviously resulting from it, must also be included in the *religion of the gospel*, as most important and essential branches of that likewise, because it is absolutely impossible that there should be *any religion at all* but what is founded on these original truths and obligations. There can in nature be *no other ground* for the authority of God over rational creatures, nor for any homage and duty to be paid him."

In 1748. Moreau de Maupertuis published his "Essai de Cosmologie." The titlepage bears this admirable

motto from the fourth book of Virgil's Æneid, *Mens
agitat molem*. In the preface he "examines the proofs
of the existence of God;" and here he sounds the first
note of that chorus of criticisms of natural theology
which marked the middle and latter part of the last
century.

He passes over three arguments, (1) the ontological,
(2) the general consent of mankind. (3) the anthropological, with a bare allusion, remarking that "they are
all very strong, but not of the kind he proposes to examine."

"In all ages proofs of the wisdom and power of him who
governs the universe have been found by those who applied
themselves to the study of it. The greater the progress in
physics, the more numerous have these proofs become. Some,
struck with amazement at the divine tokens which we behold
every moment in nature, others through a zeal misnamed religious. have given certain proofs greater weight than they
ought to have, and sometimes taken for proof that which
was not conclusive."

He thinks the genuine arguments are numerous and
strong enough, without the attempt to multiply them
by an overstrained zeal.

He passes over the argument "which the ancients
drew from the beauty, order, and arrangement of the
cosmos," with the remark, "I attach myself to a philosophy which, by its grand discoveries, is far more competent to judge of those marvels, and whose reasonings
are far more precise than theirs." One of these "grand
discoveries," of which Maupertuis was very proud, was
the oblateness of the spheroidal form of the earth. He
was chairman of a committee of the Academy which
measured a degree of longitude, and thence deduced
this conclusion, — an achievement for which, or on ac-

count of his vanity about it, Voltaire ridiculed him
most unmercifully, styling him the "flattener of the
earth."

The argument of the ancients thus summarily disposed of was eutaxiological. He immediately passes
on to criticise the views of Sir Isaac Newton, apparently without recognizing them as of the same piece
with the eutaxiology of the ancients: —

"That great man believed that the movements of the
celestial bodies sufficiently demonstrate the existence of
Him who governs them: such uniformity must result from
the will of a Supreme Being. The sublimest objects seem
to have furnished him with the strongest arguments."

To this he proposes two objections: First, though
the probabilities that chance governed the forms of the
orbits and the relative distances of the planets is very
small (he figures out the ratio 1419856:1; and he was
a great mathematician), still chance has some chance
left. He handles this objection very gingerly, as if he
knew how light a missile it was against a weighty argument. Secondly, there may be a physical cause for all
the celestial phenomena. This, of course, Newton
would admit; but the next question would be whether
all the physical causes were not dominated by mind.
This objection only shifts the ground of the controversy.

Respecting Newton's argument from morphological
symmetry among animals, Maupertuis' criticisms simply
show that he did not comprehend it. He thought that
Newton claimed a uniformity of animal structures
throughout.

"If the uniformity which one observes in many animals
is one proof, is that not overthrown by the infinite diversity
which one observes in others?"

And so away he goes on a false scent, comparing an eagle with a fly, a stag with a snail, etc., to overthrow the idea of uniformity.

"The argument drawn from the fitness of the different organs of animals for their uses appears stronger. Were not their feet made for walking, their wings for flying, their mouths for eating, their eyes for seeing, their other parts for reproduction? Does not all that indicate an intelligence and a purpose which has presided in their construction? That argument struck the ancients as it did Newton; and it is in vain that the enemy of Providence replies that the function was not intentional, but followed from the construction of the organs; that chance formed eyes, ears, and tongue, from which resulted sight, hearing, and speech."

He seems to think there is a good deal in teleology, if it is properly handled. But he immediately falls afoul of its advocates for their mismanagement and abuse of it: —

"Almost all the modern authors in physics and natural history have done little else than *expand* the proofs drawn from the organization of animals and plants, and push them in the small details of nature. . . . A crowd of physicists since Newton have found God in stars, in insects, in plants, and in water; not to mention those who find him in the wrinkles of the rhinoceros's hide. . . . Leave such *bagatelles* to those who do not perceive their folly."

His foot-notes enable us to see that these telling shots were aimed at Derham, in part at least. He quite as pointedly condemns all who go to the opposite extreme of denying all *final causes*.

"Those see intelligence everywhere; these nowhere. They think a blind mechanism has been able to form the bodies of animals and plants, and to produce all the wonders we see in the cosmos.

" It must be confessed that these proofs have been abused. Some have given them greater weight than they deserve ; others have expanded them too much. Natural theology is full of such stuff as this : Observe the hatching of a fly or an ant ; admire the care of Providence for the eggs of insects, for the nurture of the young, for the chrysalis so long shut up in its case, for the metamorphoses of insects, etc.

" The bodies of animals and plants are machines too complex, whose obscure parts too easily escape us, whose use and end we too little understand, to be able to judge of the wisdom and power needed for their construction."

No one ever claimed that we could determine precisely how much wisdom and power were needful, — certainly a great deal more than man is able to command, or even to comprehend. Maupertuis dwells somewhat upon the topic of the evils and imperfections in the world. Some animals are highly perfect in structure, others very rude and sketchy beings. Some are wholly useless ; some injurious, as serpents for example ; but these are furnished with all that is needful, and cared for by Providence precisely like the most beautiful and useful creatures. Suffering, disorder, and crime abound : how are all these things to be reconciled with a beneficent Providence ? " Some to preserve His wisdom seem to limit His power, saying that he made the world as well as He could." Here the reference is to Leibnitz, who does say something like that in his " Theodicy." Maupertuis stirs up these doubts and objections respecting evil, and leaves them so.

" I review the proofs drawn from the contemplation of nature, and I add a reflection : it is, that those which have greatest strength have not been sufficiently examined as regards their validity and extent. That the cosmos presents trains of agencies converging to an end on a thousand occasions, is no proof of intelligence and design: it is in the purpose of these contrivances that we must search for wisdom. Skill in the execution is not sufficient: the purpose must be rational.

"It is not in petty details, but in those phenomena whose universality suffers no exception, and whose simplicity is such that they are wholly within our comprehension, that we are to search for the proofs of a Supreme Being. It is true that this research will be more difficult than that which consists in the examination of an insect, a flower, or something else of that sort. . . . The organization of animals, the multiplicity and minuteness of the parts of insects, the immensity of celestial bodies, their distances and revolutions, are better suited to astonish the mind than to enlighten it. . . . Let us search for Him in the fundamental laws of the cosmos, in those universal principles of order which underlie the whole, rather than in the complicated results of those laws."

This "reflection," which he appends to his review of the reasonings in natural theology, is for the most part eminently sound and judicious. After reading it we turn with new interest to see what sort of an argument Maupertuis himself is going to make, after slashing about so freely at those of other people. His method is peculiar, and our eagerness speedily turns to disappointment. He frames a definition of the Supreme Intelligence, and then deduces from this a suite of cosmical laws. Comparing these with the actual laws of nature, and finding them to agree, he infers that the Being from whom his laws were deduced has a real existence, and is the Author of the actual cosmos. His method is so manifestly foredoomed to failure that it is not necessary to follow him through, and point out the very spot where he stumbled.

CHAPTER VIII.

REIMARUS, KANT, HUME, AND REID.

HERMANN SAMUEL REIMARUS, professor at Hamburg, published at various times, about the middle of the eighteenth century, ten essays on the " Principal Truths of Natural Religion." They were collected, and published in book-form, in 1754. Reimarus is a thoughtful and suggestive writer. Kant gives him a very appreciative notice in his " Enquiry into the Grounds of Proof for the Existence of God." Kant's work was critical, and mostly of the nature of destructive criticism. Comparing his own with the work of Reimarus, he gives the palm to the latter for practical value; its merit consisting " in an unartificial use of a sound and fine reason."

The first four essays contain his transcendental theology, or the arguments from à priori conceptions, and the causal argument. The fifth is teleological. In this he dwells especially upon animal instincts: —

" But what shall we say of the chamois and mountain goat? No cliff too high or too steep for them to ascend, and thence to make the most astonishing leaps to some other point hanging in the abyss. Who has given them that exact estimation of the distance, so that they neither overleap nor fall short of the mark ? Who has taught them to break the fall with their horns when they make a long leap downwards? Who has instructed them that it was within their power to whirl over backwards in mid-air in such an unnatural fashion, and still preserve the equilibrium of their bodies? Who has made them so courageous and daring that they shrink at no abyss, fear no fall, but, like the elements, trust themselves to their untried skill ?

" Is there not a marvellous diversity of wise contrivances which all minister to one grand purpose, — the propagation and perpetuation of the species of animals? In what school of life have animals acquired so many artful expedients and devices? Or how is it that each one has chosen that which was most suitable and brought it to perfection? Do not say Nature has taught them: that expression has no meaning. . . . I should become tedious if I touched upon all the modes of propagation of the various orders, — with what art and circumspection birds construct nests beforehand for their eggs and young; with what foresight insects deposit their eggs, sometimes in a lump when the young are gregarious, sometimes, on the contrary, scattering them one by one, gluing them fast here, shoving them in yonder, wherever their offspring will find its natural element and proper nutriment, although the mother may not be at all accustomed to that element or nutriment, and gives herself not the slightest concern about her eggs after they are laid ; how fishes seek the fresh and shallow waters when they spawn, and deposit the roe among the reeds at the water's edge, or in a shallow nest at the bottom ; how some aquatic animals and birds lay their eggs in the bare sand, to be hatched by the sun, while others keep them warm and hatch them in nests, and then most tenderly cherish their young, feeding them from their own crops, or bringing food to them ; how among bees, wasps, and ants neither father nor mother, but the sterile females, busy themselves with the nursing and feeding of the young ; to make no mention of many other expedients and contrivances of animals which contribute to the preservation, defence, pleasure, and welfare of themselves or their species. A man must be very perverse if he will not see that these

things are so contrived for a wise purpose, and that they
have their origin in an infinite mind and will.''

Immanuel Kant's "Enquiry, Critical and Metaphysical, into the Grounds of Proof of the Existence of
God," was published in 1763. To him belongs the
merit of systematizing and naming the arguments for
the existence of God. He is not, however, entirely
consistent in his nomenclature. He first distinguishes
between the ontological argument, "that by which
the internal possibility of all things is considered as
something that gives to presuppose some one existence," and the cosmological, in which "the proof is
given by the properties perceived in the things of the
world and the casual order of the universe." Here he
includes under the term "cosmological," not only the argument for a First Cause, but all design-arguments, and
all arguments whatever which are drawn "from what
experience teaches us of existing things;" in other
words, all *à posteriori* arguments are cosmological.

That this is true, especially as regards design-arguments being included under the term "cosmological,"
appears further from the following quotation: —

"In our humble opinion this cosmological proof is as old
as the reason of man. It is so natural, so engaging, and
enlarges our reflection so much with the progress of our insights, that it must last as long as there exists anywhere a
rational creature who wishes to partake of the noble contemplation of knowing God by his works. In this respect
the endeavors of Derham, Nieuwentyt, and many others,
though they sometimes betray much vanity in giving all sorts
of physical insights or even chimeras a venerable semblance
by the signal of religious zeal, do human reason honor."

But in Part VIII. of this "Enquiry" he separates the
design-arguments of physico-theology from the cosmo-

logical argument, leaving the latter term to apply only to the causal argument : —

"There can be but three sorts of proof of the existence of God from speculative reason, — the physico-theological, in which we begin with the determinate experience and the thereby known peculiar quality of our sensible world, and mount from it, according to laws of causation, to the very Supreme Cause out of the world ; the cosmological, in which we lay indeterminate experience only, that is, any one existence, empirically as a ground ; and the ontological."

It is true that this statement alone gives but a faint notion of what he means to include under each argument; but it shows, at all events, that he has abandoned his first position of including all *à posteriori* arguments under the term " cosmological." Turning over to the more careful statement of each argument just before he proceeds to his destructive criticism of it, we get further light upon his meaning. Speaking of the cosmological proof, he says, —

" It runs thus : If something exists, an absolutely necessary Being must exist. Now I, at least, exist myself : therefore an absolutely necessary Being exists.

" The main points of the physico-theological proof are as follows : 1. Everywhere in the world there are distinct marks of an arrangement according to a determined design, executed with great wisdom, and in a whole of indescribable variety, as well as of unbounded greatness of sphere. 2. This arrangement, so answerable to the end, is quite foreign to the things of the world, and adheres to them fortuitously only ; that is, the nature of the different agencies could not agree of its own accord in determinate designs by so various uniting means, were it not chosen and disposed for that purpose entirely by a rational Principle ordering it according to ideas laid as a foundation. 3. Therefore there exists a

sublime and wise Cause (or more of them), which must be
that of the world, not only as blind, working all-powerful
nature by fertility, but, as an intelligence, by liberty.
4. This Cause's unity may be inferred from the unity of the
reciprocal reference of the parts of the world as members
of an artificial structure, in that to which our observation
reaches with certainty [that is, inferred with certainty.
These Germans thrust so many clauses and qualifications
between subject and predicate, that one must have a long
memory and a clear head if he will keep track of the relation between the beginning and the end of one of their sen-
tences], but farther, on all the principles of analogy, with
probability." [That is, the analogical inference carries us
beyond the sphere of observation, but gives only a probability instead of a certainty.]

I have quoted more than was needed to show that
his physico-theology is co-extensive with design-arguments, or with eutaxiology and teleology; and that,
although he first included these under the cosmological
proof, he has here excluded them. That is one point I
wish to establish; but I shall use the quotation for other
purposes also, and hence have extended it more than
would have been otherwise necessary. Upon this first
point, however, I wish to remark, that those theologians
who have adopted the later classification of Kant, in
which he restricts the term "cosmological" to the argument for a First Cause, have, in so doing, followed his
worse, rather than his better, thought. The design-
arguments are both unquestionably cosmological, in
that they draw their facts from external nature; and
the eutaxiological proof is *the* cosmological one *par excellence*, because the principle of order is of the very
essence of a cosmos as distinguished from a chaos.

A singular fact appears in the above quotation: Kant

resolves the design-arguments into causal arguments. This is all the more remarkable, because he excludes them, in this part of his treatise, from a place under the term " cosmological." That is a causal argument as he employs it here; and, if the design-arguments also proceed according to the law of cause and effect, it would seem that he had an additional reason in this fact for adhering to his first plan of including them all under one name. But the resolution of design-arguments into cause-and-effect arguments is a part of his general plan of attack. He turns them all into one, in order to sweep them all away at one stroke. He resolves the physico-theological proof into the cosmological, the cosmological into the ontological, and then proceeds to demolish the ontological proof. One is reminded of that rural practitioner whose first step in every case was to throw the patient into convulsions, because, while he was ignorant of the proper remedies for other diseases, he knew how to cure " fits."

I am not concerned about the attack upon the ontological proof: let others defend that if they choose. But I contend that the design-arguments are distinct lines of reasoning, not capable of being resolved into any other. The first step in proving the existence of God by means of them is to establish the proposition that intelligence has been concerned in the orderly disposition of the cosmos. The farther steps from an intelligent World-Orderer to an infinite God (steps which are generally ignored, but which are quite as necessary as the first) I shall not discuss at present. But how are we to take the first step? Kant says, by proceeding upon the principle of cause and effect. The order of nature is an effect whose cause must be intelligent. I say that we need not resort to the principle of causation at all. The reasoning properly proceeds (I speak of that one of the design-arguments which I have named eutaxiological) upon the principle of identification by means of *marks*. The quality *a* is a *mark*, an invariable attribute of the substance A: therefore the presence of *a* enables us to infer the presence of A. Now, mind has its marks, one of which is order. The order of the cosmos therefore justifies the inference of an intelligent World-Orderer.

But it may be answered, that the principle of causation is there, whether you bring it out in the statement of the proof or not. Intelligence was the cause of order. That I cannot deny, but there are some considerations which set this undeniable fact in a new light. The principle of causation is involved in precisely the same way and to the same extent *in all reasoning*. Suppose a lawyer is trying to convict a man of murder by means of certain stains upon a knife in his possession when he was arrested. He claims that they are *blood-marks;* and, very likely, the reasoning will be conclusive enough to convince the court and jury that the man ought to be hung. Here the law of cause and effect is involved. Blood was the cause of the marks. But does that make it a causal argument? Suppose the advocate for the defence should claim that it was a causal argument, and proceed to throw doubt upon it by rehearsing the metaphysical disputes respecting causation. Is the judgment that every event has a cause, an intuition, or an induction from experience? May it please the court, gentlemen of the jury, Hume says this about it, and Reid says that. The case of Mill *v.* McCosh must be thoroughly examined before we hang this man. How long would the judge permit that sort of quibbling to go on? But it would be just as reason-

able as it is to resolve design-arguments into causal
arguments, because, forsooth, the principle of causation
underlies them, or, more accurately speaking, the *nexus*
between order and intelligence may be viewed as causal
if we choose to do so.

Why should we not so choose? It seems from what
has been said, that it is *possible* to resolve design-arguments into causal arguments, — possible upon just the
same grounds that would apply to all sorts of reasoning. The considerations thus far urged go to show
only that it is not *necessary* to do it. If there is an
option in the matter, what objection is there to this
resolution of these arguments, — a course which tends
to simplify the whole problem of theology? Simplicity
is certainly a good thing in most cases. It depends
somewhat upon circumstances, however, whether this
party or that is to be benefited by it. For the tyrant
who wished to behead all his subjects at one blow, the
resolution of all necks into one would have been a
capital thing; but not so for his subjects. So it might
be a capital thing for the atheists to reduce all theistic
arguments into one, but not a good thing for the opposite party.

Eutaxiology is, in fact, a distinct argument; and every
attempt to resolve it into some other form of proof is
of the nature of legal quibbling. The inference from
mind-marks to mind is direct and certain. It does not
at all depend upon the principle of· causation. That
may be a matter of intuition or a matter of experience:
it is entirely a matter of indifference which it is, so far as
this order-argument is concerned. So of any other difficulties which the causal argument encounters: whether
they are trivial or fatal, it matters not to eutaxiology,
because that stands upon its own independent basis.

Kant, as we all know, was far from being an atheist. How did it happen, then, that he assailed theistic arguments with such energy? I suppose it resulted from his peculiar psychology. He parcelled out the mind into sharply defined faculties, and walled them off in separate compartments. He had his "speculative" reason and his "practical" reason. It was by the light of the former that he framed his destructive criticism of the proofs of God's existence. But his practical reason accepted these very arguments as valid, and enabled him to look up with all reverence and Christian humility to a heavenly Father. If one's speculative and practical reason were really so distinct as he made them, might it not happen that the one should bring up at the wrong port in eternity, while the other came out all right?

But let us be thankful that Kant had a practical reason as well as a speculative one; for by means of it he was enabled, not only to be a good Christian, but to make some very sound suggestions respecting the strengthening and improvement of design-arguments. The most remarkable thing in these suggestions is, that, although he did not distinguish eutaxiology from teleology so far as to give it a distinct name, he pitches upon the order of nature for especial emphasis at the very beginning, and holds it forth prominently to the very end. Manifestly his physico-theology is mostly eutaxiology, while that of his predecessors and contemporaries was mostly teleology.

"The following considerations, then, may tend to improve this method (namely, the physico-theological proof). Order and harmony, though they are necessary, denote an intelligent Author. Nothing can be more disadvantageous to the thought of a Divine Author of the universe, or more irrational, than always to be ready to ascribe a great fertile rule of regularity, of utility, and of harmony, to accident. The *klinomen* of atoms in the systems of Democritus and Epicurus is of this nature. Without dwelling on the absurdity and the premeditated illusion of this way of judging, as they are already made sufficiently evident by others, we have to observe, that the perceived necessity in the reference of things to regular connections, and the coherence of useful laws with a necessary unity, yield, as well as the casual and arbitrable arrangement, a proof of a wise Author, though the dependence upon him in this point of view must be represented in another way. In order to see this properly, we perceive that order and various advantageous harmonies in general denote, even before we reflect whether this reference is necessary or casual to the things, an intelligent Author. According to the judgments of common, sane reason, the course of the alterations of the world, or that connection in whose stead another is possible, has, though it affords a clear proof of casualty, little effect in occasioning the understanding of the presumption of an author. Thereto philosophy is required, and even its use in this case implicated and uncertain ; whereas great regularity and harmony in a great multifarious whole astonish, and common reason itself never can find them possible without an intelligent Author. Let the things themselves be necessary or contingent, let the one rule of regularity essentially lie in the other or be arbitrariously conjoined with it, it is directly found impossible that order and regularity should thus have place of themselves (*sponte*) either by accident, or among many things which have their separate existence ; for the possibility of extensive harmony or agreement without an intelligent ground never is sufficiently given.''

Kant's thought is not easy to follow, either in the above or in the next quotation. It is not all on the surface : it is subtile and deep, not to say a trifle muddy sometimes. One key to the comprehension of his suggestions for the improvement of design-arguments is to observe his antithesis between what is "necessary" and what is "casual and arbitrable." He has a profound comprehension of the contrast between that which is settled, fixed, unbending, and 'universal in the cosmos, and that which is flexible and tends to specialization. In other words, he knew the difference between eutaxiology and teleology; and it is a pity that he did not emphasize it more, and nail it down by giving each argument a distinct name. The attempt to distinguish the one as "necessary," and the other as "casual," besides its awkwardness, is open to several other objections. It is not essential to eutaxiology to admit fatality to the extent which he seems willing to grant. But, although these terms are not the best, they serve to distinguish the two arguments after a fashion, and to show what prominence Kant gives to eutaxiology.

With these hints to aid in their interpretation, I hope the reader may ponder Kant's six "rules" with as much profit and satisfaction as I have : —

"We shall comprise the improved method of physico-theology in the following short rules : Guided by a confidence in the fertility of the universal laws of nature, because of their dependence upon the Divine Being, let us —

"1. Seek the causes of even the most advantageous constitutions in universal laws, which, with a necessary unity, bear, besides other regular consequences, a reference to the productions of these effects.

"2. Observe what is *necessary*, in this connection of various fitnesses in one ground ; because the way of thence concluding the existence of God is distinct from that which has the artificial and chosen unity in view, as well as the consequence according to constant and necessary laws is to be distinguished from accident.[1]

"3. Presume greater necessary unity than is directly obvious, not only in unorganized but in organized bodies ; for even in the structure of an animal it is presumable that a single predisposition has a productive fitness for many useful consequences, for which we at first might find various particular arrangements necessary. This attention is very suitable to philosophy, as well as advantageous to the physico-theological consequence.

"4. Make use of the manifestly artificial order thence to infer the wisdom of an Author as a ground ; but, of the essential and necessary unity in the laws of nature, thence to conclude a wise Being by means, not of his wisdom, but of that in him which must accord with it.

"5. From the casual combinations in the world conclude of the Author of the way in which the universe is composed ; but, from the necessary unity, of the very same Being as the author of matter itself, or of the very elemental or constituent parts of all the things of nature. And let us —

"6. Enlarge this method by universal rules which can render intelligible the grounds of the regularity of what is mechanically or even geometrically necessary, and not neglect to consider under this point of view the properties of space, and from the unity of its great multifariousness to illustrate the same chief conception."

David Hume's "Dialogues concerning Natural Religion" appeared in 1779, three years after the death of the author. His motive in adopting the form of a dialogue is thus stated : —

"There are some subjects, however, to which dialogue-writing is peculiarly adapted, and where it is still preferable to the direct and simple method of composition.

---

[1] In this rule he is pulling hard towards a clear distinction between eutaxiology and teleology; but his keel sticks a little in the gravel.

" Any point of doctrine which is so *obvious* that it scarcely admits of dispute, but at the same time so *important* that it cannot be too often inculcated, seems to require some such method of handling it, — where the novelty of the manner may compensate the triteness of the subject, where the vivacity of the conversation may enforce the precept, and where the variety of lights, presented by various personages and characters, may appear neither tedious nor redundant.

" Any question of philosophy, on the other hand, which is so *obscure* and *uncertain* that human reason can reach no fixed determination with regard to it, if it should be treated at all, seems to lead us naturally into the style of dialogue and conversation. Reasonable men may be allowed to differ where no one can reasonably be positive. Opposite sentiments, even without any decision, afford an agreeable amusement; and, if the subject be curious and interesting, the book carries us, in a manner, into company, and unites the two greatest and purest pleasures of human life, — study and society.

" Happily all these circumstances are to be found in the subject of Natural Religion. What truth so obvious, so certain, as the *being* of God, which the most ignorant ages have acknowledged, for which the most refined geniuses have ambitiously striven to produce new proofs and arguments? What truth so important as this, which is the ground of all our hope, the surest foundation of morality, the firmest support of society, and the only principle which ought never for a moment to be absent from our thoughts and meditations? But, in treating of this obvious and important truth, what obscure questions occur concerning the *nature* of that Divine Being, — his attributes, his decrees, his plan of providence? These have been always subjected to the disputations of men. Concerning these, human nature has not reached any certain determination. But these are topics so interesting that we cannot restrain our restless inquiry with regard to them, though nothing but doubt, uncertainty, and contradiction

have, as yet, been the result of our most accurate researches."

The conversational method was certainly well suited
to Hume's genius. He was vain of his fertility in
raising objections, and this method gave him the opportunity to display that faculty without incurring the
opprobrium of being personally responsible for opinions
he puts into the mouth of some dashing sceptic in the
dialogue. It gave him even the opportunity, which he
did not fail to improve, of complimenting himself in his
own book! His Cleanthes praises his Philo for "the
fertility of his invention in raising doubts and objections." As these are mere imaginary personages invented to carry out the form of a dialogue, this is
simply Hume praising Hume.

Another reason why the dialogue form suited Hume
was, that it furnished an excuse for leaving many things
unsettled. Something is said on both sides of every
controversy raised. This gives a double opportunity for
brilliant writing, first on one side, and then on the
other; but, when all is done, you are wholly in the dark
as to what Hume himself believed. It is doubtful
whether he knew himself what he believed. What he
advances with apparent conviction in one essay, he
overthrows in another. We have an illustration of this
in respect to the very topic of these dialogues. In the
"Natural History of Religion," published in 1757, he
speaks of design-arguments as presenting "invincible
reasons" for the inference that there is "one Supreme
Deity;" while in the "Dialogues" he raises all manner
of doubts and objections against them.

The parties to the conversation are Demea, who represents a sturdy orthodoxy; Cleanthes, who personates

a sober and reverent rationalism ; and Philo, a brilliant, dashing, and reckless sceptic. At the end Pamphilus, who records the dialogue, says, —

"Upon a serious review of the whole, I cannot but think that Philo's principles are more probable than Demea's, but that those of Cleanthes approach still nearer to the truth."

That is to say, Hume wished it to be understood that Cleanthes most nearly expressed his own opinions, while, at the same time, he recalled with complacency the brilliant conversational exploits of Philo.

Cleanthes is the spokesman for teleology ; and, singularly enough, the ultra-orthodox Demea and the ultra-sceptical Philo unite their forces against Cleanthes. Demea does this because the rational proofs of God's existence yield only a probability, and not a certainty, of it ; and he is shocked at the audacity of even starting such an inquiry. He thinks "that each man feels, in a manner, the truth of religion within his own breast." The only proper question to be raised pertains not to "the being but the nature of God." And even on this question silent adoration is the proper attitude of the mind, for God's nature is "altogether incomprehensible and unknown to us." Philo, the sceptic, of course chimes in with this opinion so far as the incomprehensibility of the Deity is concerned, though he is not so strong on the point of silent adoration. He and Demea go on together in a very lovely manner for a time, having the demolition of the teleology of Cleanthes for a common object and point of sympathy ; but finally his ribald scepticism proves too much for the orthodox champion, and Demea retires in disgust.

The teleological proof is thus stated by Cleanthes : —

" Look round the world ; contemplate the whole and every part of it : you will find it to be nothing but one great machine, subdivided into an infinite number of lesser machines, which again admit of subdivisions to a degree beyond what human faculties can trace and explain. All these various machines, and even their most minute parts, are adjusted to each other with an accuracy which ravishes into admiration all men who have ever contemplated them. The curious adapting of means to ends resembles exactly, though it much exceeds, the productions of human contrivance, of human designs, thought, wisdom, and intelligence. Since, therefore, the effects resemble each other, we are led to infer, by all the rules of analogy, that the causes also resemble, and that the Author of nature is somewhat similar to the mind of man, though possessed of much larger faculties proportioned to the grandeur of the work which he has executed. By this argument *à posteriori*, and by this argument alone, do we prove at once the existence of a Deity, and his similarity to human mind and intelligence."

The first point in this argument which Philo selects for his attack is the logical method. He claims that the *analogy* is a very weak one because of the dissimilarity of the productions of art and nature.

" After having experienced the circulation of the blood in human creatures, we make no doubt that it takes place in Titius and Mævius. [But that is not a case of analogy at all : it is an induction.] But from its circulation in frogs and fishes, it is only a presumption, though a strong one, from analogy, that it takes place in men and other animals. The analogical reasoning is much weaker when we infer the circulation of sap in vegetables from our experience that the blood circulates in animals ; and those who hastily followed that imperfect analogy are found, by more accurate experiments, to have been mistaken. [Not entirely mistaken : the sap does circulate.] If we see a house, Cleanthes, we conclude, with the greatest certainty, that it had an architect or builder, because that is precisely that species of effect which we have experienced to proceed from that species of cause. But surely you will not affirm that the universe bears such a resemblance to a house that we can with the same certainty infer a similar cause, or that the analogy is here entire and perfect. The dissimilitude is so striking that the utmost you can here pretend to is a guess, a conjecture, a presumption, concerning a similar cause; and how that pretension will be received in the world, I leave you to consider.

" When two species of objects have always been observed to be conjoined together, I can infer. by custom, the existence of one wherever I see the existence of the other; and this I call an argument from experience. But how this argument can have place where the objects, as in the present case, are single, individual, without parallel, or specific resemblance, may be difficult to explain. And will any man tell me, with a serious countenance, that an orderly universe must arise from some thought and art. like the human, because we have experience of it? To ascertain [he means *verify*] this reasoning, it were requisite that we had experience of the origin of worlds; and it is not sufficient, surely, that we have seen ships and cities arise from human art and contrivance."

In the last quotation he passes from the first to the second point of attack. The animus of this is to be found in his principles of psychology. He belonged to the *sensational* school, admitting no innate or intuitive elements of mind, but holding that all knowledge comes from without through the senses. But let him state this for himself: —

" All the perceptions of the human mind resolve themselves into two distinct kinds, which I shall call *Impressions* and *Ideas*. The difference betwixt these consists in the degrees of force and liveliness with which they strike upon the mind, and make their way into our thought or consciousness. Those perceptions which enter with most force and violence we may name *impressions;* and under this name I comprehend all our sensations, passions, and emotions, as they make their first appearance in the soul. By *ideas* I mean the faint images of these in thinking and reasoning." [1]

As he held that all knowledge comes through experience by the channel of the senses, it was inevitable that he should deny any possibility of inferring an intelligent world-builder unless we had actually witnessed the process of world-building. Reid took a clever turn upon him at this point by showing, that, on this ground, he could not know that any mind at all existed, even of his most intimate and gifted companions! He could not obtain any knowledge of it through the senses; and, according to his own principles, he could not therefore be sure of the existence of any intelligence except his own.

Hume himself, speaking through Cleanthes, indicates the wild and boundless sweep of such a style of objections. Upon the same grounds that we reject any inference of intelligence in the structure of worlds unless we had seen their origin, it would be impossible for us to receive any revelation of God's existence conveyed in any manner whatsoever.

" ' Suppose,' says Cleanthes, ' that an articulate voice were heard in the clouds, much louder and more melodious than any which human art could ever reach ; suppose that this voice were extended in the same instant over all nations, and spoke to each nation in its own language and dialect ; suppose that the words delivered, not only contain a just sense and meaning, but convey some instruction alto-

---

[1] Treatise on Human Nature, *initio.*

gether worthy of a benevolent being, superior to mankind : could you possibly hesitate a moment concerning the cause of this voice, and must you not instantly ascribe it to some design or purpose? Yet I cannot see but all the same objections (if they merit that appellation) which lie against the system of theism may also be produced against this inference. Might you not say that all conclusions concerning fact were founded on experience ; that when we hear an articulate voice in the dark, and thence infer a man, it is only the resemblance of the effects which leads us to conclude that there is a like resemblance in the cause? But this extraordinary voice. by its loudness. extent, and flexibility to all languages, bears so little analogy to any human voice. that we have no reason to suppose any analogy in their causes ; and consequently that a rational, wise, coherent speech proceeded, you know not whence, from some accidental whistling of the winds, not from any divine reason or intelligence. You see clearly your own objections in these cavils ; and I hope, too, you see clearly that they cannot possibly have more force in the one case than in the other.' "

Very true : we should have to reject the testimony of God himself speaking in an audible voice from heaven on Philo's principles. The recoil of such a style of objection does more damage than its projectile force.

It should be observed that Cleanthes' statement of the teleological argument contains little of the strength, but all the vices and weakness, of the teleology current in Hume's day. It is grossly *mechanical :* the world is "one great machine. subdivided into an infinite number of lesser machines, which again admit of subdivisions." It proceeds by analogy, whereas the fundamental propositions of physico-theology are reached by induction. The causal element is constantly thrust forward. "Like effects prove like causes," is the text of his discourse. Philo takes this up, and easily shows that it leads to anthropomorphism ; that, the effects being finite, the cause is also finite ; that as there are slips, evils, and monstrosities in nature, so there must be in God; and that it is impossible to infer the unity of the Deity, since in human production a ship, for example, is the work of many hands. Having such a feeble and vicious statement of teleology to attack, it is no wonder that Philo makes more havoc than Cleanthes is able to repair. The whole matter is finally hammered down to this insignificant conclusion : —

" The whole of natural theology resolves itself into this proposition, *That the cause or causes of order in the universe probably bear some remote analogy to human intelligence.*"

Thomas Reid, D.D., published his " Essays on the Intellectual Powers of Man " in 1785. In this he gives some space to teleology with particular reference to Hume's attack upon it : —

" The argument from final causes, when reduced to a syllogism, has these two premises : *First*, That design and intelligence in the cause may, with certainty, be inferred from marks or signs of it in the effect. This is the principle we have been considering, and we may call it the *major* proposition of the argument. The *second*, which we call the *minor* proposition, is, that there are in fact the clearest marks of design and wisdom in the works of nature ; and the *conclusion* is, that the works of nature are the effects of a wise and intelligent Cause."

This argument would be much stronger if stated without any reference to the principle of cause and effect. Mind may be inferred from mind-marks wherever and in whatsoever these may be found. The only question is, whether they are mind-marks ; and,

in the determination of that, the law of causation is
not concerned in any way or degree whatever.

Reid says that the ancients denied the minor premise; but "the gradual advancement made in the
knowledge of nature hath put this opinion quite out
of countenance. When the structure of the human
body was much less known than it is now, the famous
Galen saw such evident marks of wise contrivance in
it, that, though he had been educated an Epicurean, he
renounced that system, and wrote his book of the use
of the parts of the human body, on purpose to convince
others of what appeared so clear to himself, that it was
impossible that such admirable contrivance should be
the effect of chance. Those, therefore, of later times,
who are dissatisfied with this argument from final
causes, have quitted the stronghold of the ancient
atheists, which had become untenable, and have chosen
rather to make a defence against the major proposition."

The method he adopts for the purpose of establishing this major premise is to assert that it is an *intuitive*
truth. Having turned Hume's position against Hume's
own objection, by showing to what absurdities it led,
he was perhaps inclined to go too far in the opposite
direction. He was not content with meeting Hume's
sensationalism by the assertion that there are some
intuitive convictions, but magnified his office of cham-
pioning intuitions by claiming some things to be intuitive which were not. The safest ground for design-
arguments is that of induction. Nevertheless, Reid's
contribution to teleology is valuable, being directed as
it is to a scrutiny of its logical validity, instead of piling
up new examples or rehearsing old ones.

CHAPTER IX.

PALEY, STEWART, AND CROMBIE.

In the "Natural Theology" of William Paley, D.D., which appeared in 1803, we are at once impressed with the exaggerated importance which he attaches to those appearances in nature which most nearly resemble the productions of human art. The *mechanical* school of teleology has in him, I was about to say, reached its culmination; but the method was too ancient to be merely in full bloom: it had gone to seed.

" I contend, therefore, that there is mechanism in animals ; that this mechanism is as properly such as it is in machines made by art; that this mechanism is intelligible and certain ; that it is not the less so because it often begins or terminates with something which is not mechanical ; that, whenever it is intelligible and certain, it demonstrates intention and contrivance as well in the works of nature as in those of art; and that it is the best demonstration which either can afford.

" Our business is with mechanism. In the *panorpa* tribe of insects, there is a forceps in the tail of the male insect, with which he catches and holds the female. Are a pair of pincers more mechanical than this provision in their structure? or is any structure more clear and certain in its design?

" For my part, I take my stand in human anatomy ; and the examples of mechanism I should be apt to draw out from the copious catalogue which it supplies are the pivot

upon which the head turns, the ligament within the socket
of the hip-joint, the pulley or trochlear muscle of the eye,
the epiglottis, the bandages which tie down the tendons of
the wrist and instep, the slit or perforated muscles at the
hands and feet, the knitting of the intestines to the mesen-
tery, the course of the chyle into the blood, and the constitution of the sexes as extended throughout the whole of the
animal creation. To these instances the reader's memory
will go back as they are severally set forth in their places.
There is not one of the number which I do not think decisive,
— not one which is not *strictly mechanical;* nor have I read or
heard of any solution of these appearances, which, in the
smallest degree, shakes the conclusion that we build upon
them.''

Probably the emphasis which he lays upon the notion
of mechanism and artificialness was partly induced by
the illustration of the watch with which he sets out,
and on account of which he has been so severely ex-
coriated as a plagiarist.

An evolutionist cannot read Paley with any patience.
The mechanical view of nature has been set aside, and
in its place we have now the *dynamical* conception.
The necessary complement of the mechanical theory,
which makes the world a vast machine made up of a
multitude of lesser machines, is a *deus ex machina*, a
God outside of the machine to set it in motion, and to
stop it, regulate it, repair it, all by abrupt intrusion of
arbitrary divine power. wholly severed from the customary action of natural forces. The dynamical conception, upon the contrary, represents natural forces as
permanently united to the divine energy as the means
by which the latter produces its results. God thus
becomes *immanent* in nature, though at the same time
transcendent above it. This view of nature is largely

the fruit of the theory of evolution; and yet it is more
widely received, and stands upon a surer foundation,
than evolution itself.   Paley is so thoroughly imbued
with the mechanical conception, that, if his work had
no other defect, this alone would render it obsolete.

In the opening of his discussion of *final causes*,
Dugald Stewart says, —

" The study of final causes may be considered in two
different points of view, — first, as subservient to the evidences of natural religion ; and, secondly, as a guide and
auxiliary in the investigation of physical laws.   Of these
views it is the latter alone which is immediately connected
with the principles of the inductive logic ; and it is to this,
accordingly, that I shall chiefly direct my attention in the
following observations."

He proceeds to fortify with elaborate argumentation
the position that teleology " has proved a powerful, and
perhaps indispensable, organ of *physical discovery*."   In
this he makes the same mistake as Whewell, of not dis-
tinguishing between *use* and *end, function* and *purpose*,
— a neglect which was indeed quite essential in order
to make out his case, but which, none the less, convicts
him of building upon a shallow fallacy.

" To understand the structure of an animal body, it is
necessary not only to examine the *conformation* of the parts,
but to consider their *functions; or, in other words, to consider their *ends* and *uses*.   Nor, indeed, does the most accurate knowledge of the former, till perfected by the discovery
of the latter, afford satisfaction to an inquisitive and scientific mind.   Every anatomist accordingly, whatever his metaphysical creed may be, proceeds in his researches upon the
maxim, that no organ exists without its appropriate destination ; and, although he may often fail in his attempts to
ascertain what this destination is, he never carries his scepti-

cism so far as for a moment to doubt the general principle. I am inclined to think, that it is in this way the most important steps in physiology have been gained ; the curiosity being constantly kept alive by some new problem in the animal machine, and at the same time checked in its wanderings by an irresistible conviction that nothing is made in vain."

To consider their functions, *or, in other words*, to consider their ends and uses! No difference whatever recognized between functions and ends! Quite easy to make out his case for the physiological value of teleology on those terms. Thus he quotes with great satisfaction : —

"If we find *one common effect* constantly produced, though in a very different way, we may safely conclude that this is the *use* or *function* of the part. This reasoning can never betray us if we are but sure of the facts."

An anatomist need only mention the use or function of an organ, and Stewart takes it as testimony to the value of teleology, just as much as if he had said *end* or *purpose*.

He is to be commended for his dislike of the term *final cause*, but not for the timidity which made him retain it, in spite of his dislike, because it had been "consecrated in the writings of Newton," nor for the method he proposed for gradually getting rid of it.

"After all, it were to be wished that the scholastic phrase *final cause* could, without affectation, be dropped from our philosophical vocabulary, and some more unexceptionable mode of speaking be substituted instead of it. In this elementary work I have not presumed to lay aside entirely a form of expression consecrated in the writings of Newton and of his most eminent followers ; but I am fully sensible of its impropriety, and am not without hopes that I may contribute something to encourage the gradual disuse of it by the indiscriminate employment of the words *ends* and *uses* to convey the same idea."

He was altogether too "indiscriminate" in the employment of the words "ends," "uses," "functions," and "purposes."

The quotations given above are from the third volume of his works, as collected and edited by Sir William Hamilton (p. 335, *seq.*). In the sixth volume of the same collection he has more teleological matter. In a chapter headed "The Evidences of Design exhibited in the Universe," he begins a section with the sentence, —

"The proof of the existence of God drawn from the order of the universe is commonly called the argument from final causes."

This shows that his notions of teleology were extremely vague. He threw in all sorts of design-arguments under *final cause.* In this, of course, he was no more to be blamed than Paley and the rest, unless by reason that his great powers of mind and high rank in metaphysical science entitle us to expect better things of him. If "final cause" ever had any legitimate meaning, it had reference to an *end, finis;* that is, its meaning was teleological. "The proof of the existence of God drawn from the order of nature" is not teleological, and therefore does not belong to the doctrine of final causes. Neither is the expression "argument *from* final causes" an accurate one.

The greater part of Stewart's design-arguments are brought into his "Philosophy of the Moral Powers" (vol. vii. of his works, edited by Hamilton). He regards teleology as resting upon the principle of causation, and accordingly spends most of his force in defending that against the opinion of Hume, that the judgment, " Every event has a cause," is a matter of experience. Stewart maintains that it is an intuition. Many of his arguments to support this view are repetitions of those advanced by Reid. In the course of this discussion he quotes with approval from Dr. Clarke an opinion which amounts to a complete denial of second causes : —

" The course of nature, truly and properly speaking, is nothing else but the will of God producing certain effects in a continued, regular, constant, and uniform manner ; which course or manner of acting, being in every moment perfectly *arbitrary*, is as easy to be *altered* at any time as to be preserved."

Besides maintaining that the law of causation is apprehended intuitively, he further follows Reid in the opinion that the inference of design from its effects is intuitive also. An *intuitive inference* is a contradiction of terms ; and Stewart guards his language so as to avoid this self-contradiction, but Reid does not. These two important judgments being, in his opinion, reached without reasoning. it follows logically that design-arguments ought not to be employed to prove God's existence. It would be nonsense to construct elaborate arguments to convince a man of that which he perceives by intuition. · Accordingly, Stewart not only declines to use design-arguments in this way, but complains of the evil consequences of such use of them by others : —

" It appears to me that the evidences of *design* in the universe are alike obvious to the savage and to the philosopher ; and that they are much more forcibly impressed on

the minds of those whose understandings have been perverted by sceptical sophistry, by *general* views of nature,
than by examining her works in detail. Or, if any person
should think otherwise, it must at least be granted that *any
one* organized and animated body furnishes just as complete
evidence of this truth (i.e., design) as could be obtained
from the most accurate examination of all the different subjects of natural history. *The proper use of such speculations
is not to refute the atheist*, but to illustrate the *wisdom* and the
unity of design displayed in the material and moral worlds ;
or rather to enlighten and exalt our own understandings by
tracing with humility and reverence the operations of a
wisdom which is infinite and divine. If there be any principle whatever which a philosopher is entitled to take for
granted, it is certainly this, that there are marks of design
in the objects around us and in our own frame ; and to write
large volumes in order to prove it, is to offer an insult to
human reason.

"I would not be understood by these remarks to detract
from the merit of the authors to whom they refer. I only
complain of the *form* in which they have presented their
observations to the world, — as demonstrations that a designing cause or designing causes exist, and not as an humble
attempt to display to those who are already impressed with
this conviction a few of those manifold indications of beneficent wisdom which the Author of all things has been pleased
for our instruction to place within the reach of our researches.
Many of the observations which they have collected in the
course of their inquiries are of inestimable value ; but they
have been frequently applied to an improper purpose, and
hence very serious inconveniences have arisen. Among these
inconveniences, there are two of such magnitude that I think
it of importance to state them explicitly.

"*First*, The size and number of the publications in question have led superficial thinkers to imagine that the existence of God was a truth which required a multiplicity of

proofs ; and in consequence of this apprehension they have found their faith in it rather weakened than confirmed. While, on the other hand, those who were already convinced of this truth have turned aside with disgust from the perusal of so tedious a demonstration leading to so obvious a conclusion. No expedient more effectual could have been devised for destroying that interest which the mind spontaneously takes in the details of natural philosophy and natural history, than to state them merely as premises subservient to the proof of the most incontestable of all propositions. Whereas, if the existence of an intelligent Cause be taken for granted, and if we study his works not as *proofs* of *design*, but as manifestations of his wisdom and revelations of his will, these branches of knowledge open inexhaustible sources of instruction and of delight to the mind. In the works of God we study the operations of his wisdom and goodness, as we study in the conduct and discourse of our fellow-creatures the peculiarities of their genius and characters ; and, in proportion as our knowledge extends, we find our acquaintance with the plans of his providence become more intimate, and our conceptions of his nature more elevated and sublime. *Secondly*, When we accumulate a number of particular observations as proofs of the existence of an intelligent Cause, we rest this important principle on a ground extremely open to the cavils of sceptics. In most cases, when we speculate concerning final causes, we are unable to do more than to suppose and to conjecture ; and we are extremely apt, by indulging imagination too far, to bring ridicule on the cause we mean to support. Sometimes, too, it has happened that conjectures which at first appeared extremely plausible have been afterwards discovered to proceed on a misapprehension of facts. Such accidents never fail to furnish matter of triumph to the sceptic, as if the mistakes to which our limited faculties are liable in studying the works of God afforded any just ground for ascribing them to chance or to an unintelligent necessity. But if, on the other hand, we acqui-

esce in those evidences of design which a *general* survey of
nature affords to the most common observer, the mistakes
we may commit in the subsequent examination of her works
will have no effect in suggesting doubts or scruples with
respect to the truths of religion ; but, impressed with a firm
conviction that nothing is made in vain, we will consider
every difficulty we meet with as a new reason of humility to
ourselves, and a new illustration of the unsearchable wisdom
displayed in the universe.

" I have thought proper to premise these general reflections
to the remarks I am now to make, in order to point out the
particular purpose to which I mean to apply them, — not as
proofs that there exist designing and intelligent causes in
nature, but as illustrations of that unity of design which
connects together things the most remote and apparently
insulated as parts of one system, and of that infinite wisdom
which contrived and which superintends the whole."

These views of the proper function of physico-theology, and of the mischiefs arising from a misconception
of it, are highly interesting and suggestive. They are
also in a considerable measure correct, but not altogether sound, as I shall try to show in a subsequent
chapter.

The argument which Stewart proceeds to construct,
having thus premised that he is arguing for the wisdom
and unity, not for the existence, of God, is chiefly
an argument of *adaptation:* —

" (1) Adaptation of the bodies and of the instincts of
animals to the laws of the material world.

" (2) Adaptation of the bodies and instincts of animals
to those particular climates and districts of the earth for
which they are destined."

This is, of course, teleological; but he employs eutaxiology also, or such elements of reasoning as properly

fall under that head, though he does not erect them into a distinct argument. Thus, for example, he brings in the facts of morphology under the head of "*analogies* which are observable in the structure of different tribes of animals:" —

" To all this we may add the analogy among many of the phenomena and laws of the material world, a satisfactory proof of which may be derived from the effects which philosophical habits and scientific pursuits have in familiarizing the mind to the *order of nature*, and in improving its penetration and sagacity in anticipating those parts of it which are yet unknown."

Having so pointedly condemned the use of design-arguments to prove the existence of God, and so emphatically declared and set forth the mischiefs resulting from such use, he seems to fear that he may himself be suspected of doing the very thing he condemns. Accordingly he puts in this disclaimer : —

" I have only to add further, before leaving this subject, that the various remarks and reasonings which I have offered on the two general principles of our nature formerly mentioned, are not to be considered as forming any part of the argument for the existence of God, which, as I have said, is an immediate and necessary consequence of those principles. What I had in view was, not to confirm this important truth by reasoning, but to obviate the sceptical cavils which have been raised against it."

The "two general principles" alluded to are the law of causation, and the perception of design by intuition. The belief in the existence of God flows out of these as " an immediate and necessary consequence ; " and he is not so foolish as to argue for the truth of an intuition. Oh, no! all he has been doing is to " obviate sceptical cavils." All the reasoning ever employed on this subject might be fairly brought under the head of answering the cavils of sceptics; for the mass of mankind have always firmly believed in God, in spite of all the illogical demonstrations of his existence, just as many people live to a good age in spite of medical quackery.

Stewart really stood in need of such a disclaimer as he makes in the last quotation. Without it no one would ever dream that he was doing any thing else than arguing for the existence of God. The whole discussion is entitled, "The Existence of God — Proof *à posteriori;*" and that is all along the running-title at the top of the page. In Section III., "Conclusion of the Argument for the Existence of God," the first sentence is, —

"The observations which have been made not only establish the *existence* of a Deity, but contain the evidences of his unity, of his power, and of his wisdom."

Was he, after all, suspicious that this vitally important truth was not an intuition? Did he, with Scotch shrewdness, think to shape matters so that it would be all right on either alternative? If it was not intuitive, he had contributed an argument for it; if it was intuitive, he had put in his disclaimer to save him from the double reproach of arguing for an intuition, and doing himself what he condemned in others.

The "Natural Theology" of the Rev. Alexander Crombie (London, 1829) is of a higher type than the majority of such works. The ontological and causal arguments are lightly esteemed by him. He makes much of the anthropological proof, and employs both of the design-arguments.

" Wherever we find order and regularity obtaining either uniformly, or in a vast majority of instances, where the possibilities of disorder are indefinitely numerous, we are justified in inferring from this fact an intelligent cause." (I. 386.)

He makes great use of the calculus of probabilities in establishing this proposition. However, he thinks that no such computation of the chances is required in the ordinary mental process of inferring intelligence from orderly arrangement. The conclusion is reached instantly by those who are incompetent to compute the probabilities.

" It may be asked, What is the ground of this belief? Why do we infer intelligence from order and regularity? Is the conclusion founded in reason, or is it the result of experience? The inference is immediate and irresistible; the perception is as clear, and the conviction as strong, as that a less number cannot be equal to a greater, — certainly, in many cases, as strong as an immeasurable preponderance of evidence can produce. It is intuitively obvious, that, out of any given number of equally possible results, the chance of one taking place in exclusion of the rest must be as 1 to the number of the others.

" It is not imagined that the inference depends on any nice calculation of the chances, nor is a scientific computation necessary to the conclusion. A person wholly unacquainted with arithmetical science may be unable to calculate the chance that the letters of the alphabet shall be accidentally thrown into their regular order, but he perceives intuitively that the chances against it prodigiously overbalance those in its favor. This is sufficient for his conviction." (I. 394)

Dr. Crombie does not fairly meet the question whether this conviction is intuitive or not. I am not greatly concerned about overthrowing his position, though I think the judgment that order is an invariable mark of mind is an induction. If it is an intuition, it is even more certain; that is, it is absolutely certain, because the marks of an intuitive truth are, that it is self-evident, necessary, and universal. But the judgment in question does not meet these conditions; and there is nothing to gain, but every thing to lose, by claiming intuitive certainty for a proposition which is only reached by induction. The manner in which Crombie makes it appear intuitive is fallacious. Even as against the alternative of chance, his own statements show that the conviction is not intuitive; for, though there may not be a rigid computation of the chances, there is, he thinks, a rough estimate of them. But the simple exclusion of chance does not establish the proposition. Many other considerations are involved in the judgment that order is a mark of intelligence, — so that it seems unwarrantable to class it as an intuition.

Crombie fairly deserves the credit of being the first of modern writers to frame a clear and unmixed eutaxiological argument.

His teleology is much the same as that of Paley. One point, however, deserves notice; namely, his attempted modification of the meaning of the word "end:"—

"The reader is here requested to observe that the term *end* is not here employed as equivalent to *purpose* or *design*, — for, in this sense, we should beg the question, — but in its strict and primitive signification, as denoting simply *issue*, or *effect*."

This is a foot-note appended to a sentence (I. 400) in which he speaks of "concurrences of means to ends," from which we may infer design.   His attempt is a failure.   Supposing that he could change the meaning of a word which, in teleology, has never had but one meaning, by simply saying that he would use it differently, still he would not thus escape from the fallacy he wishes to avoid, because the correlative "means" would have to be emasculated of its usual sense as well as *end*.   Whenever these two words are coupled together, a teleological force is imparted to both of them. The mental contemplation of something as a means involves the correlative notion of an end to be accomplished.   Hence the "concurrence of means" is just as dangerous an expression alone, or with some other ending than "to an end," as it is with this ending, and leaving the ordinary teleological force of "end" to attach to it.

Crombie deserves credit for making this attempt, although it was a failure.   It is an evidence that he felt conscious of a radical difficulty in the logic of the old teleology.   He criticises Paley's expression , " Design implies a designer," and he saw that his own proposition was subject to the same condemnation unless he used the terms in some unusual sense.   So he proposes to give this new force to the word *end*.   The remedy is ineffectual : it is a shallow device, whereas the evil it was aimed at was deeply seated.   The true solution of this whole problem of the logic of teleology will be found in the seventeenth chapter of this volume.   In the mean time let us give Crombie due praise for being one of the first to suspect the existence of some radical vice in the logic of teleology, although his diagnosis was incomplete, and his remedy only skin-deep.

CHAPTER X.

THE BRIDGEWATER TREATISES.

THE Bridgewater Treatises were produced under the following circumstances: —

"The Right Hon. and Rev. Francis Henry, Earl of Bridgewater, died in the month of February, 1829; and by his last will and testament, bearing date the 25th of February, 1825, he directed certain trustees, therein named, to invest in the public funds the sum of eight thousand pounds sterling; this sum, with the accruing dividends thereon, to be held at the disposal of the president, for the time being, of the Royal Society of London, to be paid to the person or persons nominated by him. The testator further directed, that the person or persons selected by the said president should be appointed to write, print, and publish one thousand copies of a work *on the power, wisdom, and goodness of God, as manifested in the creation; illustrating such work by all reasonable arguments, as, for instance, the variety and formation of God's creatures in the animal, vegetable, and mineral kingdoms; the effect of digestion, and thereby of conversion; the construction of the hand of man, and an infinite variety of other arguments; as also by discoveries, ancient and modern, in arts, sciences, and the whole extent of literature.*"

Eight treatises were the result of this bequest of eight thousand pounds sterling. The writers were Thomas Chalmers, D.D., John Kidd, M.D., William

Whewell, M.A., Sir Charles Bell, K.H., Peter M. Roget, M.D., William Buckland, D.D., Rev. William Kirby, and William Prout, M.D.

Chalmers had previously published his "Astronomical Discourses." These were not of the nature of design-arguments. The existence of God is assumed, and the tone is hortatory and sentimental. The following sentence (p. 227–8) gives a fair notion of the aim of these discourses, "to regale the imagination," "to waft the soul," and "raise it to an elevated calm." It also gives a fair example of the style of Chalmers, which has been much praised for its eloquence and sublimity, but is somewhat turgid withal.

"The sublime and interesting topic which has engaged us, however feebly it may have been handled; however inadequately it may have been put in all its worth and in all its magnitude before you; however short the representation of the speaker or the conception of the hearers may have been of that richness, and that greatness, and that loftiness, which belong to it, — possesses in itself a charm to fix the attention, and to regale the imagination, and to subdue the whole man into a delighted reverence; and, in a word, to beget such a solemnity of thought and emotion as may occupy and enlarge the soul for hours together, as may waft it away from the grossness of ordinary life, and raise it to a kind of elevated calm above all its vulgarities and all its vexations."

Neither does his Bridgewater Treatise on "The Adaptation of External Nature to the Moral and Intellectual Constitution of Man," contain any physico-theology properly speaking. It is a somewhat rambling discourse on moral philosophy chiefly, though he meanders freely in the fields of political science and sociology. The vague and general title of his treatise gave him license for diffuseness, and a sort of justification for it. Quite unexpectedly he takes "external nature," chiefly in the sense of *society*, as surrounding the individual man. Thus his first instance of adaptation of external nature to the moral constitution of man is, that the voice of individual conscience is re-echoed by society.

"And first, in regard to the power and sensibility of conscience, there is a most important influence brought to bear on each individual possessor of this faculty from without, and by his fellow-men." (I. 162.)

It is in Book II. of his "Institutes of Theology" that we find a characteristic development of the views of Dr. Chalmers on natural theology. At the beginning of his discussion he condemns the ontological and causal arguments, and rests his case upon teleology.

"Such dispositions are innumerable. Every animal and vegetable structure teems with them. Among the first that occur, let me instance the eyelashes, of the greatest use where they are placed, and which they could be nowhere else, for the protection of this delicate organ ; and the nails, in the very position where they are most serviceable, instead of being protruded as useless excrescences on other parts of the body ; and the thumb in relation to its counterpart fingers for the purposes of holding ; and the cutters and grinders, which, were they to change places, would be far less commodious for the act of eating ; and a countless host of other collocations, whether in plants or in bodies of living creatures, — all of indispensable utility, and all of which are most obviously distinguishable from laws. Now, what we affirm is, that even though we should admit matter, with all its laws, to be eternal, if ever these dispositions had a beginning, it is not the laws, the blind headlong forces or laws, which could ever have originated them ; or, on the other hand, should these dispositions ever be destroyed, it is not the laws which can replace them. Herein lies the main strength of our argument for a God as furnished by the contemplation of external nature."

The antithesis which he sets up between collocations and laws is extremely unfortunate. It would condemn his argument at once in the mind of all evolutionists; whereas there is really a valuable thought in his doctrine of collocations if he had given it a different expression, not setting it up in contrast to law. Most of the collocations or dispositions of matter, which he specifies as exceptions to law, have since been shown to conform to law; and, if there are others which have not been, perhaps can never be, as Mr. J. S. Mill supposes probable in respect to certain collocations of forces in astronomy, the proof of intelligence is none the less conclusive in the cases which have been reduced under law, and no more conclusive in those cases which have not been reduced under law.

Chalmers thought little of the causal argument; and the distinction he set up between matter with its laws and the arbitrary dispositions of matter, had for its aim the avoidance of any necessity of proving the non-eternity of matter.

" This distinction of ours between the dispositions of matter and its laws serves for a mighty disencumbrance of the whole argument, relieving it of much that is weak and obscure and questionable. We affirm not the eternity of matter, save for the purpose of bringing out our conclusion. When reasoning on the present order of things, we do not need to prove its non-eternity, — an attempt on which a deal of most unsatisfactory metaphysics has been expended."

The last remark is quite true; and every sound and healthy mind must sympathize with Chalmers in his desire to avoid the necessity of such speculations. But, in avoiding one questionable thing, he involved the argument in another difficulty not less fatal, but rather more so. The proof of the non-eternity of matter is not quite a forlorn hope, while the antithesis of collocations to laws makes Chalmers's argument very much like a mass of scoria heaved up by a submarine eruption, —the waves are eating it away hour by hour, and the only question of its entire demolition is whether there is any core of hardened lava in the centre. Every collocation which yields before the march of law is so much lost to his argument in the form in which he cast it. If there are original adjustments of matter which can never be explained, but must ever stand simply as ultimate facts, these have no additional force imparted to them by contrasting them with law and order; while the antithesis is ruinous to the argument in so far as it rests upon collocations which are explicable by natural laws.

Dr. Kidd's treatise is " On the Adaptation of External Nature to the Physical Condition of Man." It is not much of a surprise to find him trenching upon the kindred topic assigned to Chalmers; but we are somewhat astonished that he did not leave Sir Charles Bell in quiet possession of that little nook in the broad domain of physico-theology which had been allotted to him, namely, *the hand*. Kidd has a whole chapter on that topic, made up chiefly of quotations from Galen. Let it not be imagined that I blame him for quoting: I commend him. He might have inserted the substance of Galen's matter without acknowledgment, which would have been worse than quoting, though not entirely without precedent.

He is not so absorbed in design-arguments but that

he can turn aside to deliver to his British audience an invective against Napoleon Bonaparte. As regards the argument itself, it will certainly do him no injustice to let him sum it up for himself: —

"This, then, is the sum of the whole argument. The Creator has so adapted the external world to the moral as well as the physical condition of man, and these two conditions act so constantly and reciprocally on each other, that, in a comprehensive view of the relation between the external world and man, we cannot easily lose sight of that most important connection."

If there is any thing disappointing in this summary, any suspicion that the sentence concludes lamely and inconsequently, it may fairly be said — however paradoxical it sounds — that, considered as a summary of Kidd's argument, it is all the better for that: otherwise it would not correspond to the argument.

The third Bridgewater Treatise is by the Rev. William Whewell. The title is "On Astronomy and General Physics." Professor Baden Powell gives the palm to this over all the other volumes in this series, especially for "vindicating, for the principle of the reduction of *facts* under *laws*, the high position it ought to occupy in the general argument."[1] This commendation is, in some measure, just. Not only in this work, but elsewhere, Whewell gives great and deserved prominence to the principles of eutaxiology. He had some notion of the order of nature as the basis of a distinct argument, yet never reached a clear conception of it, and never thought of making it independent of teleology. There was constant reference to some *purpose* or *aim*. Thus, in the "Philosophy of the Inductive Sciences" (I. 628), he says, —

[1] Order of Nature, p. 200.

" It has appeared to some persons, that the mere aspect of order and symmetry in the works of nature — the contemplation of comprehensive and consistent law — is sufficient to lead us to the conception of a design and intelligence producing the order, and carrying into effect the law. Without here attempting to decide whether this is true. we may discern, after what has been said, that the conception of design arrived at in this manner is altogether different from that idea of design which is suggested to us by organized bodies, and which we describe as the doctrine of final causes. The regular form of a crystal, whatever beautiful symmetry it may exhibit, whatever general laws it may exemplify, does not prove design in the same manner in which design is proved by the provisions for the preservation and growth of the seeds of plants and of the young of animals. The law of universal gravitation, however wide and simple, does not impress us with the belief of a *purpose* as does that propensity by which the two sexes of each animal are brought together. If it could be shown that the symmetrical structure of a flower results from laws of the same kind as those which determine the regular forms of crystals, or the motions of the planets, the discovery might be very striking and important ; but it would not at all come under our idea of final cause."

Certainly not: the principles of eutaxiology are radically different from those of teleology, and quite stubbornly refuse to " come under our idea of final cause," although the whole army of teleologists have been trying for ages to dragoon them into their service. This quotation shows clearly enough that Whewell saw a difference between the two lines of argument; but it shows, too, that he was so much enamoured of teleology, that he would not suffer any rival to claim his regard. The whole passage is disparaging to the proposed proof from the order of nature. And from Whewell's point

of view the depreciation of it is inevitable: he wanted
to reduce every thing under "our idea of final cause,"
and those phenomena which resisted his desire were
naturally regarded with less favor. A universal law,
as gravitation, or celestial harmony, as in "the motions
of the planets," was of less consequence to him than
the sexual instinct. because, forsooth, they do not so
strongly "impress with the belief of a *purpose;*" that is,
they are not so teleological.

Whewell's sensitiveness about bringing in any thing
else as a rival to teleology, and his horror of any thing
hostile to it, prevented him from entertaining a just
view of the relations of morphology to teleology: whatever was non-teleological he took to be anti-teleological.
If it could be tortured into the service of teleology in
some way, well and good; if not, he would have none
of it. The following is from his "Philosophy of the
Inductive Sciences" (I. 630): —

"The opinions which have been put forward in opposition to the principle of final causes have, for the most part,
been stated vaguely and ambiguously. Among the most
definite of such principles is that, which, in the history of
the subject, I have termed 'the principle of metamorphosed
and developed symmetry,' upon which has been founded the
science of morphology. The reality and importance of this
principle are not to be denied by us. We have shown how
they are proved by its application in various sciences. and
especially in botany. But those advocates of this principle
who have placed it in antithesis to the doctrine of final
causes have, by this means, done far more injustice to their
own favorite doctrine than damage to the one which they
opposed. The adaptation of the bones of the skeleton to
the muscles; the provision of fulcrums, projecting processes,
channels, so that the motions and forces shall be such as the

needs of life require, — cannot possibly become less striking and convincing from any discovery of general analogies of one animal frame with another, or of laws connecting the development of different parts. Whenever such laws are discovered, we can only consider them as the means of producing that adaptation which we so much admire. Our conviction that the artist works intelligently is not destroyed, though it may be modified and transferred, when we obtain a sight of his tools. Our discovery of laws cannot contradict our persuasion of ends : our morphology cannot prejudice our teleology."

This is all sound and true, except that he insists on making morphology the mere servant of teleology. The "typical forms" have no meaning to him, except as they do service to "special ends;" that is, while he sees a difference in the ideas, he refuses, in this instance, to give to the notion of order " the high position it ought to occupy in the general argument." He regards the placing of morphology " in antithesis to the doctrine of final causes" as an act of hostility, perhaps of treachery; whereas they are in fact antithetical, without any regard to what their advocates do or neglect to do.

His tender regard for teleology prevented him from seeing the whole bearing of the discussion between Cuvier and Geoffroy Saint-Hilaire respecting " unity of plan " in the animal kingdom. All he could make out of it was a hostile movement against his favorite final causes; and it did indeed touch them, but it had wider issues, which kept widening until Charles Darwin summed them up in one comprehensive formula of evolution.

We have seen in the Introduction what exaggerated views of the value of teleology in physiological research Whewell entertained. His strong instance for the confirmation of this view was that of Harvey's great discovery. On that he was impregnable; because he had Harvey's own word for it, as reported by Boyle. But in another famous instance it is not so clear that he got any real support. I refer to the case of Baron Cuvier. Whewell claims that his method of recovering or reconstructing the whole animal by means of a minute fossil fragment was an illustration of the value of teleology. When we attempt to affix a definite value to this claim by referring to the statements of Cuvier himself, we find, in the first place, that his notion of what are "vulgarly called final causes" is somewhat wide and flexible.

"Zoölogy has a principle of reasoning which is peculiar to it, and which it employs with advantage on many occasions: this is the principle of *the conditions of existence*, vulgarly called the principle of *final causes*." [1]

Remarking, as we pass on, that "the conditions of existence" is a thoroughly Darwinian and anti-Whewellian phrase, we want to see, in the next place, how he applies "the principle of the conditions of existence, vulgarly called the principle of final causes," in that special research which has done more than any other for his fame as a naturalist. Turning to his "Researches on Fossil Bones," we find that his "peculiar principle" has there resolved itself into the law of correlation of structures.

"In a word, the formation of the tooth bespeaks the structure of the articulation of the jaw, that of the scapula that of the claws, just as the equation of the curve involves all its properties; and, in taking each property separately as

<hr>

[1] Animal Kingdom, p. 5.

the basis of a particular equation, we should find again both the ordinary equation and all the other certain properties : so the claw, the scapula, the articulation of the jaw, the thigh-bone, and all the other bones separately considered, require the certain tooth, or the tooth requires them reciprocally ; and, beginning with any one, he who possessed a knowledge of the laws of organic economy would detect the whole animal " (p. 62).

" It is by this method alone that we have been guided, and have always found it sufficient to classify each bone with its species, when it was a living species ; to its genus, when it was an unknown species ; to its order, when it was of a new genus ; and, finally, to its class, when it belonged to an order not yet established " (p. 65).

Now, this law of correlation has somewhat mixed affinities. The modification of the organ A, in re-sponse to some special condition of existence, might be viewed as teleological ; and if the organs B and C also varied with an obvious reference to the same con-dition, or series of conditions, which determined the form of A, the whole group of changes would be as much teleological as if one organ only were concerned. But if, as is sometimes the case, the organs B and C vary without any reference to external conditions, but simply because A has varied, then it would seem to be in response to some inner principle of sympathy or symmetry. But that is only the dynamical side of the problem: the statical elements of it have still less to do with teleology. There is an original correspond-ence of the parts in an animal, independent of any question of their varying together or separately. This primitive harmony in the animal frame is a matter of morphology, not of teleology ; and, as re-gards coincident and sympathetic variations of different organs, that also, if not clearly morphological, is certainly eutaxiological : so that the preponderance of relations in this affair is decidedly in the direction of eutaxiology rather than teleology.   There is, therefore, no sufficient ground for Whewell's claim, that teleology furnished to Cuvier the clew tŏ the complex labyrinth of fossil remains.

Turning now to Whewell's Bridgewater Treatise, we note, in the first place, his divisions : —

"The two portions of the subject may be treated as cosmical arrangements and terrestrial adaptations. We shall begin with the latter class of adaptations ; because in treating of these the facts are more familiar and tangible, and the reasonings less abstract and technical, than in the other division of the subject. Moreover, in this case men have no difficulty in recognizing as desirable the end which is answered by such adaptations, and they therefore the more readily *consider it as an end.*"

He sounds the teleological note at the start.   While he does indeed, as Powell says, make much of the phenomena of law and order, it is all by way of subordination to teleology.   In his discussion of terrestrial adaptations he covered much of the same ground which Kidd also traversed.

"The length of the year is so determined as to be adapted to the constitution of most vegetables ; or the construction of vegetables is so adjusted as to be suited to the length which the year really has, and unsuited to a duration longer or shorter by any considerable portion. The vegetable clock-work is so set as to go for a year."

He regards each of these adjustments as independent of the other, and the coincidence of the two as a strong proof of wisdom.

"In the existing state of things the duration of the earth's revolution round the sun, and the duration of the revolution of the vegetable functions of most plants, are equal. These two periods are adjusted to each other. . . . Now, such an adjustment must surely be accepted as a proof of design exercised in the formation of the world" (p. 28).

"The same kind of argument might be applied to the animal creation. The pairing, nesting, hatching, fledging, and flight of birds, for instance, occupy each its peculiar time of the year" (p. 32).

In like manner he shows that the functions and habits of plants and animals are adjusted to the alternations of day and night. He rejects with scorn, as "an arbitrary and baseless assumption," the suggestion "that the astronomical cycle has occasioned the physiological one" (p. 37). Nevertheless, that is probably the true explanation.

On p. 142 he enumerates nineteen examples of terrestrial adaptation, which have been often quoted. One writer names them as absolutely essential conditions, any one of which failing, the whole population of the earth would instantly perish. Whewell is much more moderate in his statement; claiming only, that by virtue of these the world "is fitted for the support of vegetables and animals in a manner in which it could not have been if the properties and quantities of the elements had been different from what they are." Which we must all admit without question: it is equivalent to the classical remark of Jack Bunsby, "Circumstances alter cases."

Book II., on "Cosmical Arrangements," is much the best part of this treatise. But also in Book III., on "Religious Views," where, reasoning from the analogy of other writers, we should expect to find only some excellent reading for a Sunday afternoon, we in fact find some of his best arguments. Here he comes nearer to a complete emancipation from his too partial attachment to teleology than anywhere else. In chapter iv. he constructs an almost purely eutaxiological argument : —

" To most persons it appears, that the mere existence of a law connecting and governing any class of phenomena implies a presiding intelligence which has preconceived and established the law. When events are regulated by precise rules of time and space, of number and measure, men conceive these rules to be the evidence of thought and mind, even without discovering in the rules any peculiar adaptations, or without supposing their purpose to be known " (p. 295).

" The connection of the laws of the material world with an intelligence which preconceived and instituted the law, which is thus, as we perceive, so generally impressed on the common apprehension of mankind, has also struck no less those who have studied nature with a more systematic attention, and with the peculiar views which belong to science. The laws which such persons learn and study seem, indeed, most naturally to lead to the conviction of an intelligence which originally gave to the law its form.

" What we call a general law is, in truth, a form of expression including a number of facts of like kind. The facts are separate : the unity of view by which we associate them, the character of generality and of law, resides in those relations which are the object of the intellect. The law, once apprehended by us, takes in our minds the place of the facts themselves, and is said to *govern* or determine them, because it determines our anticipations of what they will be. But we cannot, it would seem, conceive a law, founded on such intelligible relations, to govern and determine the facts themselves, any otherwise than by supposing also an intelligence by which these relations are contemplated and these consequences realized. We cannot, then, represent to ourselves the universe governed by general laws, otherwise than by conceiving an intelligent and conscious Deity, by whom these laws were originally contemplated, established, and applied.

" This, perhaps, will appear more clear when it is considered that the laws of which we speak are often of an abstruse and complex kind, depending upon relations of space, time, number, and other properties which we perceive by great attention and thought. These relations are often combined so variously and curiously, that the most subtle reasonings and calculations which we can form are requisite in order to trace their results. Can such laws be conceived to be instituted without any exercise of knowledge and intelligence? Can material objects apply geometry and calculation to themselves?" (300).

This is a fair specimen of eutaxiology. But in chapter vii. he returns to his first love, "final causes." In his effort to turn to their advantage even Bacon's irreverent simile, he fairly "rises into poetry," as another author has remarked.

" Bacon's comparison of final causes to the vestal virgins is one of those poignant sayings, so frequent in his writings, which it is not easy to forget. ' Like them,' he says, ' they are dedicated to God, and are barren.' But to any one who reads his work it will appear in what spirit this was meant. ' Not because those final causes are not true, and worthy to be inquired, being kept within their own province.' If he had had occasion to develop his simile, full of latent meaning as his similes so often are, he would probably have said, that to these final causes barrenness was no reproach, seeing they ought to be, not the mothers, but the daughters, of our natural sciences ; and that they were barren, not by imperfection of their nature, but in order that they might be kept pure and undefiled, and so fit ministers in the temple of God."

The character of the work of Sir Charles Bell on " The Hand: Its Mechanism and Vital Endowments as evincing Design," is sufficiently indicated in his own words at the close of the first chapter: —

" In the following pages I shall treat the subject comparatively, and exhibit a view of the bones of the arm, descending from the human hand to the fin of a fish. I shall, in the next place, review the actions of the muscles of the arm and hand ; then, proceeding to the vital properties, I shall advance to the subject of sensibility, leading to that of touch ; afterwards I shall show the necessity of combining the muscular action with the exercise of the senses, and especially with that of touch, to constitute in the hand what has been called ' the geometrical sense.' I shall describe the organ of touch, the cuticle and skin, and arrange the nerves of the hand according to their functions. I shall then inquire into the correspondence between the capacities and endowments of the mind and the external organs, and more especially the properties of the hand ; and conclude by showing that animals have been created with a reference to the globe they inhabit ; that all their endowments and various organization bear a relation to their state of existence and to the elements around them ; that there is a plan universal extending through all animated nature, and which has prevailed in the earliest condition of the world ; and that, finally, in the most minute or most comprehensive study of those things we everywhere see prospective design."

It appears that Peter Mark Roget, M.D., has a double aim in his Bridgewater Treatise ; viz., to teach science and natural theology both at the same time : —

" My endeavors have been directed to give to the subject that unity of design and that scientific form which are generally wanting in books professedly treating of natural theology published prior to the present series, not excepting even the unrivalled and immortal work of Paley. By furnishing those general principles on which all accurate and extensive knowledge must substantially be founded, I am not without a hope that this compendium will prove a useful introduction to the study of natural history; the pursuit of which will be found not only to supply inexhaustible sources of intellectual gratification, but also to furnish to contemplative minds a rich fountain of religious instruction."

He appears to have counted very largely upon the "contemplative mind" of his reader for the theological or religious effect of his work. It is the most voluminous of the Bridgewater Treatises, but all the natural theology in it is comprised in the introductory and closing chapters. The rest is a compendium or text-book of "Animal and Vegetable Physiology."

The Rev. William Buckland, D.D., was fortunate in the assignment of his subject. Geology was an almost untrodden field for the theologian. He had indeed a difficulty to encounter at the start, from the fact that the new science was making sad havoc with the old chronology. He had to reconcile geology and Genesis. This he does by injecting a long period between the first and second verse of the first chapter of Genesis. Matter was first created, and it passed through all the long catalogue of changes recorded in historical geology; then some cataclysm threw it into the confusion which is described in the second verse; then followed the creation in six literal days of twenty-four hours each. This mode of reconciliation was the favorite one for a long time after Buckland's treatise appeared.

Now, this preliminary obstacle being removed, there was a whole "new world" to conquer. In truth, there were several new worlds, — a long, receding series of terrestrial and marine faunas and floras, each replete with brand-new (notwithstanding they were so old) illustrations of design. There were the dinotherium and the megatherium and the paleotherium, and the ichthyosaurs and the plesiosaurs and the megalosaurs, and the pterodactyls, and the ammonites and the belemnites and the ichthyodorulites, and the foraminated polythalmous shells; to say nothing of the lepidodendrids, sigillarids, and equisetaceæ. All these, and many more, appear in their due order; and their long-resounding and almost jaw-breaking names impart a novel flavor to physico-theology.

It is not surprising that Buckland's book made a strong impression, — the greatest perhaps of any of the Bridgewater Treatises. Besides an attractive style, he was handling new matter in a new field. Of course it would be asking too much of one man to contribute a new method as well as new matter. Accordingly we find that his argument is the same old mechanical one which Paley used. One feature, however, of really great importance appears in his work, — not to be credited especially to him though, for it was due to the prominence assumed by geology at this period. The new science compelled theologians to take more account of the element of time than they had previously done. The long æons of historical geology offered a striking contrast to the six literal days of the old scheme, and led to broader and truer views of creation.

The seventh treatise is by the Rev. William Kirby, on "The History, Habits, and Instincts of Animals." He takes the account of the Deluge literally, and frames a bold hypothesis to help the animals of America and Australia back into their respective countries after their

voyage with Noah. He supposes " that, immediately
subsequent to the Deluge, America and New Holland,
and the various other islands that are inhabited by
peculiar animals, were once connected with Asia and
Africa by the intervention of lands that have since
been submerged." The indefinite " once " and the
definite " immediately subsequent to the Deluge," do
not exactly harmonize; but we will not be captious
about that. We ought to be generous in the matter of
time with a hard-pressed theologian who is heaving
up a continent to serve as a bridge for his diluvian
creatures.

He argues at length against the geological doctrine
that there was once an age of reptiles : —

" I have been led into this discussion by Mr. Mantell's
hypothesis of an *age of reptiles*, which I have seen only
in an extract from one of the Sussex advertisers for last
year, which he was so kind as to send me, in which he
supposes that the saurians were the mighty masters, as well
as monsters, of the primeval animal kingdom, and the lords
of the creation before the existence of the human race.
Since this hypothesis, as stated in the above extract, cannot
be reconciled with the account of the creation of animals as
given in the first chapter of Genesis, I shall not be wandering from the purpose of the present essay if I devote a few
pages to the consideration of it. . . . Setting aside these
arguments upon the uncertain facts on which this hypothesis
is built, if we turn our attention to the reason of the thing,
who can think that a Being of unbounded power, wisdom,
and goodness, should create a world merely for the habitation
of a race of monsters, without a single rational being in
it to serve and glorify him? The supposition that these
animals were a separate creation, independent of man, and
occupying his eminent station and throne upon our globe
long before he was brought into existence, interrupts the

harmony between the different members of the animal kingdom, and dislocates the beautiful and entire system recorded with so much sublimity and majestic brevity in the first chapter of Genesis." (I. 39.)

When Mr. Kirby thus attempted to sit down upon and crush out of existence Mr. Mantell's big reptiles, he must have found it an unpleasant seat: for the said reptiles are, so to speak, still alive and sprawling upon the pages of every text-book of geology; while Mr. Kirby's book has passed into an oblivion which is well deserved, since it is the most worthless of the Bridgewater series.

If Dr. Buckland was fortunate in his subject, William Prout, M.D., the last of the eight, seems to have been rather unfortunate. The title "Chemistry, Meteorology, and Digestion" looks somewhat mixed and heterogeneous as an assignment of a subject, — apparently the scraps and ends of the business. His notion of his function as a natural theologian is similar to that of Dr. Roget. He makes an almost purely scientific treatise, and relies upon the "contemplative mind" of the reader for the natural theology. However, he gives an example of how it should be done in his introduction : —

"Animals in cold climates have been provided with a covering of fur. Men in such climates cover themselves with that fur. In both cases, whatever may have been the end or intention, no one can deny that the *effect* at least is precisely the same : the animal and the man are alike protected from the cold. Now, since the animal did not clothe itself, but must have been clothed by another, it follows that whoever clothed the animal apparently knew what the man knows, and reasoned like the man ; that is to say, the clother of the animal knew that the climate in which the animal is placed is a cold climate, and that a covering of fur is one of the best means of warding off the cold : he therefore clothed his creature in this very appropriate material.

"The man who clothes himself in fur to keep off the cold performs an act directed to a certain end ; in short, an act of *design*. So whoever, directly or indirectly, caused the animal to be clothed with fur to keep off the cold, must likewise have performed an act of *design*. But under the circumstances the clother of the animal must be admitted to have been also the *creator* of the animal ; and, by extending the argument, the creator of man himself, — of the universe. Moreover, the intelligence the Creator has displayed in clothing the animal, he has deigned to impart to man, who is thus enabled to recognize his Creator's design."

He uses " design " usually in the sense of " adaptation of means to an end." The topic of his introduction makes them synonymous : " Of the Leading Argument of Natural Theology, that Design, or the Adaptation of Means to an End, exists in Nature." Remembering this synonymy, I wish the reader to note his " classes of objects," all of which, he thinks, prove design ; that is, adaptation of means to an end : —

" The argument of design, therefore, in its general sense, embraces at least three classes of objects : —
" 1. Those objects regarding which the reasoning of man coincides with the reasoning evinced by his Creator, as in the simple adaptation of clothing above mentioned ; or those objects in which man is able to trace, to a certain extent, his Creator's designs, as in the various phenomena amenable to the laws of quantity ; viz., mechanics, etc."

This first class includes two divisions, — first, those cases where the means and end are both in plain sight ; and, secondly, those in which they are not so clear : but we are still " able to trace the Creator's designs to a certain extent." This subdivision runs into his second division : —

" 2. Those objects in which man sees no more than the preliminaries and the results, or the end and design accomplished, without being able to trace, through their details, the means of that accomplishment; as in all the phenomena and operations of chemistry.

" 3. Those objects in which design is inferred, but in which the design, as well as the means by which it is accomplished, are alike concealed; as in the existence of fixed stars, of comets, of organic life, and indeed in all the great and more recondite phenomena of nature."

His three classes are not well defined; but it would seem that he means something like this: in one class of those objects upon which the argument of design is based, we see plainly both the end and the means; in another, the end only; and, in the third, neither the end nor the means is ascertainable. Now, remembering that he associates "design" with teleology exclusively, we have here a remarkable example of the principles by which teleologists managed to bring all possible phenomena under teleology. Prout thinks we can apply the teleological method in cases where we see only the result without knowing the means of its accomplishment; and — still more astonishing — he will bring in also those cases where means and end " are alike concealed." The old teleologists quite generally acted upon such principles, but Prout distinctly avows them.

That is, he will bring all these classes of objects under teleology, provided we are right about what he meant by "design." He certainly starts out with the meaning "adaptation of means to an end," as in the heading of his introduction given above. But in his definition of the second class of objects embraced in design-arguments, where he speaks of the design being "accomplished," he evidently means *purpose;* and the same meaning applies best in the definition of the third class, — that or *end,* — which would answer just as well as *purpose.*   So we have here a fine example of the ambiguities of *design.*   But these ambiguities do not defeat the conclusion that he associated *design* with *teleology;* for, notwithstanding the shifting senses in which he used that word, the associated words "means" and "ends" give the teleological flavor to all his three classes.   Therefore it is indubitable that Prout considered stars, comets, "and indeed all the great and more recondite phenomena of nature," good material for teleology, notwithstanding the fact that the end of their existence might be wholly unknown, as well as the means by which that end was accomplished.

Now, when we remember that "fitness in the adaptation of means to an end" was considered the strong point of teleology by all its advocates of the old school, we are curious to know what they could make of the argument when either the means or the end was unknown, much more when both "are alike concealed." We know that they did often make a lame attempt to frame arguments from such examples as are included in Prout's third class; but, if we attempt to discover the logic of their reasoning, it baffles all our research. Most of them, as we have seen, thought it sufficient to recite the facts, and then exclaim, "How admirable is all this!"

Of course the grand mistake under which Prout was laboring was the failure to distinguish between eutaxiology and teleology, and the attempt which grew out of that to force the facts of eutaxy into the service of teleology; and this mistake crippled the efforts of design-advocates for centuries. It appears more or less distinctly in all of the Bridgewater Treatises, even in that of Whewell, the ablest man among them, and the only one who came anywhere near framing a distinct eutaxiological argument.

Another fact about these treatises, regarding them collectively, is that the writers seem to be in some degree uncertain whether their aim is to prove God's existence, or simply his "power, wisdom, and goodness." It was the latter they were appointed to do; and in doing that the first point would be included, provided they did not assume his existence in order to prove his attributes; in that case it would not follow that they accomplished both things by one effort. However, it seems that they did suppose they had done both. Dr. Prout, apparently speaking for them all, says, —

"The intention of these treatises is to point out the various evidences of design among the objects of creation, and to deduce from them the existence and the attributes of the Creator."

Still they do not, any of them, attack the problem of proving his existence with specific directness. They seem to think their proofs of his attributes involve the point of his existence, and establish it indirectly.

The whole Bridgewater series answers in the aggregate to that conception of a "natural theology" which Derham, Nieuwentyt, and Paley entertained, and which they attempted to realize in their respective works. That conception or ideal was to "digest all the science of their day into a system of natural theology." What each of them attempted singly the eight Bridgewater essayists united their strength to accomplish. What was the result? We have seen, that, in the case of those who singly attempted the whole task, the product was very indifferent, considered either as science or as theology. Is it any better when eight men join hands in the work? Candidly, we cannot say it is. The conception is radically wrong, and the results of working upon a false ideal can never be very valuable.

Wherein was the conception at fault? Chiefly in the assumption that the argument is strengthened by every added example of design. That is true only within very narrow limits. Ten examples are better than one, and a hundred better still. But, when it comes to an indefinitely great number of similar examples, all comprised under the same logical formula of argumentation, the vast unwieldy mass is a burden rather than a help. But to digest all the science of a given generation into a system of natural theology is simply a process of piling up endless examples and illustrations all of the same kind.

But are they all alike? Does not the march of science constantly open new fields? Did not Buckland strike an entirely new vein by reason of the erection of geology into a science? So he did; and there is something still to be done in that direction by popular writers applying old formulas to new facts. That is really an inviting field for those who like that kind of work. But at bottom it is only a process of piling up new examples where we have already millions at hand ·for each one that can really be of any use. Design-arguments can be constructed just as well upon the basis of a single science as upon a whole encyclopædia of the sciences. What is needed is a reconstruction of the logic of design, instead of a new batch of illustrations.

There is every indication that the Bridgewater essayists were working to the very ideal of which I have

just endeavored to show the error. In the aggregate
they cover the field of science with tolerable completeness; and the scrappy mixture of topics which fell to
the eighth man looks as if he had to take what was
deemed necessary to make the work exhaustive. It is
to be hoped that a similar attempt will never be made
again. There is a sameness, a dead level of monotony,
about these eight treatises which is seldom realized,
because only two or three of them are well known, but
which becomes painful when they are all examined
together. There is an individuality about the style;
but there is the same general undertone, the same suspicion of a set task, the same kind of argument, and
the same conclusion, in all of them.

Did they not do some good in their day? Unquestionably: as did also the similar efforts of their predecessors. Several of these "Natural Theologies" were
extremely popular, and brought much fame and some
money to their authors. That was certainly a good
thing for them, and their readers were benefited also.
They were good books in their day, and of their kind;
but the kind is happily obsolete. They did some harm
as well as good. That conception of teleology which
Whewell presented under the name of the doctrine of
final causes, was provocative of that wave of hostility to
teleology among men of science which is just now sub-
siding, and which swept many of them into infidelity.
The repetition of a similar style of argument in this
generation would be wholly mischievous. According
to Dugald Stewart, the multiplication of such works
was mischievous even in their own day, by reason that
they created an impression of God's existence as being
a very doubtful question, which required a great deal
of argument to establish.

The " Ninth Brigewater Treatise," by Charles Babbage, Esq., seems to have been inspired by the desire of the author to prove that a man of high attainments in pure mathematics could write on natural theology. Whewell had spoken disparagingly of " mechanical philosophers and mathematicians," as being less likely than men engaged in other pursuits " to make any clear advance towards such a subject of speculation." Babbage's argument is a singular one, and is illustrated by means of the " Calculating Engine."

CHAPTER XI.

BROUGHAM, IRONS, AND THE BURNETT PRIZES.

HENRY LORD BROUGHAM published his "Discourse of Natural Theology" in 1835.

"This discourse is not a treatise of natural theology: it has not for its design an exposition of the doctrines whereof natural theology consists. But its object is, first, to explain the nature of the evidence upon which it rests, — to show that it is a science, the truths of which are discovered by induction, like the truths of natural and moral philosophy; that it is a branch of science partaking of the nature of each of those great divisions of human knowledge, and not merely closely allied to them both. Secondly, the object of the discourse is to explain the advantages attending this study. The work, therefore, is a *logical* one."

Here is one man at last who is going to look into the logic of design, instead of piling up new examples, or warming over the old ones. We are especially interested in his opinion that design-arguments rest upon induction. How does he make this out?

"But let us examine further this matter. The position which we reach by a strict process of induction is common to natural philosophy and natural theology; namely, that a given organ performs a given function, or a given arrangement possesses a certain stability by its adaptation to mechanical laws. We have said that the process of reasoning is short and easy, by which we arrive at the doctrine more peculiar to natural theology; namely. that some power, acquainted with and acting upon the knowledge of those laws, fashioned the organ with the intention of having the function performed, or constructed the system so that it might endure. Is not this last process as much one of strict induction as the other? It is plainly only a generalization of many particular facts. — a reasoning from things known to things unknown; an inference of a new or unknown relation from other relations formerly observed and known. . . . When we see that a certain effect — namely, distinct vision — is performed by an achromatic instrument, the eye, why do we infer that some one must have made it? Because we nowhere and at no time have had any experience of any one thing fashioning itself, and indeed cannot form to ourselves any distinct idea of what such a process as self-creation means; and, further, because when we ourselves would produce a similar result, we have recourse to like means. Again, when we perceive the adaptation of natural objects and operations to a perceived end, and from thence infer design in the maker of these objects and superintender of these operations, why do we draw this conclusion? Because we know by experience, that, if we ourselves desired to accomplish a similar purpose, we should do so by the like adaptation. We know by experience that this is design in us, and that our proceedings are the result of such design. We know that if some of our works were seen by others, who neither were aware of our having made them, nor of the intention with which we made them, they would be right should they, from seeing and examining them, both infer that we had made them, and conjecture why we had made them. The same reasoning, by the help of experience, from what we know to what we cannot know, is manifestly the foundation of the inference, that the members of the body were fashioned for certain uses by a maker acquainted with their operations, and willing that those uses should be served."

The whole matter would be much clearer if Brougham
had framed a definite proposition embodying the results
of the inductive process which he claims to be involved
in design-arguments. Let us note the fact, however,
that he has here proposed an entirely new view of the
logic of design. All the old writers made it a process
of analogy.

He uses "design" and other colloquial expressions in
the same loose way as previous writers had done. Setting out as he did to write a *logical* discourse, a little
sharp analysis and discrimination in the use of terms
would have been entirely in order. He did not discriminate at all between the argument from *order* and
the argument from *ends*, or between *eutaxiology* and *teleology:* he makes *design* synonymous with *teleology*. One
thing, however, he did which comports well with his
logical ideal: he drew the distinction between natural
theology and natural religion, which, as he remarks,
all the older authors had neglected. As regards the
boundaries of natural theology, he includes in it the
moral or anthropological argument. In this he is undoubtedly correct. Several previous writers had done
the same, — Sebonde, for instance, whose example has the
more value because he was the first to use the term
"natural theology." Brougham's comments on the work
of his predecessors in this respect, and frank expressions about Paley's plagiarism, are worth quoting : —

"Hitherto our argument has rested upon a comparison of
the truths of natural theology with those of physical science.
But the evidences of design presented by the universe are
not merely those which the material world affords. The intellectual system is equally fruitful in proofs of an intelligent
cause, although these have occupied little of the philosopher's
attention, and may, indeed, be said never to have found a

place among the speculations of the natural theologian. Nothing is more remarkable than the care with which all the writers on this subject, at least among the moderns, have confined themselves to the proofs afforded by the visible and sensible works of nature, while the evidence furnished by the mind and its operations has been wholly neglected. The celebrated book of Ray on 'The Wonders of Creation'[1] seems to assume that the human soul has no separate existence, — that it forms no part of the created system.[2] Derham has written upon astro-theology and physico-theology as if the heavens *alone* proclaimed the glory of God, and the earth *only* showed forth his handiwork; for his only mention of intellectual nature is in the single chapter of the 'Physico-Theology' on the soul, in which he is content with two observations, — one on the variety of man's inclinations, and another on his inventive powers — giving nothing which precisely proves design. Dr. Paley, whose work is chiefly taken from the writings of Derham, deriving from them its whole plan and much of its substance, but clothing the harsher statements of his original in an attractive and popular style, had so little of scientific habits, so moderate a power of generalizing, that he never once mentions the mind, [truly a strange reason to give for his neglect to mention the mind!] or any of the intellectual phenomena, nor ever appears to consider them as forming a portion of the works or operations of nature."

Brougham is mistaken in the opinion that "all the writers on this subject, at least among the moderns, have confined themselves to the proofs afforded by

---

[1] A very loose citation of a title. "The Wisdom of God manifested in the Works of Creation" is the book he referred to.

[2] Entirely too severe. Ray had some queer notions, — that of the "plastic nature," for example, — and some of his expressions are unguarded; but he was no materialist. The fact that he did not frame any arguments from the human faculties is no proof that he did not believe in their "separate existence."

the visible and sensible works of nature, while the evidence furnished by the mind and its operations has been wholly neglected." Socrates, Sebonde, More, Cudworth, Wollaston, and Crombie employed the anthropological argument; and Kant laid great emphasis upon it. Even Lord Brougham set up for a natural theologian, without knowing much about what had already been done in that field.

" The Whole Doctrine of Final Causes," by William J. Irons, Curate of St. Mary's, appeared in 1836. After the *flood* of Bridgewater Treatises, it might be expected that there would be an *ebb* in the tide. Irons makes an elaborate attack upon final causes, but in the interest of theism and revealed religion. He denies that natural theology can add any thing to our knowledge of God : —

" I venture to affirm, that, although natural conscience may lead a man to feel the want of some religion, it will not teach him the precise nature of religious obligation; neither will natural reasoning be able to prove, with certainty, *any single theological truth*, even the unity or personality of God, or the reasonableness of worship, — all which points are indispensable to religion " (p. 34) .

" I conclude, therefore, that though, without a revelation, we might arrive at a certain knowledge that there was a cause (or causes) for all things in nature, yet we could never tell whether there was only one cause, or whether there were many. We could not know even the personality of any such cause, nor the moral character of it : we *must* disbelieve either in its wisdom, its goodness, or its power. So that not one truth of theology could by any possibility be arrived at on natural principles " (p. 143).

He maintains that the teleologists have reversed the doctrine of final causes as it was propounded by Aristotle, and used by the ancients generally. Their aim was to discover the ultimate tendencies of things, the *end*, by an induction of facts; and they never thought of starting with the end, and thence deducing a Supreme First Cause. But the latter method is the one adopted by the moderns; so that the teleologists start with the end in order to reach the beginning, while the ancients started with an induction of facts in order to reach the end, where, says Irons, they stopped contented.

This is only partially true. The ancients did not rest content always with the discovery of the end, but sought to make inferences beyond that, using it as the ground of further deductions; and the modern teleologists did not neglect the induction of facts by any means. They piled up facts mountain high to prove design, in order that thence they might prove a designer.

But does "design imply a designer"? Irons attacks this truism of Paley's with fatal effect. The similar expression, "There cannot be contrivance without a contriver," shares the same fate. But, when he comes to the declaration of Paley, that there cannot be "order without choice," he resorts to an *evasion*.

"I prefer to bring this, as well as every other matter, to every man's individual knowledge and experience; and I ask whether the 'order' of a man's actions is *always* the result of 'choice.' No! the truth seems to be, that this proposition has been linked to two or three evident truisms, and has passed as one itself."

The "order of a man's actions" is simply the *sequence* of them: that is quite a different notion from the eutaxy, the established order of the cosmos. The order of nature *might* mean the sequences of nature: *possibly*

Paley meant that, but it is not at all likely. Irons was dealing with a very different proposition here from those " easy " ones, — easy to demolish, — " Design implies a designer," etc. He ought not to have supposed he could demolish it with a wave of the hand, simply because he found it associated with certain patent and easily demonstrated fallacies.

It will be observed that he speaks of God uniformly as a cause. He makes all design-arguments causal, just as Kant, Reid, Stewart, and McCosh do ; and he does not entertain the conception of any other design-argument than teleology. If he had not been so summary with the statement that order implies choice in its establishment, he might have been led to a more respectful view of natural theology. His criticisms are very damaging to the teleology of Paley and the Bridgewater Treatises, but they do not touch eutaxiology at all. The only point he makes which could have any bearing that way is, the *evasion* of turning the widespread and deep harmonies of the cosmos into a mere sequence of events.

He thinks, notwithstanding all its fallacies, there is some use for the doctrine of final causes, if you keep it within due bounds, and in the hands of proper persons. He shows that Voltaire and other infidels thought favorably of design-arguments. They would be glad to set up natural religion as a rival to supplant revealed religion, knowing that man will have a religion of some sort. To all such persons who want thus to employ teleology, he sternly cries, " Hands off ! "

" The believer in revelation alone has any right to entertain the doctrine of design. When, on higher and more substantial grounds. the Christian has embraced his holy religion, this doctrine may be brought forward to *illustrate* the revealed character of God."

The Burnett prizes were provided for by the bequest of John Burnett, Esq., a merchant of Aberdeen. They were to be awarded, at intervals of forty years, to the authors of the two best treatises upon the evidence of God's existence, and the refutation of objections against his wisdom and goodness. Upon the first occasion of their award, in 1815, the first prize of £1,200 was obtained by William Laurence Brown, D.D.; and the second prize was obtained by the Rev. John Bird Sumner, afterwards Archbishop of Canterbury. Upon the second occasion of their award, in 1855, the first prize of £1,800 was adjudged to the Rev. R. A. Thompson, and the second prize of £600 was adjudged to the Rev. John Tulloch, D.D.

Dr. Brown's treatise is entitled " An Essay on the Existence of a Supreme Creator." Some expressions in his introduction imply that he was but slightly acquainted with the large body of literature already in existence upon the subject he was about to handle : —

" Of the many systems of Christian theology which have been communicated to the public, comparatively few unfold, in a clear and detailed manner, the proofs of the *existence* and *attributes* of the Deity. . . . Young persons are hurried into the particular doctrines of Christianity, and generally into the particular tenets of that church or sect of which they are destined to be members. These points they are taught to consider as much more interesting than the fundamentals of all religion ; and, accordingly, in this channel religious study and improvement are directed in succeeding life. Hence, while a considerable number know the chief differferences between Papists and Protestants, Calvinists and

Lutherans, Presbyterians and Episcopalians, Trinitarians and Unitarians, the Church of Scotland and Seceders, comparatively few are capable of offering a judicious and solid answer to the objections of a deist or of an atheist" (I. ix.).

It is no doubt true, that sectarian differences are better understood, and more frequently form the topic of conversation among Christians, than the proofs of God's existence. But this does not surely result from any dearth of treatises on the latter subject. Sectarian controversies are living and lively issues, and they are level to the comprehension of all; while the paucity of real atheists, and the secure confidence in the inherent strength of their position felt by all theists, make that issue theoretical and speculative rather than practical. The fundamental and vital importance of theism is not able to prevent the contest over it from being a languid and bloodless one, as compared with the hot and fierce skirmishes between rival sects. It is not only that there are few atheists, and that theists feel the ground very solid under their feet no matter how the speculative battle may turn, but theistic arguments must in the nature of things always be in a high degree abstruse, recondite, and to be thoroughly comprehended by a relatively small number of persons.

Dr. Brown relies almost wholly upon the ontological, causal, and moral arguments, referring the reader to " Payley (*sic*), Ray, and Derham " for design-arguments.

Sumner's Burnett prize essay is simply an apology, or treatise upon the evidences of Christianity.

The Burnett prize-essay of the Rev. R. A. Thompson is entitled " Christian Theism : the Testimony of Reason and Revelation to the Existence and Character of the Supreme Being." Book I., on " First Principles of

Knowledge," is psychological and metaphysical. Book II., on " The Direct Evidences of Natural Theism," is the one in which we are specially interested. He regards the physico-theological argument as complementary to the causal or cosmological.

" The cosmological proof states the procedure of the mind in giving its first matter to this empty conception, and raises it to the positive conception of the source of all being and power. It is where this proof ends that the physico-theological proof, or argument from design, has its commencement. The cosmological, when properly stated, infers a Cause of causes, a Source of all reality, from the knowledge of the world as a unity of diversities. The physico-theological examines the nature of these diversities; and from their harmnoy, their beauty, their marvellous adaptations to ends, in the order of the material, the intellectual, and the moral worlds, draws its conclusions respecting the nature and attributes of that Eternal Power who is the source of all being " (I. 293).

As regards this attempt to link causal and design arguments together, I have nothing to say but to commend it. Thompson maintains, that there is but *one* proof of the existence of God, that each of the several arguments contributes something to this, and that the correct treatment of them all is to link them together into one consecutive argument. This is an interesting and commendable suggestion; though as to its practicability, and as to the details of the scheme, — which argument is fundamental, and which are subsidiary; what does this proof contribute to the whole result, and how shall it be linked with that proof, — there would be room for wide differences of opinion. And we care less about how Mr. Thompson himself would carry out his suggestion when we observe how vague and confused are his notions of physico-theology. He speaks of it as the argument *from* design; he mixes eutaxiology and teleology together in the expression "marvellous *adaptations to ends* in the *order*" of the world, and makes the bald truism, "Design implies a designer," the major premise of his argument. "It is the argument of natural theology, that design must imply a designer, and that that which designs is mind" (I. 303).

The Burnett prize-treatise of the Rev. John Tulloch, D.D., was published in 1855.

His argument is more distinctly eutaxiological than that of any other writer before or since. His syllogistic statement of it is, —

"Order universally proves mind. The works of nature discover order. Therefore the works of nature prove mind."

This is well enough to start with; but what is inscrutable to an ordinary mind is the motive which led him almost to ignore his syllogism, and ramble off on a long discussion of the principle of causation. The only plausible solution is, that, like Stewart and others, he held that causation underlies the whole argument, though he does not say so. He thinks, with Reid and Stewart, that the fundamental inference is an intuition.

"Why is it that we apprehend everywhere in phenomena of order the operation of a rational will or mind? Simply because we cannot help doing so; because the laws of our rational being compel us to do so. These will not permit us to rest short of mind as the ultimate explanation of such phenomena. The theistic position, therefore, is based on an inherent rational necessity."

If the perception that "order universally proves mind" is intuitive, what is the need of resting the argument upon the law of causation, or bringing that in at all? But Tulloch spoils his eutaxiology, not only by this gratuitous delivery of it over to the law of cause and effect, with all the doubtful issues which attach to that law, but also by retaining the term *final cause*, which he fails to comprehend, and by using the word *design* with all its fertile ambiguities. In his discussion of causation he arrives at the same conclusion with Irons; viz., that mind is the only cause. What, then, is the difference between *efficient* and *final* causes if both are mental? No one could ever find out from Tulloch. In his whole discussion of final cause he is perfectly contented when he has traced it to mind; but, having traced all efficient cause to the same point, one would suppose he would tell us the difference between these two mental causes.

A fundamental obtuseness to the meaning of terms appears in the fact, that, making his argument rest upon the order of nature as he does, he still brings it under the doctrine of final causes, which always has reference to an end (*finis*), nor is he any more discriminating in the use of the word "design." In commenting upon the passage which I have quoted from Whewell[1] respecting the perception of "design" from "the mere aspect of order and symmetry in the works of nature," as compared with the perception of it "which is suggested to us by organized bodies," he, like Whewell, seems to be groping in the twilight, dimly conscious that there is a difference in the two cases, but unable to comprehend it clearly or state it precisely. If the reader will refer to the analyses of *eutaxiology* and *teleology* in my Introduction, and to the discussion of the word "design," he will find the distinction which Whewell and Tul-

[1] P. 249 of this work.

loch were groping after. The teleological meaning of
design is "adaptation of means to an end: " its meaning
in eutaxiology is *plan*. Tulloch differs from Whewell
in this, that he thinks the evidence of design is just as
clear in one case as in the other, while Whewell's comments are wholly disparaging to eutaxiology. In respect to the just appreciation of this line of argument,
Tulloch is therefore clear in advance of any previous
writer. But inasmuch as he, like the others, was still •
entangled in the ambiguities of design, which prevented
him from making the clear distinction between teleology
and eutaxiology, the praise which we might otherwise
bestow without qualification must be expressed with
some reserve.

We have had frequent illustrations in the course of
this historical review of the fact that theological discussion is apt to take tone and coloring from some
dominant antagonism. In the seventeenth century
teleology was anti-Cartesian ; in the eighteenth century
Hume was the objective point of the antagonistic animus, and still continued to be in the early part of
the nineteenth century. But, when Tulloch wrote his
" Theism," a new target for polemic theology had been
furnished by the philosophy of positivism ; and his
treatise takes its tone from that, as does also that of
his colleague, Mr. Thompson.

•

CHAPTER XII.

McCOSH, POWELL, AND COOKE.

"TYPICAL Forms and Special Ends in Creation," by James McCosh, LL.D., and George Dickie, M.D., Edinburgh, 1856, is the most admirable design-argument ever produced. The motto is τύπος καὶ τέλος, "Type and End." The two grand principles of order and adaptation, eutaxy and teleology, are carried along side by side throughout the work. This fact is illustrated by the section-headings, — "I. Traces of Order in the Organs of Plants." "II. Traces of Special Adaptation in the Organs of Plants." "I. Order in the Number, Form, and Structure of Teeth." "II. Special Adaptations in the Number, Form, and Structure of Teeth." Thus it runs through the whole of Book II., which is the special contribution of Dr. Dickie. But Dr. McCosh, the author of Books I. and III., is probably responsible for the fundamental ideas of the book, Dickie's function being to furnish the facts. I shall take the liberty, therefore, of speaking of the principles of the work as those of McCosh.

In the "Analysis of the Order of Nature" he brings out the elements of *number*, *time*, *color*, and *form*. The latter element assumes very great importance in the book, from the fact that so large a part of it is biological, the doctrine of morphology being thus brought to the front. But there is a chapter on terres-

trial bodies, and one on " The Heavens;" so that the
principle of order takes a wider range than that expressed by the word "morphology," and requires, therefore, a more generic term. For this purpose he again
proposes the word "cosmology," and without that reserve which marked his first suggestion of this term:
" We need a word to embrace the whole, and we propose that this be cosmology ; that is, the science of the
order in the universe."

In my Introduction I have given reasons which seem
to me sufficient to prevent the acceptance of this suggestion ; and I have proposed the term "eutaxiology,"
instead of "cosmology." It is a matter of regret that
McCosh's suggestion could not be accepted without
danger of involving the order-argument in some confu-
sions of the same kind which have beset teleology from
the use of ambiguous terms. Next to Professor Owen,
who has done more for the morphological phase of
eutaxiology than any other living man, McCosh would
be the fittest godfather to name the new argument
which he employed with such skill. He has indeed
named it, as we have seen ; but he made the suggestion
very gingerly in the first place ;[1] and, though he repeats
it more confidently in the volume before us, still he did
not have the courage of his convictions sufficiently to
use it himself.

And, in regard to the use of terms, it is to be regretted
that he did not rid his teleology of the ambiguities incident to the word "design" and the phrase "final cause."
He saw the fallacy of the truism, " Design implies a
designer " (p. 89); but he uses the word himself without
discriminating between its teleological and its eutaxiological meanings. One of the infelicities of "final

_____
[1] Meth. of Div. Gov., 1850. See also p. 4 of this volume.

cause" appears in the following sentence: "Every organic object is constructed after a type, and is, at the same time, made to accomplish a final cause." How awkwardly it sounds to speak of *accomplishing* a *cause!*

McCosh agrees with Kant, Reid, and Stewart in making the whole argument from nature rest ultimately upon the principle of causation; and, like Reid and Stewart, he thinks the judgment that every event has a cause is intuitive. He differs from these authors, however, in not regarding the existence of God as an intuition. He regards teleology and eutaxiology both as good proofs of the divine existence, but is inclined to subordinate the latter to the former. He has not escaped wholly from the old prejudice in favor of teleology; for he attempts to resolve his order-argument into a sort of higher teleology: "Every thing has, after all, a final cause. The general order pervading nature is just a final cause of a higher and more archetypal character" (440).

His special notion of what the "final cause" of morphology is may be gathered from the following:—

"While the special modifications or adaptations investigated so carefully by Cuvier are intended to promote the well-being of the particular species of animal, the archetypal plan investigated by Owen is fitted to make the animal intelligible by the intelligent creation. Owen has developed— to some extent perhaps unconsciously, but to a far greater extent consciously— a teleology of a higher order than Cuvier" (441).

It is only in a vague, rhetorical metaphor that you can thus transform morphology into teleology; and, without adverting to some stronger reasons for avoiding such expressions, which will appear in the sequel, the mischievous effect of them is obvious enough when we connect them with the persistent abuse of teleology all through its history in the matter of wild, conjectural purposes assigned to this or that thing, in order to construct a teleological argument upon it. That, of course, was not the doctor's object in this case: he was not really trying to transform eutaxiology into teleology, but only to harmonize them. That can be done, however, without reducing one to a form of the other.

In commenting upon the doctrine of "collocations" of Dr. Chalmers, I expressed the opinion that there was something valuable in it if divorced from the antithesis to natural law. McCosh's appreciation of eutaxiology as a distinct argument ought to have enabled him to set that doctrine in its true light, and to develop all that was useful in it. And he has undoubtedly improved very decidedly upon the previous statement of it. He does not make it the antithesis of natural law.

" It will be necessary in this place to state an important distinction which Dr. Chalmers had the merit of introducing into natural theology in a formal manner. He calls on us to notice how, the laws of matter being as they are, the results might have been different if a different set of collocations had been made of the bodies obeying these laws. Thus the law of gravitation still being as it is, the planetary bodies would have been moving in a very different manner from what they do, had they been differently situated with reference to the sun and to one another. Had they not, for example, revolved in nearly one plane, they might in their revolutions have come into violent and destructive collision with each other. This is prevented by their being so disposed that their spheres can never intersect each other; that is, by their skilful collocation. Dr. Chalmers thinks that the argument in favor of the existence of God should be founded on the collocations of matter rather than the laws of matter. The distinction is undoubtedly a sound one."

Here he seems to take the doctrine just as Chalmers left it, the antithesis to law included. But, being really dispossessed of the prejudice in favor of arbitrary interferences as the only proof of divine activity, he avoids the antithesis to law by introducing a distinction between original properties of matter and derivative laws, the latter being the results of collocations.

"If these remarks be just, we are entitled to argue, that there has been adaptation, not only in two or more bodies being so arranged as to produce an isolated effect of a benign character, but also in their being so disposed as to produce general laws or general results, these being wide-spread and continuous, stretching through extensive regions of space, and prolonged through many successive ages, such as the seasons, and the regular forms and periods of plants and animals. These — indeed, all the principles of order in respect of number, time, color, and form — are entitled to be called laws. But they are not original: they are derivative laws, not simple but composite, and the result of arrangements."

This distinction between original properties and the laws resulting from collocations was convenient for the purpose of rescuing the doctrine of Chalmers from its fatal opposition to natural law; but otherwise it has little value in physico-theology. It is not essential to draw the line between what was originally imparted to matter, and what flowed as a consequence from this; and, if it were essential, it would, in the present state of science, be practically impossible.

If Dr. McCosh erred in the direction of giving too

high a place to teleology in relation to eutaxiology, Professor Baden Powell was inclined to the opposite extreme of ignoring teleology altogether.

"The argument, as popularly pursued, proceeds upon the analogy of a personal agent, whose contrivances are limited by the conditions of the case and the nature of his materials, and pursued by steps corresponding to those of human plans and operations, — an argument leading only to the most unworthy and anthropomorphic conceptions. Yet such have been the now confessedly injudicious modes of expression adopted by some approved writers on the subject. The satisfactory view of the whole case can only be found in those more enlarged conceptions which are furnished by the grand contemplation of cosmical order and unity, and which do not refer to inferences of the *past*, but to proofs of the *ever-present* mind and reason in nature." [1]

The last point in this quotation is obscure: it seems impossible to separate the tokens of "ever-present," active intelligence from "inferences of the past." One element of the order of nature is time. An orderly sequence of events is as striking a proof of intelligent arrangement as those orderly dispositions of matter which exist simultaneously. If we are studying the celestial harmonies, we can have no indications of intelligent adjustments which do not, in strictness, refer to the past; for the light of those bodies, by which alone we can learn any thing about them, may have been millions of years on its way to us. The whole of nature is so linked together, that every token of present intelligence must be linked with inferences of the past.

But the main point of the quotation is clear enough. Powell relies upon the principle of order rather than that of special adaptation. This appears in many forms

[1] Order of Nature, 237.

and in numberless passages, besides dominating the whole plan and tone of his books.

"The instances in which we can trace a *use* and a *purpose* in nature, striking as they are, after all, constitute but a very small and subordinate portion of the vast scheme of universal order and harmony of design which pervades and connects the whole. Throughout the immensely greater part of nature we can trace *symmetry* and *arrangement*, but not the *end* for which the adjustment is made. But this is in no way a less powerful proof of design and intelligence than the former. The most exact and recondite adaptation of means to accomplish an obvious end is no more peculiarly an evidence of design, than the universal arrangement according to determinate laws which pervades the depths of cosmical space, where we are least able to trace any end. Symmetry and beauty are results of mind of at least as high an order as mechanical efficiency. A mere numerical relation invariably preserved, but no further connected with any imaginable purpose, or a systematic arrangement of useless parts or abortive organs on a regular plan, are just as forcible indications of intelligence as any results of immediate practical utility.[1]

"The old and limited view of final causes will not meet the increasing demands of scientific enlightenment. It will not suffice now to argue solely on the adaptation of means to a known purpose, or a practical design evinced, and an obvious end answered. We may speak of 'design' with reference solely to 'order' and 'arrangement,' without looking to the idea of practical utility. Such modes of expression are far preferable, as not leading the mind to any undue expectation of what it will not realize.

"Paley expressly held that the mechanism of the heavens was a branch of science the least susceptible of this kind of application [that is, least fitted to serve as the basis of de-

[1] Unity of Worlds, 135.

sign-arguments]. According to the principles here advocated, it forms the highest and most satisfactory.

"But a more special argument has been raised on the
ground that the planetary perturbations have been shown so
to compensate each other, that no permanent derangement
can arise ; and La Place pointed out that this stability of the
planetary system is the necessary consequence of certain
conditions, *not themselves necessary;* namely, the smallness
of the inclinations and eccentricities, the motions of all in
the same direction, the comparatively vast mass of the sun,
and the incommensurability of the periods.

" Professor Playfair justly enlarges upon this as an argument for *design;* but, if the conditions thus assigned were
necessary (i.e., *necessary consequences* of each other or something else), he thinks we could not infer *design.* They, however, are not *necessary:* each *might be* otherwise, the rest remaining. Their existence then, he argues, not arising from
necessity, nor from *mechanical causes,* nor from *chance,* must
be from *design* and intelligence.

" But I would ask, suppose *they were necessary* consequences of each other or of some higher principle, or did
arise from mechanical causes, would not that higher principle, or those causes so arranged as to produce them, be an
equal proof of *design,* or even a *higher?* So singularly deep-
seated is the prejudice, that design can only be inferred
when we cease to trace *laws,* or when conditions appear *arbitrary* " (142).

This passage shows his thorough-paced reliance upon
law and order. Not only does he take these as the best
manifestations of intelligence, but he thinks every in-
terruption and anomaly obscures the evidence instead
of making it stronger.

" To speak of apparent anomalies and interruptions as
special indications of the Deity, is altogether a mistake. In
truth, so far as the *anomalous* character of any phenomenon

can affect the inference of presiding intelligence at all, it
would rather tend to *diminish* and detract from that evidence."

Manifestly, Powell's *beau idéal* mark of intelligence
is universal, unchanging, inflexible law. With such an
ideal we can understand a fact which would otherwise
be rather surprising. He wrote before the publication
of Darwin's " Origin of Species," and yet he was ready
to accept evolution. Whatever extended the reign of
law as distinguished from the sphere of special interventions was welcome to him.

Powell devotes a large part of his latest volume to a
historical sketch of the progress of the human mind
towards a broad and just conception of the order of
nature. This is admirably conceived as an introduction
to cutaxiology; and the conception is well carried out
on the whole. But in a few points his statements are
inaccurate. Speaking of the natural theology of the
seventeenth and of the early part of the eighteenth
century, he says it was "of the abstract, *à priori* cast,
typified in the writings of Locke, S. Clarke, Cudworth,
and Wollaston, who, setting out from high, abstruse,
first principles, attempted a deductive system of technical and formal propositions, embodying precise views
of the divine nature and attributes, and thence the
moral scheme of man's relation to his Creator, and of
his condition in this life to that in another." [1]

I should give More, Boyle, Ray, Derham, and Nieuwentyt as typical expounders of the natural theology
of that period, rather than those he mentions. He says
that Boyle " believed the whole universe subservient to
the well-being of man ; " citing a passage in " The Use-

[1] Order of Nature, 123.

fulness of Experimental Natural Philosophy," published in 1664, but not quoting Boyle's exact language. Turning to the place in question (p. 24), we find this: " That much of this visible world was made for the use of man may appear not only from the time of his creation, etc." " Much of this visible world," and the " whole universe," are not quite equivalent terms. Still, Boyle advanced in his views on this point in the course of a quarter of a century; for, when he published his work on " Final Causes " in 1688, he had thoroughly out-grown the vulgar notion that all things were made for man, and even indulges in a little satire at the expense of a certain learned divine who thought the earth was made for the sake of man in his travelling condition, and would therefore be destroyed after the Day of Judgment. In the earlier work he speaks of " God's making those noble and vast luminaries, and other bodies that adorn the sky, to give light upon the earth;" and this may account for his vacillating course in his " Disquisition," where he first excludes the fixed stars as unsuitable material for teleology, and subsequently retracts that sound opinion. Some desire to be consistent with himself may have influenced this change for the worse.

Barring these slight inaccuracies, Powell's showing of the progress of the human mind towards a full comprehension of the order of nature is not only deeply interesting, but exceedingly valuable. It shows plainly that the data for the construction of eutaxiology have been slowly and gradually accumulated as the various sciences were created and perfected.

" Religion and Chemistry," by Professor Josiah P. Cooke of Harvard University, presents fair examples of eutaxiological reasoning : —

" The illustrations of the attributes of God which may be drawn from the constitution of matter are conveniently divided into two classes, — first, those which appear in the adaptation of various means to a particular end; and, second, those which are to be found in the unity of plan, according to which the whole frame of nature has been constructed. The first class are exhibited by the properties of matter, the second by the so-called physical laws and forces " (p. 5.)

This distinction is essentially the same as that between teleology and eutaxiology. It is noteworthy, that he does not use either kind of reasoning to prove the existence of God, but simply as "illustrations of his attributes."

It is not entirely clear which kind of proof he regards as the best. In the following passage it seems to be the eutaxiological : —

"We can see that each property of water has been designed for some specific purpose. . . . [But] the strength of our argument lies not so much in the fact that each property has been skilfully adjusted to some specific end, as it does in the harmonious working of all the separate details.

" To me the *laws* of nature afford the strongest evidences of the existence of a God ; and in their uniformity I see merely the constant action of an omnipotent Creator, who acts with perfect regularity because he acts consistently with infinite wisdom. I believe that all parts of nature are correlated by laws, and that the wider our knowledge becomes the more universal these laws will appear. I do not, therefore, regard the constitution of water as something apart from law [he has reference more especially to the exceptional property of expansion near and at the freezing-point, which theologians have often cited as a wonderful proof of design because of its anomalous character], and as the evidence of a power coming down as it were upon law to make an exception to it" (161).

Notwithstanding these strong expressions of appreciation of those elements of his argument which are plainly eutaxiological, the ancient and deep-seated prejudice in favor of teleology still sways his mind: —

"I do not, of course, regard analogies as proofs, nor do I believe that this argument from general plan could supply the place of the great argument from design. The last lies at the basis of natural theology, and all the rest is merely subsidiary to the great central light."

That he means teleology by the phrase "argument from design," appears from the marginal note: "It is subsidiary to the argument from special adaptation" (318).

How disappointing, not to say provoking, to see a man construct a good piece of eutaxiology, and then give it all away by making it subsidiary to teleology! He thinks the latter is not only the "great central light" of natural theology, but also that it is simpler and easier to comprehend than the argument from general plan.

"Moreover, while the argument from design comes home to every man's understanding, these analogies appeal with their full force only to the few who are able to study the processes of nature for themselves, as they alone are familiar with the phenomena in which the resemblances are seen. But to the student whose life has been passed in successful investigation, and whose soul has been brought into sympathy with the harmonies of nature, these tokens are constantly assuring him of the presence of his God. Every discoverer feels — when in the presence of a great truth he cannot resist the feeling — that in discovering a law he has been brought nearer, not to a blind agency, but to Omnipotence itself."

Great discoverers may have a monopoly of great emotions of that sort; but, happily, the perception that mind has produced the order of nature is not limited to them. This passage, as well as the last, suggests the point that Cooke uses the word "analogy" in some very recondite and unusual sense. He says the argument from design is based on analogy, in which he is, of course, sustained by a host of teleologists; but he also declares that "all scientific *generalization* is based on analogy" (249). It must be that he uses analogy to designate that process which is usually called *induction*. In the practical development of his eutaxiology, or "argument from general plan," he makes much of the phenomena of crystallization as an example of symmetry, also of combining proportions in chemistry and phyllotaxy in botany.

He adopts the theory that all force is a manifestation of the divine will.

" According to this view, the energy which sustains the universe is the will of God, and the law of conservation is only the manifestation of his immutable being, — 'the same yesterday, and to-day, and forever' " (340).

He thinks that "the existence of an intelligent author of nature, infinite in wisdom and absolute in power, may be proved from the phenomena of the material world with as much certainty as can any general truth of science." But he is not so clear about proving personality, and is positive that the goodness of the Deity *cannot* be proved from nature.

" I do not believe, however, in any sense, that nature proves the goodness of God. . . . So prominent, indeed, is the evil in nature, and so insidiously and mysteriously does it prevade the whole system, that an argument to prove the malignity of God could be made to appear quite as plausible as the arguments which are frequently urged to prove his pure beneficence.

"God is love; but nature could not prove it, and the Lamb was 'slain from the foundation of the world' to attest it."

CHAPTER XIII.

RESULTS OF THE HISTORICAL REVIEW.

RECENT publications on natural theology have all hinged more or less closely upon Darwinism and evolution. As I propose to devote a chapter to each of those topics, it will be convenient to range the later productions on the one side or the other of the question of hostility or amicable relations to these very striking and revolutionary doctrines of biology, instead of treating them in the form of a historical review, as I have done with previous writers. That portion of my task which consists in showing what had been done in natural theology up to about that time when the "Origin of Species" appeared, is completed. I have not attempted to make it exhaustive; and even considering that fact, considering that my aim was only to mention the leading writers and delineate the most characteristic phases of theological speculation, I am painfully conscious how imperfectly this purpose has been accomplished. Still, the data for certain conclusions respecting the course and development of physico-theology have been furnished by the preceding chapters; and it is now desirable to gather these up, and present them in a connected view, in order to fix and crystallize the impressions which they may have made.

One impression, which took a deep hold upon my own mind in this investigation, was the proficiency of the ancients in natural theology. That portion of my sketch has less pretensions to exhaustiveness than any other; and yet it exhibits a range and accuracy of thought, and a practical skill and judgment in the management and application of the reasoning, which may well challenge comparison with any thing in modern theology. So that a very pertinent question is sprung upon us at the very threshold of our inquiry into the results of the historical review: this, namely, Has there been any real growth of natural theology through all these centuries?

When we consider the fact, that there has been a tiresome and almost nauseating repetition of arguments and illustrations, it might seem justifiable to answer this question in the negative. But that would be a superficial view of the matter. Amid all this monotonous harping upon the well-worn strings, there has been, after all, a real improvement in the music. In order to verify this statement, let us consider, in the first place, the charge brought against teleology by Spinoza, that its advocates regarded the whole universe with reference to its utility to man.

The ancients undoubtedly did look upon every natural object, terrestrial or celestial, with an eye to human uses; and up to a certain period we find the same tendency very strong among modern theologians. That period coincides very closely with the time when Spinoza's criticism appeared; and this may be taken as an illustration of the value of criticism, even when its animus is hostile. Indeed, it is questionable whether friendly criticism is ever so efficacious, even when it is very searching. Some men will never be reformed by any thing short of the whipping-post; and some reasoners will never wake up to the consciousness of their fallacies till the lash is laid on in good, downright earnest.

A recent writer on natural theology,[1] with reference to its relations to evolution, repeats Spinoza's criticism, charging the fault in question upon the Bridgewater Treatises, and upon natural theology in general : —

" An ichneumon fly, had it reasoning powers, might easily conclude that caterpillars were beneficently designed for its use as being the place where it should lay its eggs. On the other hand, the caterpillar would have a very different view of the beneficence of that Being who made both itself and the ichneumon. I repeat, therefore, to bring forward instances of advantages, or even blessings to one creature, even if we select man, as proofs of the wisdom and beneficence of God, is, and must be, a partial and one-sided view of creation ; and this, if I understand them aright, is an unmistakably weak point in the arguments of the Bridgewater Treatises, and of natural theologians in general " (p. 161).

This is one more example of a sweeping and wholesale accusation brought by one natural theologian against all the rest, without having made a careful examination of the facts. No doubt some of the Bridgewater essayists were, in a measure, involved in this strong tendency even to deny the existence of that which was not obviously useful to mankind. The case of the Rev. Mr. Kirby's hostility to Mantell's theory of an age of reptiles will recur to the reader's memory.

[1] " The Theory of Evolution of Living Things," by the Rev. George Henslow. This is another prize essay. Writers on natural theology have had considerable stimulus of this kind. Hannah Acton gave £1,000, from the income of which £105 is to be given every seven years for "the best essay illustrative of the wisdom and beneficence of the Almighty in such department of science as the committee of managers shall in their discretion select."

But Kirby is the least advanced, the least representative, the most mediæval, of that group. The rest are quite as enlightened upon the point in question as the majority of intelligent people of the present generation, — as much so, in fact, as Mr. Henslow himself. For, after such a criticism of "natural theologians in general," we are really amazed at his own conclusion respecting the purpose and aim of this sublunary world : —

" This phenomenon of the existence of a mixture of good and evil, which is of very wide application, is a result of that struggle for existence which is a well-recognized law of nature, and is applicable to all kinds of life. To a partial or restricted view this law may appear as a ' fatal ' result of undirected natural forces ; but I maintain, though God chose to establish such laws as a condition of life on the earth, *he had a motive in so doing;* and that motive was, in its ultimate bearings, to surround man with inideal[1] circumstances, and so render his life on earth probationary in every way."

That is about as comprehensive a scheme for bringing the whole world under that point of view which makes it all have reference to man, as we can find anywhere among the ancients or moderns; and, if Mr. Henslow is to stand as the type of a modern natural theologian, I should have to recant my opinion that there has been any real growth in this particular. In his view all the physical evils which affect the brute creation, and have harassed them with pain and suffering, and done them to death by millions during long ages before man appeared upon the scene, — all this was for the sake of surrounding man with inideal circumstances. This may

---

[1] "Inideal" is a word of Henslow's coining, and means *relatively* perfect, as opposed to *ideally* perfect.

be very orthodox theology, but it is derived from some other source than nature.

And this raises the question how far it is an unseemly prejudice which ought to be outgrown, and how far it is really true, that things were made for the benefit of man. Spinoza's criticism was just in this respect, that theologians were too prone to ascribe human utilities to all objects with a view to teleological argumentation. The ascription was often a dubious one to start with; and, when they proceeded to build an argument upon such a foundation, the ridiculous flimsiness of the whole fabric was obvious to all but themselves. For illustration, let us take this doctrine propounded by Henslow, that the whole world has been made a scene of mixed good and evil, in order that it might be a perfect place of probation for man. Moral probation is the end; the mixture of good and evil, of joy, comfort, hope, and gladness, with sin, disease, crime, despair, and death, is the means. And the theologian proceeds to argue from the fitness in the adaptation of the means to the end, that there is a God! The absurdity of it — one absurdity, for there are several — is, that almost any rational being would accept the conclusion quicker than he would the premises. But precisely the same thing is true of a great deal of teleological reasoning. The end assigned to this or that thing is far more doubtful than the existence of God.

But detach such speculations respecting the purpose of this world from teleology, make no attempt to use them for any ulterior purpose of argument, then they assume a more reasonable phase. So far as the earth is concerned, there can be no doubt that much of its present condition and past history finds its true explanation in its occupation by a rational animal. So the charge of referring often to human uses may have very little condemnation in it, though sustained by the facts. Since the time of Robert Boyle, writers on physico-theology have been reasonably cautious in this particular. Derham is especially severe upon the vulgar prejudice that celestial bodies were all made for our benefit.

Indeed it is unquestionably true that these writers have been in advance of the sentiments even of well-informed people in the general community in their own day, or even at the present moment. Since I have been engaged in writing this book, several persons have suggested examples of what they regarded as good proofs of design; and invariably the end was one which had reference to human utilities, and not always of the highest order. Upon the whole, there has been a decided advance in natural theology since the time of Cicero, not only as regards this human prejudice in favor of humanity, but also as regards the degree of caution exercised in the general interpretation of the Creator's intentions. The very thought of asserting that this or the other was God's purpose ought to make men go slow, and tread softly; and they *have* learned a little caution in the course of ages.

In the matter of selecting examples to illustrate their doctrine, the course of teleologists has been a devious one. Instead of a steady improvement, there was an actual retrogression, and then a very great advance. Nothing in Socrates, Cicero, or Galen is so ridiculous as Dr. More's argument from the "signatures" of plants. Derham was an improvement on More; but his argument from volcanoes was not an eminent success. Nieuwentyt has some very feeble examples, such as the size of a man's bite, and the wisdom of making the food pass over the glottis on its way to the pharynx. Paley, with all his *panorpa* forceps and woodpeckers' tongues (borrowed ones: Ray was the first to introduce that example), was more judicious in his selection; and more recent writers have gone beyond him in the dignified good taste they have exhibited in their illustrations.

It would have been more unpardonable in them than in writers a century ago not to have done so, considering the wealth of good material which advancing scientific discovery was constantly pouring upon them. Whatever improvement there has been in the sifting and selection of illustrations may be traced directly to the growth of physical science. Science has taken the lead in every instance and in every particular; and not only has physico-theology been a follower, instead of a leader, but it has been in some particulars a lagging and far-distant follower.

Especially has this been true in respect to its nomenclature, and the analysis of its arguments. Long Greek compounds are not agreeable to the ear; and there is always a smack of pedantry about them when first introduced, which continues, indeed, until they are thoroughly naturalized and acclimated. (It is with a full consciousness of this fact that I have ventured to launch a new name for the order-argument.) But they are indispensable to every true science. Accuracy, not elegance or euphony, is the grand desideratum; and this can only be attained by the use of technical terms, — that is, words selected from the classical languages, of appropriate primitive meaning, but, above all, accurately defined when first introduced, and then rigidly restricted to their technical and uniform sense. Kant was the first who attempted to equip theology with a complete technical nomenclature. His terms have been largely adopted; but in one case, where he used the same term ("cosmological") in two different senses, the less accurate one was selected.

Not only have there been delay and partial failure in the matter of furnishing an equipment of good technical terms, but there has been the ambiguous use of common words such as "design," and the distorted application of scholastic phrases such as "final cause." In respect to the latter, there has been an improvement. Many of the later authors who use it do so with expressions of regret and dissatisfaction. But in regard to "design," while several have detected the fallacy of the proposition that "design implies a designer," not one has pointed out the ambiguity of the word itself, or made any discrimination in respect to its teleological and its eutaxiological meaning.

But the halting movement and desultory course of development of physico-theology, in comparison with other sciences, is at no point more conspicuous than in the analysis and use of its arguments. The elements of eutaxiology and teleology have been more or less involved in the arguments of physico-theology from the earliest time to the latest; but, while this is especially true of the ancients, they failed utterly to distinguish these elements, or to give them separate names and a distinct treatment. For a long time the order-argument was almost ignored, though not so completely ignored as the remark of Dr. McCosh, in his "Method of Divine Government," would imply. During the present century, through the labors of Crombie, Tulloch, Powell, McCosh, and Cooke, eutaxiology has been in a measure advanced to its true position. But

even some of these have seemed half ashamed of it,
and ready to merge it into " the great central light " of
teleology. So feebly has it been set forth, that I seriously question whether the average theologian is at this
moment conscious of the existence of but one kind of
design-argument, and that one is teleology.

But supposing that eutaxiology had been fully developed by the middle of the present century, while it
would have been most opportune in relation to the
spread of Darwinism, it would have still been a century too late in relation to scientific progress. From
the time when Copernicus announced the true theory
of the solar system, and Galileo made his discoveries in
physics, thus affording a new and broader view of celestial harmonies and terrestrial order, — from that time,
three centuries ago, eutaxiology ought to have dated
its birth, or its resurrection if we grant that the ancients developed a true and distinct argument for the
existence of God from the order of nature. And, from
the time when Newton discovered the law of gravitation, the order-argument ought to date its full development.

It should not be forgotten, that the two great minds
of the last century, Newton and Kant, did make use of
this argument. But theologians in general were too
much absorbed in the subtilities of the doctrine of
final causes, even to perceive the new departure, much
less to appreciate its significance.

Being so enamoured of teleology we should expect
that they would at least know all about that. But,
on the contrary, they made no analysis of the conceptions involved in it ; no logical scrutiny of its validity
and its limitations ; no discrimination in the use of its
leading terms ; and, finally, they are wholly uncertain,

and all at loggerheads among themselves, about the proper use to be made of teleology when they have once got it constructed after a bungling fashion. Shall we use teleology to prove God's existence, or use his assumed existence to prove his intentions, — that is, to prove that there is such a thing as teleology? One cries one thing, and another cries another thing. There is no uniformity either in opinion or practice. In the seventeenth century we find More taking the first alternative, and Boyle the second. In the eighteenth century Derham and Nieuwentyt use teleology to prove God's existence, as do nearly all the writers of the present century except Stewart, who declines to do so, because he thinks that truth is intuitive and needs no proof, and Irons, who thinks that nobody but a theist and a Christian has any business with teleology anyhow.

But of those who take the first alternative, and set out to prove God's existence, we have observed that they generally assume that truth after all, and practically do nothing more than to illustrate his attributes. Nor do those who take the second alternative stick to their text much better. Boyle sets out to prove the existence of teleology; but much of his argument is so framed that he seems to be attempting the more ambitious achievement of demonstrating divine existence. Even so late and excellent a writer as Professor Cooke sets out with some modest "illustrations of the attributes of God," but ends with the declaration that "the existence of an intelligent Author of nature may be proved from the phenomena of the material world with as much certainty as can any general truth of science."

What is the reason of all this vacillation and uncertainty about the true use of teleology? What *is* the true use of it? Does God's existence need proving so much as teleology itself needs it? Harassed by its enemies and abused by its advocates, foes and fightings without, and fallacies and frailties within, is not that doctrine *in extremis*, and more in need of God than he of it? Will not the ambitious programme of demonstrating God's existence by means of teleology have to be laid aside for a little, till we ascertain whether there is any such thing in existence as teleology? The answers to these questions I reserve until after I have finished the critique of teleology in a subsequent chapter.

CHAPTER XIV.

DARWINISM AND DESIGN.

DARWINISM is a theory of evolution, and yet the two are not identical. I propose to discuss the bearing of each upon physico-theology in separate chapters, not only because they are not precisely identical, — evolution may be a general truth of nature independent of natural selection, which is the characteristic thing in Darwinism, — but also because there are certain, so to speak, personal issues respecting Darwinism which justify a separate treatment. In these chapters on Darwinism and evolution, while I have dropped the form of a historical review under which I have delineated the productions of the earlier authors, I shall still preserve the spirit of the historian or reviewer, rather than that of the essayist. I shall state what others have said about the effect of Darwinism and evolution upon design-arguments, rather than to elaborate my own views, though I shall make no effort to conceal them.

I shall, in the first place, mention some opinions upon the anti-Darwinian side, to the effect that Darwinism is fatal to natural theology, and indeed to every good thing. Such opinions might be multiplied indefinitely were there any need of it.

" Essays on Religion and Literature," edited by Henry Edward, Archbishop of Westminster, London,

1874, contains an essay entitled "Darwinism brought to Book," by the Rev. F. H. Laing, D.D. This is as fierce and intemperate a diatribe as was ever penned. Considering the high auspices under which it appeared, it had almost the semblance of an official anathema. But now, in less than ten years from its publication, I have seen this same Charles Darwin laid to rest, with all the honors and sacred rites of the church, in this very Abbey whose archbishop lent his name to such an assault upon him while living.

Eight years, however, is a long time in this busy age. Let us see what a very recent writer has to say. "The Creed of Science," by William Graham, 1881, contains this : —

" But now it appears that Darwin has at last enabled the extreme materialist to attempt and carry the design-argument, the last and hitherto impregnable fortress, behind which natural theology had intrenched herself " (319).

Then, after an illustration of this statement, showing the effect of the Darwinian explanation of the process by which the eye has been evolved, he says, —

" This is the whole story. And here the design-argument as formerly understood loses its point and force, apparent design being explained by, and resolved into, a natural process and the fact of inheritance. What we mistook for a preconception of an infinite Mind, realized by an Almighty and skilful hand, is a most excellent result that chance has spared, and that natural selection has brought to the front " (322).

The most elaborate attempt to prove that Darwinism and design are mutually destructive was made by Dr. Hodge of Princeton : [1] —

[1] What is Darwinism ? New York, 1874.

"It appears that Darwinism includes three distinct elements. First, evolution, or the assumption that all organic forms, vegetable and animal, have been evolved or developed from one or a few primordial living germs ; second, that this evolution has been effected by natural selection, or the survival of the fittest ; and third, and by far the most important and only distinctive element of his theory, that this natural selection is without design, being conducted by unintelligent physical causes " (48).

"It is, however, neither evolution nor natural selection which gives Darwinism its peculiar character and importance. It is that Darwin rejects all teleology, or the doctrine of final causes " (52).

We and all the world have been much in the dark about Darwinism, it seems. We honestly thought the important and distinctive thing in it was evolution by natural selection. In our great simplicity we imagined that he was to take a high rank among the great thinkers and discoverers on account of his work in biology. But that, says Hodge, was a very trifling incident of his career. The great thing to remember about him, " the only distinctive thing," is that he rejects all teleology!

But does he reject all teleology? How does Hodge make it out that this thing, which he regards as the only distinctive thing about Darwin, really attaches to him at all? Let us see : —

" The sources of evidence on this point are, 1st, Mr. Darwin's own writings. 2d, The expositions of his theory, given by its advocates. 3d, The character of the objections urged by its opponents " (52).

Queer sources of proof truly, especially the third. Dr. Hodge is going to prove what Darwin believes by citing what Darwin's enemies say he believes! The first source is the only legitimate one; and it is worthy of note that he occupies only eleven pages with "Darwin's own testimony," including also Hodge's comments on it, thirty-two pages with the "Testimony of the Advocates of the Theory," and *eighty-two* pages with the "Testimony of the Opponents of Darwinism." Well may he say at the end, "We have *thus* arrived at the answer to our question, What is Darwinism? It is atheism" (177). In order to get Darwin just where he wanted him, so that he could hit him fair and hard, he summoned the whole host of his enemies and a goodly array of his over-zealous and too radical friends, by whose combined aid he at last got him fairly planted before his loaded howitzer yclept atheist-exterminator, and then blazed away!

But to the one legitimate source of proof. Let us examine his quotations from Darwin *seriatim.* I give the pages from the sixth London edition of the "Origin of Species:" —

"Nothing can be more hopeless than to attempt to explain this similarity of pattern in members of the same class by utility or the doctrine of final causes" (382).

"Similarity of pattern in members of the same class" is simply a typical form, or an example of morphology; and morphology is a distinct thing from teleology. No scientist and no *well-informed* design-advocate has any desire to explain the facts of morphology "by utility or the doctrine of final causes." They would never dream of such a thing, and yet they may be thorough-going teleologists. This quotation lacks two things of showing that Darwinism is death to design. In the first place, it would not follow that Darwin rejected teleology because he could not use it to explain every thing in heaven and earth; and, in the second place, teleology is not the only design-argument. Hodge seemed to think it was; and this fact forms a curious comment upon the state of physico-theology when the issue of Darwinism was sprung upon it. If eutaxiology had been properly developed and brought to the front, Darwinism and design would have been good friends from the start.

Hodge's second quotation from the "Origin of Species" is the following : —

"It is interesting to contemplate a tangled bank, clothed with many plants of many kinds, with birds singing on the bushes, with various insects flitting about, and with worms crawling through the damp earth, and to reflect that these elaborately constructed forms, so different from each other, and dependent on each other in so complex a manner, have all been produced by laws acting around us. These laws, taken in the largest sense, being growth, inheritance, which is almost implied by reproduction [this clause about "inheritance" was omitted by Hodge], variability from the indirect and direct action of the conditions of life, and from use and disuse ; a ratio of increase so high as to lead to a struggle for life, and as a consequence to natural selection, entailing divergence of character and extinction of less improved forms. Thus, from the war of nature, from famine and death, the most exalted object which we are capable of conceiving, the production of the higher animals follows. There is a grandeur in this view of life with its several powers, having been originally breathed by the Creator into a few forms, or into one ; and that whilst this planet has gone cycling on, according to the fixed law of gravity, from so simple a beginning, endless forms most beautiful and most wonderful have been, and are being, evolved" (429).

Dr. Hodge comments copiously on most of the quotations from Darwin, but offers not a word on this passage; so that we are left wholly to conjecture how he made out a denial of teleology from it. Most likely it was from the words, "that these forms have all been produced by the laws acting around us." That is simply a denial of special creation. It is probable that Hodge did not distinguish in his own thought between the denial of special creation and the denial of teleology. If he did, he was in advance of the majority of theologians. To such a mind this quotation would be conclusive evidence that Darwin rejected teleology.

But Darwin simply inscribed on his last page what his whole book was intended to prove; viz., that animals and plants are not special creations. And we can even see a sort of teleology in this very passage. "The most exalted object we are capable of conceiving, the production of the higher animals," seems to lie in his thought as an *end* accomplished by means of natural selection. And he justly conceives that "there is a grandeur in this view" of a purpose so long cherished by the Creator, and so patiently wrought out while "this planet has gone cycling on according to the fixed law of gravity." All that seems to be entirely proper; indeed, not only harmless, but devout, and worthy to stand as the closing sentence of a grand book written by a man who was at once a great scientist and a good Christian.

The teleological import of this quotation is confirmed by some sentences in the preceding paragraph.

" To my mind it accords better with what we know of the laws impressed on matter by the Creator, that the production and extinction of the past and present inhabitants of the world should have been due to secondary causes, like those determining the birth and death of the individual. When I view all beings not as special creations, but as the lineal descendants of some few beings which lived long before the first bed of the silurian system was deposited, they seem to me to become ennobled. . . . And, as natural selection works solely by and for the good of each being, all corporeal and mental endowments will tend to progress towards perfection.''

In his opinion natural laws were "impressed on matter by the Creator;" and one of them, natural selection, is the means, by reason of its working "solely by and for the good of each being," of accomplishing this most excellent, most exalted end, that "all corporeal and mental endowments will tend to progress towards perfection."

Hodge's third quotation is the following: —

"Did He ordain that the crop and tail feathers of the pigeon should vary in order that the fancier might make his grotesque pouter and fantail breeds? Did He cause the frame and mental qualities of the dog to vary in order that a breed might be formed of indomitable ferocity, with jaws fitted to pin down the bull for man's brutal sport? But if we give up the principle in one case, — if we do not admit that the variations of the primeval dog were intentionally guided in order that the greyhound, for instance, that perfect image of symmetry and vigor, might be formed, — no shadow of reason can be assigned for the belief that variations, alike in nature and the result of the same general laws, which have been the groundwork through natural selection of the formation of the most perfectly adapted animals in the world, man included, were intentionally and specially guided. However much we may wish it, we can hardly follow Professor Asa Gray in his belief ' that variation has been led along certain beneficial lines,' like a stream ' along definite and useful lines of irrigation. ' " [1]

[1] Variation of Animals and Plants under Domestication, ii. 431. Hodge omitted to tell his readers where this passage was to be found.

At first view this passage seems much more to the point, that Darwin rejected teleology, than either of the previous quotations. He implies a negation by the form of his questions; and in such cases the interrogative form, if it carries a negative force at all, amounts to an *emphatic* negation. So we may say that Darwin strongly denies that variations have been "intentionally and specially guided." There is one plain landmark for us in our attempt to find out what Darwin really thought about teleological purposes in nature; and this, be it known, is our main purpose. It matters less whether Hodge truly represented or misrepresented his views, than what his opinions really were. And this one landmark which we have reached in our investigation does seem to point to the conclusion that he rejected teleology.

It often happens, however, that an author's true meaning shines in new light when we examine the context of any quotation. This will be seen to be true in the present instance; but, before resorting to that means of reaching the truth about Darwin's opinions, let us observe closely the precise thing which he emphatically denies in the passage just as Hodge gave it. He denies that *variations* have been intentionally guided. It is quite possible that *progress* accomplished by the selection of beneficial variations has been intentionally and specially guided, notwithstanding the variations were purely accidental with respect to the results actually realized, though not accidental in any other sense. If this is what Darwin meant, there is no denial of teleology in the passage: progress *has* been guided "along certain beneficial lines," though variation has not, but on the contrary has been pushing out this way and that indiscriminately, without any reference to useful results. The whole tenor of his theory of natural selection makes it inherently probable that this is precisely what he meant; and this probability is distinctly and emphatically confirmed by the context of Hodge's third quotation. I shall quote extensively from this context, but I bespeak a careful perusal of the whole. The passage combines a spirit of reverence with a profound philosophy worthy of Bishop Butler, — not unlike the " Analogy " indeed, in that it discloses a difficulty in natural religion precisely parallel to one in revealed religion. It ought to put to the blush any one who asserts that Darwinism is atheism.

" The long-continued accumulation of beneficial variations will infallibly lead to structures as diversified, as beautifully adapted to various purposes, and as excellently co-ordinated, as we see in the animals and plants all around us. Hence I have spoken of selection as the paramount power, whether applied by man to the formation of domestic breeds, or by nature to the production of species. I may recur to the metaphor given in a former chapter : if an architect were to rear a noble and commodious edifice, without the use of cut stone, by selecting from the fragments at the base of a precipice wedge-formed stones for his arches, elongated stones for his lintels, and flat stones for his roof, we should admire his skill, and regard him as the paramount power. Now, the fragments of stone, though indispensable to the architect, bear to the edifice built by him the same relation which the fluctuating variations of each organic being bear to the varied and admirable structures ultimately acquired by its modified descendants.

" Some authors have declared that natural selection explains nothing, unless the precise cause of each slight individual difference be made clear. Now, if it were explained to a savage utterly ignorant of the art of building, how the edifice has been raised stone upon stone, and why wedge-formed fragments were used for the arches, flat stones for the roof, etc. ; and, if the use of each part and of the whole building were pointed out, it would be unreasonable if he declared that nothing had been made clear to him because the cause of the precise shape of each fragment could not be given. But this is a nearly parallel case with the objection that selection explains nothing because we know not the cause of each individual difference in the structure of each being.

" The shape of the fragments of stone at the base of our precipice may be called accidental : but this is not strictly correct ; for the shape of each depends on a long sequence of events, all obeying natural laws, — on the nature of the rock, on the lines of deposition or cleavage, on the form of the mountain which depends on its upheaval and subsequent denudation, and lastly on the storm or earthquake which threw down the fragments. But, in regard to the use to which the fragments may be put, their shape may be strictly said to be accidental. And here we are led to face a great difficulty, in alluding to which I am aware that I am travelling beyond my proper province. An omniscient Creator must have foreseen every consequence which results from the laws imposed by Him. But can it be reasonably maintained that the Creator intentionally ordered, if we use the words in any ordinary sense, that certain fragments of rock should assume certain shapes so that the builder might erect his edifice? If the various laws which have determined the shape of each fragment were not predetermined for the builder's sake, can it with any greater probability be maintained that He specially ordained, for the sake of the breeder, each of the innumerable variations in our domestic animals and plants ; many of these variations being of no service to man, and not beneficial, far more often injurious, to the creatures themselves? Did He ordain that the crop and tail feathers of the pigeon should vary in order that the fancier might make his grotesque pouter and fantail breeds? Did

He cause the frame and mental qualities of the dog to vary in order that a breed might be formed of indomitable ferocity, with jaws fitted to pin down the bull for man's brutal sport? But if we give up the principle in one case, — if we do not admit that the variations of the primeval dog were intentionally guided in order that the greyhound, for instance, that perfect image of symmetry and vigor, might be formed, — no shadow of reason can be assigned for the belief that variations, alike in nature and the result of the same general laws, which have been the groundwork through natural selection of the formation of the most perfectly adapted animals in the world, man included, were intentionally and specially guided. However much we may wish it, we can hardly follow Professor Asa Gray in his belief 'that variation has been led along certain beneficial lines,' like a stream 'along definite and useful lines of irrigation.' If we assume that each particular variation was from the beginning of all time pre-ordained, the plasticity of organization which leads to many injurious deviations of structure, as well as that redundant power of reproduction which inevitably leads to a struggle for existence, and, as a consequence, to the natural selection or survival of the fittest, must appear to us superfluous laws of nature. On the other hand, an omnipotent and omniscient Creator ordains every thing and foresees every thing. Thus we are brought face to face with a difficulty as insoluble as is that of free will and pre-destination.''

I am dealing, first of all, with personal issues in this chapter; and here is one between Darwin and Gray which demands an explanation. This issue is not, however, precisely what Hodge represented it to be; viz., that between the denial of teleology by Darwin and its acceptance by Gray. The utmost that can be made of it is, that Gray says *variations* have been guided in useful lines, while Darwin says that *progress* has been guided in

useful lines by the constant selection of beneficial variations, these variations being "strictly accidental" in relation to the use made of them, but not at all accidental
in another sense. Here is a difference truly; but, in
my opinion, it arose from an infelicity of expression in
those articles which Gray published in "The Atlantic
Monthly" magazine at an early stage of the Darwinian
controversy. In his "Darwiniana" Gray compares
natural selection to the rudder which guides the ship,
while variation is the wind that "bloweth where it
listeth." This indicates that he came round to Darwin's view "of selection as the paramount power,
whether applied by man to the formation of domestic
breeds, or by nature to the production of species."

It is proper to note the fact, that, although Gray seems
to have receded from his earlier view, there are some
evolutionists who still diverge widely from Darwin's
doctrine of the paramount power of selection, and give
more weight to inherent tendencies of organic structure
than he did. But this is a question of detail, which may
be settled either this way or that without the slightest
damage or disparagement to teleology or theism.

In the second place, here is a personal issue between
Darwin and Hodge. "My notion," says Darwin, "of the
process of natural selection and variation is illustrated
by the architect choosing his materials from a heap of
natural fragments, instead of cutting each stone for its
place." How could the most ardent teleologist frame a
better illustration for his purpose? "Ah," says Hodge,
"Darwin doesn't say God selects, but nature selects.
Selection is a natural force." "Very true," says Darwin, "it is one of the 'laws impressed on matter by the
Creator.'" "But," says Hodge, "do you think God
intended that law to work as you say it does?" "Cer-

tainly," answers Darwin, "'an omnipotent and omniscient Creator ordains every thing and foresees every
thing.' 'An omniscient Creator must have foreseen
every consequence of the laws imposed by him.'"
"Well," says Hodge, "in view of such declarations
I can't very well say that you are an atheist, however
much I would like to do so ; but I do say that Darwinism is atheism." [1] That is very much as if one should
tell a man, "I will not call you a liar, sir; that is not
a polite expression, and I never use it : but I do say
that your statement is a damnable falsehood."

In respect to this "insoluble difficulty" in natural
theology, which Darwin thinks is on a par with that of
divine sovereignty and human freedom in dogmatic
theology, the gist of it is the antithesis of particular
providence and universal law. Dr. McCosh and the
Duke of Argyll have attempted to throw some light
upon this problem, but I suppose neither of them would
claim that they have really solved it. It does unquestionably present grave difficulties, — so grave that the
practical man will be apt to take the same course with
it that Darwin did ; that is, to consider it insoluble, and
give himself no further concern about it. To his mind
there were two such insoluble problems, but his faith
did not stagger under either. He believed the will was
free, though he could not reconcile that with divine
sovereignty ; he believed in special providences, in an
"omnipotent and omniscient Creator foreseeing and
ordaining every thing," though he could not reconcile
that with his deep conviction of the universal reign of
natural laws.

[1] " We have thus arrived at the answer to our question, What is Darwinism ? It is atheism. This does not mean, as before said, that Mr.
Darwin himself and all who adopt his views are atheists; but it means
that his theory is atheistic." — *What is Darwinism?* p. 177.

If we were disposed to press his architectural illustration to the full extent of its possible application, a very strong case might be made out for his belief in teleology. The parallelism between it and the process of selection which he intended it to illustrate, can only be carried out by the supposition of an intelligent Author of nature guiding all the processes concerned in the production of species. Some expressions employed by him in the chapter where he first brought in this illustration throw additional light upon this view of it:—

"If our architect succeeded in rearing a noble edifice, using the rough, wedge-shaped fragments for the arches, the longer stones for the lintels, and so forth, we should admire his skill even in a higher degree than if he had used stones shaped for the purpose. So it is with selection, whether applied by man or by nature : for though variability is indispensably necessary, yet when we look at some highly complex and excellently adapted organism, variability sinks to a quite subordinate position in importance in comparison with selection, in the same manner as the shape of each fragment used by our supposed architect is unimportant in comparison with his skill." [1]

Hodge's fourth quotation is as follows : —

"Nothing, at first sight, can appear more difficult to believe than that the more complex organs and instincts have been perfected, not by means superior to, though analogous with, human reason, but by the accumulation of innumerable slight variations, each good for the individual possessor. Nevertheless, this difficulty, though appearing to our imagination insuperably great, cannot be considered real if we admit the following propositions : namely, that all parts of the organization and instincts offer at least individual differences ; that

[1] Var. of An. and Plants under Dom., ii. 249.

there is a struggle for existence leading to the preservation of profitable deviations of structure or instinct; and, lastly, that gradations in the state of perfection of each organ may have existed, each good of its kind " (404).

This passage will have to go for what it is worth, without any explanation so far as I am concerned. It seems to bear the interpretation which Hodge would put upon it; but it is the only one which sustains his view, and it is inconsistent with the general tone of Darwin's writings. It is strikingly discordant with his architectural illustration, which exalts the skill requisite for the process of natural selection, to say that the means by which "the more complex organs and instincts have been perfected" are not "superior to, though analogous with, human reason." There is a slight obscurity in the grammatical construction which makes it hazardous either to affirm or deny very positively just what Darwin meant in this instance.

Hodge's fifth and last quotation is the Darwinian explanation of the development of the eye : —

" To suppose that the eye, with all its inimitable contrivances for adjusting the focus to different distances, for admitting different amounts of light, and for the correction of spherical and chromatic aberration, could have been formed by natural selection, seems, I freely confess, absurd in the highest degree " (143).

" It is scarcely possible to avoid comparing the eye with a telescope. We know that this instrument has been perfected by the long-continued efforts of the highest human intellects, and we naturally infer that the eye has been formed by a somewhat analogous process. But may not this inference be presumptuous? Have we any right to assume that the Creator works by intellectual powers like those of man? If we must compare the eye to an optical instrument, we ought, in imagination, to take a thick layer of transparent tissue, with spaces filled with fluid, and with a nerve sensitive to light beneath, and then suppose every part of this layer to be continually changing slowly in density, so as to separate into layers of different densities and thicknesses, placed at different distances from each other, and with the surfaces of each layer slowly changing in form. Further, we must suppose that there is a power, represented by natural selection or the survival of the fittest, always intently watching each slight alteration in the transparent layers, and carefully preserving each which, under varied circumstances, in any way or in any degree tends to produce a distincter image. We must suppose each new state of the instrument to be multiplied by the million, each to be preserved until a better one is produced, and then the .old ones to be all destroyed. In living bodies variation will cause the slight alterations, generation will multiply them almost infinitely, and natural selection will pick out with unerring skill each improvement." (147.)

"Let this process," says Hodge, "go on for millions of years," and we shall at last have a perfect eye. The last sentence of the paragraph, which Hodge slurs over instead of quoting, contains an expression which seems to throw the whole process into the province of intelligent creative action, though it is creation by law. The doctor was not only quite skilful in selecting the point to begin quoting, but he was always careful to stop just in the nick of time. Here is the sentence which he omitted: " Let this process go on for millions of years, and, during each year, on millions of individuals of many kinds, and may we not believe that a living optical instrument might thus be formed as superior to one of glass as the works of the Creator are to those of man?" Darwin thought the eye was a work of the Creator if natural selection was the means of its production.

The whole paragraph is simply a protest against that mechanical view of natural processes which makes them akin to the methods of an instrument-maker, picking up his brass here and his glass there, shaping the one into tubes and the other into lenses, polishing, fitting, adjusting focus, mounting, and finishing up. No, says Darwin, that is not the way God works. It is by a far slower and less mechanical process, — a process as different from that of the optician as the "living optical instrument" is more perfect than the one of glass. It has been denied that the eye is more perfect than a telescope, — nay, the denial of excellence goes much farther than that.[1] In the point of mere nicety and precision of mechanical adjustments, this is all true; but I have not heard of any telescope or microscope which could *see*. *That* is a considerable difference between the eye and the finest optical instrument of human construction, — a difference which rebukes equally these croakers about the imperfections of the eye on the one hand, and the mechanical school of teleologists on the other. What pertinence is there in the comparison of the eye to an optical instrument, when there is this fundamental contrast, that the one is a living thing, which, in conjunction with the nervous system, has the power of vision, while the other is a piece of dead mechanism? The parallelism upon which the teleological inference rests fails at the vital point; and this weakness becomes the more striking and fatal when we consider that the dead machinery has been put together piece by piece, while the living organ has reached its

[1] "It shall suffice us to say here, that any optician who should manufacture an instrument as grossly imperfect as the human eye, would be hooted from the trade as an ignoramus and a bungler." — Article on "Design in Nature," Westminster Review, July, 1875. See also Helmholtz's "Popular Lectures on Scientific Subjects."

present form and proportions by growth and development.

But, if the mechanical parallelism were exact and complete, the conclusion would assimilate God to a mere craftsman, and a poor one at that, since in the matter of mere mechanism the eye is inferior to some optical instruments. Darwin was wiser than the teleologists of the school of Paley in declining to look upon the works of God in that way. But Dr. Hodge belonged to the very school which was thus condemned. Read his discussion of the teleological argument in the first volume of his "Systematic Theology," and you will see that he begins with Paley's truism, " Design implies a designer," pursues the argument in the stereotyped fashion of the Bridgewater Treatises, and closes it up with this over-whelming syllogism from Philo : " No work of art is self-made. The world is the most perfect work of art. Therefore the world was made by a good and most perfect author." To this astonishing syllogism he appends the still more astonishing remark, " All the Christian fathers and subsequent theologians have reasoned in the same way." Sad if true.

Such is the sum and substance of " Darwin's own testimony " on the point of his denial of design in nature. An acute and experienced critic scans the whole field of his productions, and culls out the passages best adapted to show that he rejected teleology, with the result shown above. When all his quotations are candidly examined together with the context, the impression produced by them is not precisely what we should expect if it is really true that " Darwinism is atheism."

We have heard three witnesses for the prosecution, — that is, for Darwin's conviction upon the charge of

hostility to teleology: let us summon an equal number
for the defence. The first is Professor Kölliker of
Würtzburg. In his "Essay upon the Darwinian Theory," he concludes that "Darwin is, in the fullest sense
of the word, a teleologist." The second is Professor
T. H. Huxley. This may be a surprise; and the truth
is, this man was first summoned for the prosecution:
but the lawyer on that side found that his testimony
was not precisely what it had been reported to be, not
just what it appeared to be at the first glance. In
short, he found that he had caught a Tartar, and that
the best thing he could do was to drop him quietly
before it came to the test of a cross-examination in
open court. So the advocate for the defence issued a
subpœna for him, and quite unexpectedly Huxley turns
up as witness for teleology. But the court, or the
reader, in order that we may drop this legal by-play,
will please to observe that it is not the teleology of
Paley, or teleology *in the ordinary sense*, but some
form of that doctrine which is consistent with evolution, which Huxley has in mind when he appears for
the defence of Darwin against the charge of hostility
to teleology.

Referring to the opinion of Professor Kölliker quoted
above, Huxley says, —

"It is singular how one and the same book will impress
different minds. That which struck the present writer most
forcibly on his first perusal of the 'Origin of Species' was
the conviction that teleology, as commonly understood, had
received its death-blow at Mr. Darwin's hands.[1]

Such expressions certainly convey an impression of
hostility to teleology; but bear in mind that he is

[1] Lay Sermons, 301.

speaking of teleology *as commonly understood,* which would be that of Paley and the Bridgewater Treatises.

"If we apprehend the spirit of the 'Origin of Species' rightly, then nothing can be more entirely and absolutely opposed to teleology, as it is commonly understood, than the Darwinian theory. So far from being 'a teleologist in the fullest sense of the word,' we should deny that he is a teleologist in the ordinary sense at all; and we should say, that, apart from his merits as a naturalist, he has rendered a most remarkable service to philosophical thought by enabling the student of nature to recognize, to the fullest extent, those adaptations to purpose which are so striking in the organic world, and which teleology has done good service in keeping before our minds, without being false to the fundamental principles of a scientific conception of the universe. The apparently diverging teachings of the teleologist and of the morphologist are reconciled by the Darwinian hypothesis."

Here we begin to get a glimpse of that "wider teleology" of which Huxley speaks in another place. "Adaptations to a purpose" is a thoroughly teleological phrase; and it appears that Darwin has, in Huxley's opinion, not only thrown new light upon these adaptations, but has done the further service to teleology of reconciling it with morphology. The famous controversy between Cuvier and Geoffroy Saint-Hilaire would never have occurred if the comprehensive principles of the "Origin of Species" had been understood in 1830.

In a later volume [1] Huxley protests against the interpretation which Haeckel puts upon Darwinism: —

"In more than one place Professor Haeckel enlarges upon the service which the 'Origin of Species' has done in favoring

---

[1] Critiques and Addresses : London, 1873, p. 305.

what he calls the 'causal or mechanical' view of living nature as opposed to the 'teleological or vitalistic' view. And
no doubt it is quite true, that the doctrine of evolution is the
most formidable opponent of all the commoner and coarser
forms of teleology. But perhaps the most remarkable service to the philosophy of biology rendered by Mr. Darwin is
the reconciliation of teleology and morphology, and the explanation of the facts of both, which his views offer."

Dr. Hodge thought the "only distinctive thing"
about Darwin was his hostility to teleology; Professor
Huxley thinks "the most remarkable service" he has
rendered is in favor of teleology. We can set off these
contrasted pieces of evidence against each other, which
may serve to give an impartial and judicial balance to
our minds, while we listen to the testimony of Professor
Asa Gray.

In his "Darwiniana" (p. 357) he says that Darwin
has "brought back teleology to natural history. In Darwinism usefulness and purpose come to the front again
as working principles of the first order. Upon them,
indeed, the whole system rests." Gray thinks that the
burdens which have become too heavy for the teleologist are due to the special-creation hypothesis; but, "in
the far-reaching teleology which may take the place of
the former narrow conceptions, organs, and even faculties, useless to the individual, find their explanation
and reason of being" (357). "Finally, Darwinian teleology has the special advantage of accounting for the
imperfections and failures as well as for successes. It
not only accounts for them, but turns them to practical account. Without the competing multitude, no
struggle for life," no selection and survival of the fittest,
no continuous adaptation to changed environment, and
no progressive improvement.

" So the most puzzling things of all to the old-school teleologists are the *principia* of the Darwinian. In this system
the forms and species, in all their variety, are not mere ends
in themselves ; but the whole is a series of means and ends,
in the contemplation of which we may obtain higher and
more comprehensive, and perhaps worthier, as well as more
consistent, views of design in nature than heretofore " (378).

Such radical differences of opinion between intelligent men and competent judges of the nature and tendency of a given theory could not exist without some
fundamental divergence in the point of view from which
each of them has taken the bearings of Darwinism.
And it is easy to see what this fundamental divergence
was in the present instance. When Dr. Hodge says
that Darwin rejected all teleology, his notion of what
teleology is differs *toto cœlo* from the notion of teleology entertained by Dr. Gray: still more does it differ
from the "wider teleology" of Professor Huxley. So
that, strictly speaking, these witnesses all agree in their
testimony. Gray and Huxley would accord perfectly
with Hodge in the opinion that Darwin rejected that
form of teleology which Hodge regarded as the only
possible form of it. But these evolutionists maintain
that there is a wider and better and more far-reaching
teleology, which, so far from being the object of Darwin's hostility, was in a sense created by him.

How far Darwin would accept such interpretations
as Gray and Huxley put upon his work is not easy to
determine. It is probable, however, that he would go
farther than Huxley on the teleological road, but not
so far as Gray. Huxley's "wider teleology," which
denies any intelligent purpose in the structure of the
eye, does not harmonize well with Darwin's notion of
an omnipotent and omniscient Creator foreseeing and

ordaining every consequence of the laws impressed upon matter by him. And, on the other hand, some of Darwin's expressions, such as that about "the more complex organs and instincts having been perfected, not by means superior to, though analogous with, human reason;" and "Have we any right to assume that the Creator works by intellectual powers like those of man?"—these expressions are not entirely consonant with the "far-reaching teleology" of Gray. Such expressions, however, may mean much or little, as you choose to interpret them. The last one does not necessarily imply a negation of intelligent creative action, but only that creative intelligence is very different from human intelligence; and the other is so framed that whoever shall assert that it means *this* will be met by a plausible claim that it means *that* or the *other*.

The personal issue respecting Darwinism and teleology is, after all, of little consequence compared with the broader issue between evolution and teleology, to which the next chapter will be devoted.

CHAPTER XV.

EVOLUTION AND PHYSICO-THEOLOGY.

THE relations of the theory of evolution to physico-theology are not only broader and more important than that of Darwinism to design, they are also more difficult to deal with. In fact, the question now before us is a different one in almost every aspect of it. In one sense it is easier instead of more difficult: there is ample room for a difference of opinion as to what Darwin's own view of the effect of his theory really was, while there is no longer any room for doubt upon the general question whether the acceptance of evolution is destructive to all design-arguments. Theologians are practically a unit in the feeling that a belief in evolution leaves theism intact. All the opinions cited in the last chapter to the effect that there is an irrepressible conflict between Darwinism and design might, it is true, be construed as expressing the same hostility between evolution and design; but those opinions do not reflect the prevailing hue of theological sentiment. On the contrary, the theory of evolution has now fairly reached the third stage in its relations to religion.

Each radical change in scientific conceptions of nature is apt to be viewed at first as hostile to Christianity: then, if it commands the approval of scientists in general, there comes a time when theologians represent it as a matter of indifference, whether it be true or false, so far it effects their creed; but finally, when it comes to be largely accepted by the world, they manage to turn it in some way to the advantage of religion, and become its zealous advocates. Such has been the case with astronomy and geology, and the history is being repeated in respect to evolution. Already it is freely resorted to for illustrative parallels to the truths of revealed religion; and the number of such illustrations is inexhaustible. Bishop Butler would find many an "analogy" now which he was not able to draw from nature by the light of that science which existed in his day.

Only two of these stages of theological opinion are legitimate. The first stage, which is largely responsible for the hostility between science and religion, is a wanton waste of time, temper, and energy, which not only might be better employed, but could not well be employed more disastrously. It is to be hoped that the attitude of neutrality will hereafter be at once assumed toward all new theories of a strictly scientific character. It may be a question whether some note of caution ought not to be sounded respecting the third stage of theological opinion. It is all well enough to draw upon the facts of any science, or even the principles of any theory, for popular illustrations; but the most enlightened friends of revealed religion will hereafter be slow to link their system with any scientific theory in such a way that it shall be disparaged in any degree by the overthrow of the latter. The great example which ought to stand as a sufficient warning for all time in this matter, is that of the ecclesiastical sanction given to the Ptolemaic as opposed to the Copernican astronomy.

We have, in this third stage of theological opinion

when carried to an undue extent, an interesting example of the meeting of extremes. The first stage is one
of hostility ; the third is one of overstrained and excessive friendship : but they play into each other because
the attachment of the cause of Christianity to a given
theory makes it hostile to a new and rival theory.

When I say that the sentiments entertained towards
the theory of evolution have passed into this third
stage, I do not wish to be understood as asserting that
it has gone so far as to identify Christianity with evolution, or even that the friendly feeling is entirely unanimous. I might present this discussion in the same form
as that of Darwinism and design ; that is, I might
give a list of theologians who maintain that there is an
irrepressible conflict between evolution and physico-
theology, and a list of those who think there is no such
conflict. But such a course would be devoid of interest or practical value, for the reason that this question
is already practically settled in favor of the latter view.

The real problem, then, in respect to the reconciliation
of evolution and physico-theology is not whether it can
be done at all, but *how* it is to be done. Must physico-
theology undergo any modifications? and, if so, what
shall they be ? Those are the real issues now on trial.
The question what evolution is, or which one of its
several forms is meant, when we say that it may be accepted without prejudice to Christianity, may also have
to be raised. So that it is clear that we have now, as
stated in the beginning, broader, more important, and
more difficult relations to deal with in this chapter than
in the last.

As regards the form of evolution to be dealt with,
most of those who have maintained that it might freely
be accepted or rejected simply upon its evidence and

its merits, like any other hypothesis, have generally had in view its most comprehensive form, or that which regards the whole of nature as one unbroken series of causes and effects dominated throughout its whole extent and its whole history by natural laws. This is the wiser course. There is no gain in dealing with it piecemeal, reconciling and adjusting physico-theology to some partial phase of it, only to be compelled to repeat the process over and over for the remaining phases. The true method is to place physcio-theology upon a basis independent of any of its possible phases, taking it in the most sweeping and comprehensive form.

Can this be done? Let us divide the question: can it, in the first place, be done with respect to eutaxiology? There can be no possibility of a negative response to this question. The facts of order in the cosmos are not changed, nor do they speak a whit less emphatically of an intelligent author of nature, by reason of the acceptance of evolution. The direct effect of evolution is to extend the reign of law, or rather to broaden our conceptions respecting its universality; and, since the reign of law is but another name for the order of nature, the obvious effect of evolution is to strengthen eutaxiology.[1] Eutaxiology needs no modification; but, in the

[1] This objection has lately been started by what may be called the "extreme left" of the evolutionists; namely, that since human intelligence itself is a product of nature, what it beholds in the order of the cosmos, and supposes to be a divine intelligence, is merely its own reflection from the orderly conditions which have evolved it. (See A Candid Examination of Theism, by *Physicus*, p. 58). The objection has greater plausibility than force. If it be true that the order of nature has evoked human intelligence, then, supposing that this order was not the product of a prior intelligence, it *may be* that the mind would catch its own reflection from it, as asserted; but, upon the other hand, if there *was* a prior intelligence, the mind would without any doubt infer its existence from the cosmos. Since the inference would certainly be made in the latter case, and not certainly in the former, and since this

modifications which physico-theology must undergo, *the recognition of eutaxiology* is the most important of all. More than a century ago the profound genius of Kant proposed an improved method of physico-theology in which the recognition of the principle of order is the most striking feature. If his suggestions had been comprehended and followed, that science would have been placed on a foundation independent of evolution long before evolution was thought of. The avoidance of a conflict with that theory would have been one advantage of this course, but not the only one. Or, to put the same statement in another form, the hostile issue which was joined between the advocates of design in nature and the advocates of evolution, was not, in and by itself, the only mischief which resulted from the ill-conditioned state of development of physico-theology. The hostility was unpleasant enough; but it was still more unpleasant to reflect, that once more there was need of patching and mending a theological system in response to a new phase of scientific speculation, — a thing which ought never to happen in any case, and was clearly needless in this case because the true

---

inference *is* made as a matter of fact, it would seem more reasonable to refer it to the certainty than to the doubt; that is, to suppose that there was a prior intelligence. Again, if the order of nature is at all a ground for inferring the existence of intelligence, it would seem that à *fortiori* it must be a valid ground if this orderly cosmos has added to all other perfections this unique and crowning one, that it has evolved the human intelligence.

The general argument of *Physicus* against eutaxiology is a colossal fallacy. He makes order spring from "the persistence of force and the primary qualities of matter." In order to do this he imparts such prodigious and mysterious energy to this "ubiquitous and illimitable *x*," this *tremendous unknown* which he calls *persistence of force*, that he makes a *deity* of it. Thus alone is he able to account for the facts which constitute the data of theism. *He sets up a god to make us believe there is no God.*

line of design-arguments had been pointed out long
before.

It is worthy of note that recent writers on natural
theology have, almost unconsciously as it seems, been
led to advance the principle of order to the front
rank in adjusting their system to evolution. I say almost unconsciously, because none of them recognize
eutaxiology except as some broader and higher sort of
teleology, or possibly some inferior and subordinate
phase of teleology. Thus Professor Cooke, whose book
was written in the early days of the agitation over
Darwinism, and who tells us in his preface that he was
influenced by the supposed damaging effect of the new
theory in biology to seek for design-arguments in
chemistry, dwells much upon his proof from "general
plan," which is clearly eutaxiological, though he regards it as quite inferior and subordinate to teleology.

Professor Joseph Le Conte[1] also employs eutaxiology
to a large extent, and with a higher appreciation of it
than Professor Cooke exhibited.

"Let us sketch the history of thought on this subject:
first the animal body was studied with reference to its wonderful *mechanism*, its admirable contrivances for *use*. This
is the domain of the *old natural theology*. Then came, by
the study of naturalists, the recognition of the strange fact,
that in the animal body there are often rudimentary and
therefore *useless* parts " (p. 53).

"Finally, by further patient study of nature, came the
recognition of *another law besides use, — a law of order
underlying and conditioning the law of use*. Organisms are,
indeed, contrived for use, but according to a pre-ordained
plan of structure, which must not be violated. This is the
domain of the *new natural theology* " (54).

[1] Religion and Science: London, 1874.

Professor Baden Powell was fully committed to the
order-argument, and consequently welcomed evolution,
even before the publication of the " Origin of Species."
Dr. McCosh also understood the difference between
eutaxiology and teleology, but it is singular that he did
not make greater use of the former in adjusting and
defining the relations of evolution to physico-theology.
He hardly alludes to it in his later works.   In his
"Christianity and Positivism " (1871), he says, "I stand
by the evidence furnished by the order and adaptation
in the universe."   This is a recognition of eutaxiology
and teleology both, but his definition of design is
wholly teleological.   "The argument from design is, that
there are evidences everywhere, in heaven and earth, in
plant and animal, of natural agents being so fitted to
each other, and so combining to produce a beneficent
end, as to show that intention must have been employed in co-ordinating and arranging them."   The same
predominance of teleology appears in " The Development Hypothesis" (1876): " We argue final cause,
i.e., design, from the collocation of efficient causes to
promote an evident end, — say the ear to hear, and the
eye to see."

There may be wide differences of opinion respecting
the validity of the conclusions drawn from the order of
nature ; but there can be but one opinion on the point
of its perfect harmony with evolution, or its complete
independence of evolution, so that it may stand or fall
on its own merits whether evolution be a true or a false
theory.   One of the design-arguments at least is secure
from any dangers arising from that direction.

How is it with teleology?   This case is not so clear,
and the unanimity respecting it is by no means perfect.
But I think a large majority of the ablest theologians

would take the view, that the establishment of evolution would not destroy teleology : certainly that sentiment would be unanimous among Christian scientists. But in respect to the further questions whether teleology must receive any modifications, and what shall be the nature of these, there is considerable difference of opinion.

Professor Le Conte seems to think that evolution makes no difference at all. He opens his argument by producing Paley's watch, not being aware, probably, that it was already second-handed, and applies the illustration thus : —

" Now, such a watch is the solar system, with its sun, planets, and moons, — infinitely more beautiful, more complex, more delicately adjusted, than any human work, — wheel within wheel, each influencing the other, and all controlled by the central sun, and marking time with the utmost exactness upon the dial-plate of heaven. Now, observe : it matters not *when* this was made, or *how* it was made, or *where the materials came from* out of which it was made. But here is something not material, but intellectual, which I perceive ; viz., the intelligent arrangement for a purpose, the *contrivance*."

He devotes the whole of Lecture II. to a comparison of the eye with a *camera obscura.* So that we may fairly say of his plan for reconciling teleology and evolution, that it amounts to this : repeat Paley's arguments, or similar ones, and append to them the statement that evolution makes no difference.

The plan of George St. Clair is somewhat different, though he also adheres to the predilection for *machinery* as the best species of illustration ; but he throws back the contrivance to the causes, instead of taking his inference directly from what he sees in the effects.

"Whatever appearance of design exists in living structures would have its corresponding appearance in the causes
if the causes could all be seen ; and whatever reason there is
for using the term 'machinery' of the one, exists also for
using it of the other." [1]

He supposes that it is not only possible to reconcile
teleology with evolution, but that it is really enriched
by the process.

"The design-argument remains unshaken, and the wisdom and beneficence of God receive new illustration."

The Rev. George Henslow coincides very nearly with
Le Conte in supposing that teleology stands just where
it did before evolution was heard of.

"The *design* seen in a structure is in fact part of and inseparable from it, pointing at once to the existence of mind,
and is quite irrespective of the *process* by which that structure was brought into existence." [2]

Henslow outdoes all the rest in his estimate of the
gain to teleology and religion by the establishment of
the theory of evolution.   He fairly reaches the extreme
of linking the fortunes of all religion to those of evolution, so that they must stand or fall together.   We
have seen in a previous chapter how he makes the ulti-
mate‑purpose of the world as a whole to be the surrounding of man with *inideal* conditions, — that is, conditions which are not ideally perfect, — so that there may
be a moral probation in this life, fitting man thus to
enter upon the ideal heavenly life.

"We do not forget that God could not only have made
man at once fitted for heaven, but have placed him there ; so

1 Darwinism and Design, by George St. Clair: London, 1873, p. 126.
2 The Theory of Evolution of Living Things: London, 1873, p. x.

that the wisdom of development and the wisdom of probation are alike synonymous with the will of God. They are
the necessary correlatives of that system of progress which
has a universal application in every class of phenomena that
admits of improvement or differentiation of any kind. Indeed, we may go a step farther, and say, that, were this not
the case, heavenly conditions could have no difference from
earthly ones ; or rather, as they might of course be different,
that, under the present limitations of our existence, we cannot conceive of any method by which heavenly conditions
should be made contingent upon earthly ones. So that *the
whole scheme which God has framed for man's existence, from
the first that was created to all eternity, collapses if the great
law of evolution be suppressed*" (214).

In contrast to these opinions, which represent teleology as unchanged in every way by the acceptance of
evolution, except that it is enriched with new illustrations, let us note the opinion of Professor Huxley,
whom we have already discovered to be a teleologist
after a fashion, but a fashion strikingly different from
that affected by Paley and his school : —

"The teleology which supposes that the eye, such as we
see it in man or one of the higher vertebrata, was made with
the precise structure which it exhibits for the purpose of
enabling the animal which possesses it to see, has undoubtedly received its death-blow. Nevertheless, it is necessary
to remember that there is a wider teleology, which is not
touched by the doctrine of evolution, but is actually based
upon the fundamental proposition of evolution. That proposition is, that the whole world, living and not living, is the
result of the mutual interaction, according to definite laws,
of the forces possessed by the molecules of which the primitive nebulosity of the universe was composed. If this be
true, it is no less certain that the existing world lay poten-
tially in the cosmic vapor ; and that a sufficient intelligence

could, from a knowledge of the properties of the molecules of that vapor, have predicted, say, the state of the fauna of Britain in 1869, with as much certainty as one can say what will happen to the vapor of the breath on a cold winter's day." [1]

He then brings in the simile of the clock inhabited by a scientific " death-watch," who sees nothing but pure mechanism, and denies that there is any purpose whatever in the structure of the clock; and a philosophical "death-watch," who is sure there is a purpose, but, influenced by his own function of monotonous ticking, concludes that the clock also was made solely for the purpose of ticking.

" The teleological and the mechanical views of nature are not necessarily mutually exclusive. On the contrary, the more purely a mechanist the speculator is, the more firmly does he assume a primordial molecular arrangement, of which all the phenomena of the universe are the consequences ; and the more completely is he thereby at the mercy of the teleologist, who can always defy him to disprove that this primordial molecular arrangement was not intended to evolve the phenomena of the universe. On the other hand, if the teleologist assert that this, that, or the other result of the working of any part of the mechanism of the universe is its purpose and final cause, the mechanist can always inquire how he knows that it is more than an unessential incident, the mere ticking of the clock, which he mistakes for its function. And there seems to be no reply to this inquiry, any more than to the further not irrational question, Why trouble one's self about matters which are out of reach when the working of the mechanism itself, which is of infinite practical importance, affords scope for all our energies?"

[1] Critiques and Addresses, 305.

This whimsical simile of the clock and the beetles cuts both ways. On the one hand, it rebukes Haeckel and all advocates of his theory, that the universe is a purely mechanical product of molecular forces inherent in matter, likening them to that beetle who saw in the clock "nothing but matter and force and pure mechanism from beginning to end." On the other hand, it was intended to be a rebuke to the advocates of the "commoner and coarser forms of teleology," as being out of their reckoning in what they assigned to be the final cause of this or that structure, as much as the beetle who thought the clock was made only to tick. There is also a fling at anthropomorphism in representing the beetle as concluding that the function of the clock was the same as his own. But would any sensible beetle ever take the first step towards that conclusion? would he ever imagine that his own function was only to make a ticking noise, when that was of no manner of use to himself, — as purely incidental to his operations as the ticking of the clock to its real function? Again, is it conceivable that seeing is "an unessential incident" in the structure of the eye?

The simile is indeed two-edged, but it cuts deepest and keenest into the materialist. He is more hopelessly out of his reckoning who denies any purpose whatever, than he who merely assigns the wrong purpose. Moreover, the probabilities are strongly in favor of the hypothesis, that the teleologist is not only right in asserting some purpose, but that he has hit a real purpose, not an unessential incident, when he asserts that eyes were made or evolved "for the purpose of enabling the animal which possesses them to see." So that the rebuke intended for him falls harmless, while that launched at the materialist strikes home with full force.

It is pleasant to know that Huxley believes in a teleology of some sort. There is a purpose in the clock, though the philosophical beetle missed it: so there is a purpose in the universe, though the old teleologists, in Huxley's opinion, may have missed their aim in assigning this or that purpose; and no one can ever tell certainly whether they did or not. He seems to think that it is a waste of time to inquire into these purposes, since the discovery of them is as much beyond human faculties as the understanding of a clock is beyond beetle faculties.

Here is a certain residual teleology which evolution has left in its career of conquest; but it will seem to most theists to be the mere ghost of teleology as they conceived it. If one ventures to assert that eyes were intended for vision, he falls at once into the condemnation of advocating one of the "commoner and coarser forms of teleology." Sensible and practical men are supposed to abjure all search for ends and purposes in nature, and confine their energies to the comprehension of "the working of the mechanism itself." And, if any one still has a lurking ambition to be a teleologist, Huxley kindly marks out for him the only possible ground for his feet, the precise spot where he must plant himself, and the exact limits of what he can do when he has taken up his position there with the determination to do or die in that "last ditch." The professor blandly invites him to take his stand upon "the primitive nebulosity," and there boldly "defy" the mechanical theorist "to *disprove* that this primordial molecular arrangement was not intended to evolve the phenomena of the universe." It does not appear that the valiant teleologist thus suspended in the cold abysses of the cosmic gas is to be allowed to *prove* any thing: his sole function is to defy somebody to *disprove* something. If he makes any positive assertions, as "that this, that, or the other result of the working of any part of the mechanism of the universe is its purpose and final cause, the mechanist can always inquire how he knows that it is more than an unessential incident,— the mere ticking of the clock."

This "wider teleology" of Huxley's is one of the results of attempting to reconcile teleology and evolution. Essentially it consists in emasculating teleology, so that there is nothing characteristic, nothing positive, nothing that smacks of vigor or virility, left of it. The contrast between this kind of reconciliation and that of Le Conte — "It matters not *when* this was made, or *how* it was made, etc." — is sufficiently striking.

Between these two extremes there are those whose plan of reconciliation admits, upon the one hand, that some modification of the old teleology is needed; but, on the other hand, does not emasculate it, does not assign to it the negative and barren function of defying somebody to disprove something. McCosh, Gray, and Gibson may be reckoned as advocates of this view. Some sentences from the last-mentioned writer will serve to show his point of view:—

"A conviction is growing up in the cultivated mind, that all phenomena are the fruit of *general law*, and not of special appointment. It is in deference to this that I would frame my modification. No doctrine, it appears to me, is so clearly taught by modern science as this, that God works by general laws. His appointments are at least *prima facie* general, not special, though it may be that every special case has been considered in making them. I do not mean here to prejudge the question, whether such exceptions to such law have ever taken place, say in original creation or subsequent miracle. But I wish to detach the argument from design altogether from these difficult questions. Looking upon nature in the light of modern science in quest of evidence for an originating mind, what we see is the co-operation of a number of general laws ; and the question for our consideration is, Does this co-operation indicate an intelligent and moral author? . . . We are not to argue from isolated facts. We cannot, like Paley, infer the divine benevolence from the gambols of shrimps. We must take account, at least, of all that we know, and endeavor to grasp the character of the universe as a whole. On the one hand, we are not to expect discernible traces of design everywhere, nor yet, on the other hand, are we to disregard such traces if they appear too often to be accounted chances ; i.e., effects for which we cannot venture to assign a cause." [1]

Gibson uses " design " in the old, loose, and ambiguous way, so that we can hardly apply this especially to teleology ; but it may be regarded as including teleology, since that is one of the design-arguments. Gibson thinks we ought to take a broad view of nature, and infer a divine purpose from wide-ranging agencies converging to some definite result. Similar to this is the " far-reaching teleology " of Professor Gray.

" In this system the forms and species, in all their variety, are not mere ends in themselves ; but the whole is a series of means and ends, in the contemplation of which we may obtain higher and more comprehensive, and perhaps worthier, as well as more consistent, views of design in nature than heretofore."

Considering the broad and profound changes which the acceptance of evolution must make in our views of the cosmos, it would seem reasonable to expect con-

[1] Religion and Science, by the Rev. Stanley T. Gibson, p. 30.

siderable modifications of the old teleology in order to harmonize it with evolution. Its mechanical elements, its hostility to natural law, and its bias in favor of arbitrary interferences, must all be eliminated. But, important as these changes may seem, we shall presently see that even more radical modifications are required in order to harmonize teleology with *sound logic* than those which are needed to bring it into friendly relations with the doctrine of evolution.

CHAPTER XVI.

THE CRITIQUE OF EUTAXIOLOGY.

THE fundamental proposition of this argument is, that *order is a mark of intelligence*. This may be taken as the major premise of a syllogism, of which the minor premise is that order exists in the universe, and the conclusion is that intelligence exists in the universe. It is hardly necessary to mention, that as the order from which intelligence is inferred exists independently of human or animal agency, so the intelligence whose existence is concluded is independent of human or animal intelligence. That might be taken as a matter of course; and yet the mention of it is not out of place, because the mere assertion that intelligence exists in the universe is capable of misconstruction. But, on the other hand, the simple mention of it is sufficient without incorporating the limiting clause, " other than human or animal intelligence," in the conclusion itself, thus making it awkward and unwieldy.

The syllogism is the weakest form in which to cast an argument. If conviction is the object in view, the safest plan is to mass your forces in solid column, — to roll up both premises and the conclusion in a single proposition, which may then be wielded with good effect. But, if the object is to test the validity of an argument, there is no better plan than to spread it out into distinct premises and conclusion. For this reason

I shall employ a different method in this chapter from that which would be most effective if my aim were to construct eutaxiology, and to act as an advocate for it.

The first point to be determined is, whether there is any illicit process or fallacy in the reasoning. Granting the truth of the premises, does the conclusion necessarily and legitimately follow ?

What is meant by saying that order is a *mark* of intelligence? Simply that it is *invariably conjoined with it.* If this be granted, and if it be conceded also that order exists in the universe aside from that produced by men and animals, then it follows necessarily and legitimately that some intelligence other than animal or human exists in the universe. The reasoning is simple and straightforward; so that any fallacy must be easily detected if it were really there, and it does not appear that there is any.

The whole matter turns, therefore, upon the truth of the premises. Of these, the minor premise, that there is in order in the universe, will hardly be disputed. The possibility of any science whatever lies in the fact that there is an established order in nature. But is it true that the presence of order is an invariable mark of mind? The fate of this argument from the order of nature is all bound up in the answer to that question.

It is desirable, in the first place, to clear this fundamental proposition of some possible misunderstandings. When we see clearly what it does *not* assert, we shall be better prepared to judge of the truth of what it does assert. It does not, for instance, assert that intelligence never produces any thing but orderly results. That may be true; but the converse of it, that every orderly result is a product of intelligence, is the fundamental proposition of eutaxiology. *This* is vital to the argument, but *that* may be either true or false without affecting it.

Secondly, it is not asserted that order is conjoined with intelligence in the relation of an effect to its cause. It may be true — nay, it is true, without any doubt — that they are conjoined in this relation ; but that is not included in the assertion, nor is it essential that it should be. The invariableness of the conjunction is the vital point in determining the validity of the inference of intelligence from order. It is wholly indifferent in what relation order may stand to intelligence, provided only that we know to a certainty that intelligence always exists wherever order appears. The argument will be just the same, however, if we do assert the relation of cause and effect, as if we do not assert it. In either case it is the *invariableness* of the relation, and not the *nature* of the relation, which gives validity to the specific inference of intelligence. If the relation is invariable, the inference is sound ; if not invariable, the inference is faulty, and this without any regard to any other circumstance or quality of the relation, except that it is invariable.

As I have remarked in reviewing Kant's physico-theology, there is a sense in which the principle of cause and effect is involved in every possible kind of reasoning. Every case in court, civil or criminal, has to do with causes and effects, with active powers and agencies producing definite results, but not in any such sense as that the validity of the decision rests upon the law of causation. So it is not denied that eutaxiology has to deal with causes and effects ; that order is, in fact, an effect of mind. But it is not admitted that the principle of cause and effect, the truth of the proposition, *every event has a cause,* or the question whether that proposition embodies the results of induction or expresses an intuition, — it is not admitted that any of these have any thing whatever to do with the soundness of the eutaxiological inference.

While it is true that the principle of causation does in a certain sense underlie all reasoning, it is never of any consequence as affecting the logical process or the validity of the inference, except in the single instance of the causal argument for the existence of God. The reasons for this are, that the judgment — every event has a cause — is so fundamental, that the disputants on the negative side never think of calling it in question; and the positive inference from it is so general, that it has no value to the affirmative party, except when the origin of the whole material universe is under consideration. In any ordinary piece of reasoning it would betoken either levity or insanity to claim that a given phenomenon — a blood-stain for example — had no cause, or came by chance. If the defendant in a trial for murder should be so reckless as to enter that plea, an appeal to the law of causation might be useful to the prosecution, but useful only in response to the affirmation of chance or causelessness. When that was cut off, the utility of this appeal would be at an end. The conclusion to be drawn from causation is simply that a certain appearance, such as a dark spot upon a knife or a floor or a garment, had *some* cause. But that is far too *general* to be of any avail in convicting the prisoner of murder. What the prosecution desire is the *specific* conclusion that human blood was the cause of these stains. The general conclusion that they had some cause is worthless to the one party, and the claim that they had no cause at all is too idle to be entertained by the other party : hence the law of causation does not enter into the argument at all.

It may be maintained, however, that, if simple causation is not the determining principle in such cases, the principle of *sufficient* cause is involved, and that this is competent to lead to a specific conclusion. No other cause than human blood is adequate to account for the spots in question. That may be true, but still the argument is not causal. It proceeds upon the principle of identification by means of marks instead of the principle of causation. Microscopic examination of the spots reveals minute disks, or corpuscles : that shows that blood caused the marks. The disks have a definite form and size : that shows that it was human blood. Such is the course of the reasoning which might be sufficient to convince a jury of intelligent men in a matter of life and death. Now, the validity of it depends wholly upon the *invariableness* of the relation between certain appearances and a certain substance. The *character* of the relation as being *causal* has nothing to do with the conclusion. Simple causation leads us to the general conclusion of some cause : the principle of sufficient cause adds one element to this general conclusion, — namely, that of some *adequate* cause ; but to make it specific we have to resort to another principle, that of invariable sequences without regard to efficient cause. And this last principle is not only the final resort, but it is really the moving principle and the life of the argument from the beginning. The law of causation not only fails us before we reach the goal, but it is of no use at any point. The invariableness of the relation between a given substance and a given phenomenon is all that is required, even against the affirmation of chance. But, granting that the law of causation might be appealed to against chance, that is at best the utmost extent of its utility in ordinary reasoning.

In arguments concerning the origin of the whole material universe the case is somewhat different. Even the general conclusion, that the universe had some cause, is not without some value ; and the added element, that this cause must have been adequate to produce such an effect, is still more to the purpose, though it does not necessarily follow that this adequate cause was no other than God. But in eutaxiology the conclusion that the order of nature had some adequate cause is of no greater value than a similar general conclusion in a legal case. The specific conclusion of intelligent agency can be reached only by the logical process of identification by means of marks upon the principle of invariable sequences. If order is a mark of intelligence, that is enough. It is what we shall have to come back to sooner or later, even if we start with causation.

Kant, Hume, Reid, Stewart, and McCosh, to say nothing of a host of lesser lights, are all agreed that the arguments of physico-theology all rest upon the principle of causation. If the matter were to be settled by authority, that list of names would be enough to end all controversy. But, since an appeal to reason is recognized as legitimate, I cannot but believe that their verdict will be set aside. It is more than a mere matter of opinion as to the classification of arguments. It will be remembered that Kant held, that the conclusions of physico-theology were invalid because they rested upon the causal argument, while that in turn rested upon the ontological argument. If it be true that eutaxiology is independent of the causal argument, Kant's reason for condemning it will disappear.

Thirdly, it is not asserted that the fundamental proposition of eutaxiology, if established, amounts to a demonstration of the existence of God. The eutaxiological conclusion is simply, that intelligence exists in the universe, and that conclusion is to be strictly construed. The old design-advocates were far too eager and ambitious. They thought to finish up the business at one grand stroke. They supposed they had demonstrated the existence of God when they had only taken the first step in that demonstration. They left prodigious gaps in their reasoning, over which they themselves glided with such ease and unconsciousness that they thought it unreasonable if all the world did not do the same. But the day is past when intelligent men can expect to reach such a tremendous conclusion at one jump. It is probably true that a rigid demonstration of God's existence can never be attained; but, if it is ever approximated, it must be by taking one step at a time, instead of attempting to leap over the whole space at one tremendous effort.

If it be granted that this problem must be solved in detail rather than in the lump, then it is obvious that the first step towards its solution must be in the direction indicated by the fundamental proposition of eutaxiology. The intelligence pervading the universe must be the first plank of that bridge by which alone we may ever hope to span the mighty abyss which lies between us and a *demonstration* that there is a God. Hence, while eutaxiology does not assume that great task alone, it does aim to make a direct contribution to it so far as it goes. And, aside from any use or value of its conclusion as contributing to that proof, this conclusion has great interest and value in itself. Order, in some aspect, either as an internal guiding principle or as an external manifestation of symmetry or beauty, is present in every atom of matter, in every nook and cranny of creation. — as well in the most minute as in the grandest phenomena of the universe. Now, if it be true that this order is a mark of intelligence, then mind permeates matter through and through. So it is no small or insignificant thing that eutaxiology aims to accomplish, though it does not, single-handed, aim at the stupendous achievement which was so lightly and rashly attempted by the earlier writers on natural theology.

Passing now from what the eutaxiologist does not assert or attempt, what of the truth of his fundamental proposition in its naked and unperverted simplicity? Is it certain that order is a mark of intelligence?

Unfortunately we have no absolute test of truth, either in men or in principles. In primitive times it was supposed that there might be a demonstration of personal truthfulness or innocence by the wager of battle, or the trial of fire or water, or the blood of a victim; and some modern metaphysicians have conceived that certain arbitrary tests might be applied to propositions in order to ascertain their validity. Herbert Spencer, for instance, has the test of "unthinkableness." Certain propositions are mercilessly slain out of hand by him because they are "unthinkable." It would be extremely convenient if we had some universal and infallible touchstone of truth. — convenient at least for honest people. All rogues and some philosophers would cry, "Good Lord, deliver us!"

In the absence of any such single and absolute test, all we can do is to turn a proposition from side to side, and inside out if we can, — to view it from different points, to observe its possible range and applications, and to determine its logical classification. In respect to the last point, the proposition in question is, without doubt, an induction. We are momently conscious of orderly results flowing from our own intelligence; and we have a wide experience of similar results issuing from the action of other intelligences. Hence, whenever we meet with any such results without any previous knowledge of their origin, we at once ascribe them to the agency of intelligence.

Suppose we find smooth stones or shells on the beach, arranged at regular intervals in a straight line, or in three straight lines to form a triangle: we should say that an intelligent being had done this. Would we not, however, particularize instead of generalizing, — that is, would not our conclusion be, a human being, instead of some intelligent being, has done this? Very likely we should; and it is further admitted that the particular conclusion — Man has done this — is of no use in eutaxiology. But the mind-marks stamped upon any geometrical figure are deeper and more ineffaceable than the merely human marks. If we found such figures in places inaccessible to men, we should have no doubt of intelligence having been concerned in their production. If we saw them upon the moon or upon any of the planets, we should at once conclude that they were inhabited by intelligent beings. Our conclusion would not refer to human agency, but simply to intelligence in general.

This is a fair illustration of the logic of eutaxiology. We see intelligence producing orderly results; and we project the inference thence derived over those cases of orderly phenomena of which we do not know the cause. The logical method is that of induction. The relation of order to intelligence is invariable so far as our observation has extended; and we should certainly have no hesitation in applying the principle to cases such as that of symmetrical forms upon other planets, where we could never verify the inference by observation. The question now arises whether it is legitimate to apply it to the order of nature. Here is the vital point in this argument.

Let us return to the case of shells or stones laid in a straight line upon the beach. If the stones were of nearly equal size, pretty accurately adjusted at equal distances, and the line approximately straight, we should make the inference of intelligence confidently. But suppose these three elements begin to vary. The sizes and intervals are less exact, and the line becomes wavy. We should begin to doubt; and at some point in this series of variations, not very far either towards entire irregularity, we should conclude it was the work of the waves.

Wave-action is an example of the operation of natural forces, and we set it in antithesis to the action of an intelligent agent. If the line is such that the waves might have made it, we no longer think of intelligence as being concerned in it. Is not this fatal to eutaxiology? Before we make that inference, let us note that it was only as the appearance of order wavered, became faint, and finally disappeared, that the notion of intelligent agency receded, became doubtful, and finally vanished. It was because we lost sight of order that we lost sight of intelligence, not because natural forces came into view. Still, it is a suspicious circumstance, that, as the appearance of order recedes, and as the notion of intelligent agency goes glimmering at the same time, the mind falls back upon the action of some natural force as the inevitable alternative. If it was not some intelligent being that did this, it was some natural force that did it. That is our conclusion; and we rest in such a conclusion with a degree of contentment which bodes no good to the higher conclusions which must be sought out in order to verify the eutaxiological inference.

Is it, however, a sufficient philosophy of nature to rest the inquiry when we have resolved any given phenomenon into an effect of intelligence or an effect of some natural force? Sufficient undoubtedly for the child or the savage or the rustic; but does it satisfy a trained mind? Is it not at least conceivable, "thinkable" as Herbert Spencer might say, that some intelligence lies back of natural forces? Else why should they produce orderly results? They do produce such results without any doubt. And it may be a mistake, a relic possibly of some superstition or prejudice, to set the order of nature in anthithesis to intellectual order.

Let us look into this very case of the action of the waves. It was because we lost sight of order that the notion of intelligence vanished. If we can bring order again into view, will the notion of intelligence also reappear, notwithstanding the fact that natural forces are the immediate agents by which that order is produced? The waves pile up sands, pebbles, bowlders, driftwood, kelp, — whatever comes to hand, — in heaps of irregular outline and extremely heterogeneous composition. The thought of any sort of order in such action would never occur to a child or a rustic. But ask the geologist whether there is any law of wave-action, and he will point out to you that there is an assortment of the materials carried by the water. To him the beach is not a jumbled mass of *detritus* heaped up pell-mell on the shore: it is a stratified deposit. Not only is there

a definite order observed in the superficial distribution
of the materials, the coarser parts being thrown well
up on the shore, the particles becoming finer as you
proceed towards the line of low water, and still finer
out under the sea; but there is also a definite order
among the elements of each thin lamina in the finer
portions of the formation.

Take up a piece of an ancient off-shore deposit which
in the course of long ages has hardened into stone.
Each surface of fracture is covered with shining plates
of mica, which are absent, or at least less abundant, between the lines of sedimentation. Each swell of the
tide brings its burden of *detritus*. The rounded and
angular particles settle at once, and form the body of
one lamina; but the mica scales, and any other light and
flaky matters, settle last of all, lie flat upon the body of
the lamina already formed, and mark the line of weakness and fracture between that and the next lamina.

Thus we begin to see that wave-action is orderly; but
do we see that it is in any sense intelligent? Certainly
not. No one would assert that the action itself was intelligent; but that is not the question at issue. It
might be that some intelligent agency was concerned
in determining the orderly character of wave-action,
though no one would think of placing that intelligence in the waves themselves. In order to determine
whether there is any reasonable ground for inferring
that intelligence is in any way concerned in their action, let us pursue the investigation of natural laws a
little farther. We have reached one law of wave-
action of considerable interest to the geologist; namely,
that there is an assortment of the materials deposited
by water. But this law is by no means an ultimate
fact. The assortment depends partly upon specific

gravity, and that depends upon chemical composition. It depends also in part upon the form rather than the weight of the particles, and this form depends upon the laws of crystallization. So that this simple fact of assortment by wave-action brings to view a long series of orderly processes, the omission of any one of which would vitiate or defeat the result.

The orderly distribution of materials is, however, but a single phase of the order which the mind is able to discover in wave-action. That one phase does by itself indeed take hold of the deepest and most intricate harmonies of nature. The facts of crystallization and chemical composition are full enough of suggestiveness. But, while the mind is thus borne inwards to the minute manifestations of order in matter, there is another phase of wave-action which bears us outward to the contemplation of harmony upon a broader scale. The tides are lunar and solar pulses, which link the earth to the rest of the cosmos, and compel us to extend our view of the orderly elements involved in the beating of the waves upon the lonely shore. As we listen to their low monotone, if we could comprehend *all* that it signifies, it would grow deeper, fuller, richer in meaning, till it rose to a full chorus of celestial harmony.

Every example of the orderly action of natural forces should be viewed in connection with the whole system of nature. The eutaxiologist does not rest his case upon any single manifestation of order, nor even upon any group or series of such manifestations. He demands that we shall take as broad a view of the cosmos as the human mind is competent to, and then inquire whether there is any intelligent meaning in it as a whole. This demand is not unreasonable; but, if

we comply with it, we shall feel the force of his assertion that the order of nature implies intelligence.

This concrete proposition — " The order of nature
implies intelligence " — is in fact stronger than the
abstract proposition, " Order implies intelligence ; " and
this illustrates the weakness of the syllogism. It is
really easier to defend the conclusion than the major
premise. When we say that order is a mark of intelligence, we seem to assert that each solitary instance of
order is conclusive. Now, there are many examples
of order which are very striking, — far more suggestive
of intelligence than the assortment of *detritus* by the
waves. That is one of the weakest examples which
could be chosen. The facts of morphology, or the doctrine of typical forms, are perhaps the strongest. But
no single class of orderly phenomena is so strong and
full of matter for eutaxiology as the connected view
of the whole series of orderly phenomena in space and
time, so far as the mind is able to grasp it.

This brings to view a singular fact in the comparison
of eutaxiology and teleology. The popular strength of
the latter argument is largely a delusion, because it is
based upon misconceptions. But eutaxiology is so far
from being strongest with the masses, that its best points
can only be apprehended by minds trained and habit-
uated to broad and profound views of nature. Thus
the doctrine of an archetypal skeleton is a highly refined and metaphysical conception ; but even that is
less difficult than those comprehensive views of the
plan of creation which may be obtained by taking the
whole connected series of cosmical phenomena. Eutaxiology properly belongs to a period in which the sciences of matter have been largely developed ; because it
is by means of them alone that we are able to connect

any concrete example of order with its related phenomena, and to form an adequate picture of the whole. In
his " Order of Nature," Professor Baden Powell has
given a very interesting account of the progressive en-
largement of the philosophy of matter, and of the
truer views and more profound comprehension of the
principle of order resulting from the advance of physical science. While it is true, as stated by Dr. McCosh,
that the ancients attended to the principles of order as·
well as to the facts of adaptation, no science of eutaxiology was possible to them in any such sense as it is
possible now that more exact principles and wider gen-
eralizations have been reached in the interpretation of
nature. The scientific spirit which delights to trace all
phenomena to some principle of order which may be
formulated as the *law* of such phenomena, is the best
soil for eutaxiology.

Is there any spirit of opposition to this scientific
spirit? any repugnance to the reduction of particular
classes of phenomena, or of phenomena in general,
under the reign of law? Unquestionably there is; and
this has been so often manifested in one quarter, that it
is not unjust to call it the theological spirit. So far as
there is any antagonism between eutaxiology and teleology, the former is the scientific and the latter the
theological argument. And there is a real antagonism
between eutaxiology and the old teleology, because this
was based upon the notion of arbitrary interferences.
But as there is no antagonism between a true and sober
scientific spirit and a broad and an enlightened theological spirit, so there is none between eutaxiology and
that modified teleology which is not set in contrast
with natural law.

We noted it as a suspicious circumstance, that the

action of natural forces is the alternative to which the mind resorts in contrast to the action of intelligence. Strictly speaking, the antithesis is between human agency and physical force; but there is an underlying tendency to carry it out to the extent of contrasting physical force with any sort of intelligence, and calling it "blind" or "brute" force. The old teleology was decidedly of this character. The conception of creation .by law, or divine energy operating in an orderly manner through and by means of natural forces, was persistently shut out. "Blind" force was set over against immediate divine agency, as if there were no common ground between them. This repugnance to natural law is as unscriptural as it is unscientific. But it has taken deep root, and is the source of the tendency to contrast the orderly effects of physical force with those of intelligence, and to rest in the shallow philosophy of accounting for any orderly phenomenon by referring it to some natural process, as if that were the end of it.

But the order of nature cannot be so easily disposed of. When we refer it to natural laws, we give no explanation or philosophy of it whatever, but merely restate the problem. These laws are themselves mere formulas of order; and, so far from explaining any thing, they need explanation as much as any other form of order; and the most reasonable explanation of them is that they were so settled and ordained by mind. Hence it appears, that the suspicious tendency to contrast the order of nature with intellectual order is no real ground of objection to eutaxiology, because that tendency is a relic of ancient prejudice. It requires mental keenness and mental breadth, both combined, to enter fully into the spirit of eutaxiology. The penetrating insight is requisite to catch the finer notes of harmony in the midst of apparent fortuities. Largeness of spirit is requisite to escape entanglement in complex and multifarious results, to rise to the contemplation of general laws, and to overcome all narrow, antiquated prejudices.

The order of nature implies intelligence, no matter whether it be regarded as flowing *necessarily* from the properties of matter, or *arbitrarily* from the collocations of matter. Chalmers introduced the doctrine of arbitrary collocations as contrasted with natural laws. As an example of what he meant by collocations, take the case of the compensation of irregularities in the solar system. This is effected by the force of gravitation in conjunction with certain conditions of planetary movement; namely, the smallness of the inclinations and eccentricities of the orbits, the motions all in the same direction, the comparatively vast mass of the sun, and the fact that the periods of revolution are incommensurable. Gravitation is regarded as flowing necessarily from the properties of matter; but these five conditions are apparently arbitrary, — that is, they might any of them have been different so far as any natural law or property of matter with which we are acquainted is concerned. Without these arbitrary conditions gravitation would destroy, instead of preserving the solar system. Hence, argues Chalmers, the evidence of intelligence lies in the arbitrary collocations.

But Professor Powell very pertinently inquires whether the established order of the solar system would be any less a mark of intelligence if these collocations should be explained by some natural law at present unknown; and another query would be, whether all results flowing from the law of gravitation directly are to be rejected from the list of marks of intelligence.

Chalmers brought in his doctrine for the purpose of

avoiding the interminable wrangle about the eternity of matter. I am entirely in sympathy with him upon that point; and I have already expressed the opinion, that there is something in these collocations, provided that the doctrine concerning them is rescued from that attitude of hostility to natural law in which its author left it. If there are dispositions of matter essential to the orderly sequences which we behold, and which cannot be resolved into any law, but must stand as ultimate facts or as arbitrary adjustments, the inference of intelligent agency in such adjustments is inevitable. But it is not any more certain because such adjustments have not yet been explained. If they were resolved into the action of natural forces, the determinate direction of those forces so combined with gravitation as to insure stability in the heavens would be as conclusive of intelligence as the arbitrary adjustments.

Even if we grant that the whole orderly and beautiful cosmos is a necessary result of the properties of matter without any arbitrary adjustments or collocations, the conjunction of intelligence with that order is none the less certain. It may appear fatal to eutaxiology to admit that order flows necessarily from the properties of matter, unless we have proved that matter is not eternal, — the very point which Chalmers wanted to dodge. But the turn which Kant gives to the argument at this point is of especial interest. He does not shrink at all from the admission of necessity. On the contrary, he says, that, if matter is so constituted that it *must* produce an orderly and beautiful world, then an intelligent being must have created matter, and endowed it with such properties. The point is well taken : eutaxiology thus raises a strong presumption at least against the eternity of matter, and lends a hand to assist in the task usually assigned to the causal argument. It is, however, still distinct from that argument; because it accounts for the origin of the cosmos, not simply as a something which exists and must therefore have a cause, but as an orderly system which implies an intelligent author of its order, and thence of its matter, provided that its order is a *necessary* result of the existence and properties of its matter.

If it can be demonstrated that matter is eternal, then the only proof we can have of a Supreme Intelligence must be from the dispositions of matter. The same is true if we dodge the issue of the eternity or non-eternity of matter as Chalmers did. In that case his arbitrary collocations are our only resource; and, as fast as they are resolved under laws in consequence of new discoveries, our argument crumbles away. A host of what he thought were good collocations have been resolved by the theory of natural selection. Some are still left, and may never be touched: still, one feels insecure upon the ground of arbitrary collocations which may turn out not to be arbitrary after all.

But the eternity of matter is not demonstrated, and we are not shut up to arbitrary collocations as the only source of evidence. Let the atheist maintain if he will, that the order of nature flows necessarily from inherent properties of matter. The logical outcome of such a claim is the intelligent authorship of the matter itself, with its properties and orderly sequences.

The notion of necessity may be extended still more without disturbing the eutaxiological inference. Suppose it be affirmed, as was actually done by Spinoza, that divine action itself is *necessary* instead of voluntary: it must still be intelligent. Bishop Butler has shown, in his "Analogy," that *fate* is, like *chance*, meaningless and impotent in itself. Admitting the utmost claim that can be made for necessity, it cannot account for any positive result, but only amounts to *a condition affecting the action of real agents.* As a condition it may be conceived as applying to human or divine action; but such action would still be intelligent, though not free. Granting the position of Spinoza, Spencer, and other fatalists, the necessity I am under to do this or that is simply a condition, — simply that I must do thus, and not otherwise; but it by no means dispenses with my intelligence in dispensing with my freedom. It is conceivable that I *must* compose and write this page, but that does not enable me to do it without the exercise of intelligence.

In like manner, if we conceive that necessity attaches to divine action, such action must still be intelligent. Fate is as much a bugbear as chance. Neither can in itself account for any thing. If it be true, that a fata necessity rules both us and God, that simply means that our and his intelligent actions cannot be other than they are; if chance rules, that simply means that some real agent acts fortuitously. The fortuitous action of real agents is conceivable; though chance is not a real agent, but a mere name for such action. In like manner, it is conceivable that certain real agents *must* act thus, and not otherwise; though fate is no more a real agent than chance, but is simply a name for the necessary action of real agents. Eutaxiology has nothing to fear either from fate or chance. So far as the latter is concerned, the order of nature gives it a most emphatic denial. Eutaxiology is the very weapon to slay chance. Necessity is equally harmless to this argument; because it may be admitted that order is a necessary result of the properties of matter, and even that the creation of matter was a necessary divine action, without in the least disparaging the inference that order implies intelligence.

An argument which is so indifferent to the fundamental doctrines of the fatalists is likely to be suspected of favoring fatalism, and there would be some degree of plausibility in such a charge. If order were the only phenomenon in nature, the universal, eternal, unbending rule of law would strongly suggest the notion of fatality. But there are other phenomena in nature, and these furnish better ground upon which to contend with the fatalists. Eutaxiology is not the argument to use against them; but it does not follow that it should be given over bodily into their hands because it cannot be used to decapitate them.

Under the admission of necessity as affecting divine action, the eutaxiological inference would of course be limited strictly to intelligence without volition. It is quite unnecessary to make that admission. I have referred to it simply to show that the most extreme fatalism does not destroy this argument, provided that its conclusion be limited strictly to intelligence. It is no doubt wiser in any case, whether necessity be admitted or denied, to keep this argument within that limit; that is, to use it only to prove intelligence. Any other of the divine attributes may be better established by some other line of reasoning. The admission of necessity, either as regards the actual order of the cosmos or the original creation of matter, is by no means essential to this argument; neither is the denial of necessity essential to it. Hence, if volition or intention in nature can be shown upon other grounds, eutaxiology is not disparaged thereby, since it is indifferent either to the affirmation or denial of necessity.

The critique of eutaxiology shows that it is a legitimate line of argument. The logic is sound: granting the truth of the premises, the conclusion necessarily follows. The degree of probability that its conclusion is true, is as high as can be expected in a field where rigid demonstration is impossible. But that conclusion falls far short of a proof of God's existence. The utmost that can be claimed from this argument alone is, that intelligence exists in the universe. A personal Supreme Being is not proved; volition is not proved; benevolence is not proved; even intelligence is not proved to be infinite. But the proof of intelligence pervading all nature is no mean result in itself, and may pave the way to further results in the direction of a reasonable proof that there is a God.

CHAPTER XVII.

THE CRITIQUE OF TELEOLOGY.

FITNESS in the means used to accomplish an end implies intelligence. This may be regarded as the major premise of the syllogism in the old teleology. Any common example of an end accomplished by suitable means, as vision by means of the eye, would form the minor premise ; and the conclusion would be, that this example implies intelligence. In this form there is as gross and patent a *petitio principii* as in the proposition, "Design implies a designer." The selection of an end, the choice of means, and the use or application of them to attain the end in view, are all highly intelligent actions. We necessarily assume intelligence the moment we speak of means and ends. We cannot give utterance to the thought contained in the subject of our major premise without assuming the existence of that very attribute whose existence we wish to prove. Hence, as in the fomer case, this major premise is an identical proposition. It amounts to saying that intelligent actions imply intelligence, or that intelligence is intelligent.

Let us, then, avoid this begging of the question, by framing our major premise somehow like this : Complex structures, well fitted in every part to produce a definite result, are the work of intelligence ; or, The convergence of many agencies or forces to produce a definite result implies intelligence. Here we avoid the words *end* and *means*, and all expressions which tend to make the proposition identical in its subject and predicate. But it is questionable whether the proposition in this form is *true*. A cancer is a complex structure well fitted in every part to produce the definite result of pain and death, and in it many forces converge to this definite result: must we, then, conclude that this exact result was intended? The same might be said of a swamp breeding malaria: it is perfectly fitted for this work. And a thousand injurious things might be mentioned, each perfectly adapted to its deadly work: were they each and all intended to do this work?

More than a century ago Maupertuis claimed that fitness of adaptation was not sufficient: the result must be a *rational* one, in order to induce the belief that it was selected as an end by a reasonable being. He framed this criticism with a view to the condemnation of those who had brought forward *trivial* examples, such as the folds in the hide of the rhinoceros. But his criticism had a deeper meaning than he perceived. It is undoubtedly true that the end must be a rational one. Teleologists have generally applied the test of utility. It was implied in their reasonings, that their inference rested upon the adaptation of suitable means to accomplish a *useful* end. This would of course exclude any of the examples of injurious structures from the list of acceptable design-illustrations. But reasonableness in the end is a higher test than utility. It includes utility, and goes beyond it. Some higher motive than utility might influence a rational being in the choice of an end, but no intelligent being would seek the accomplishment of an irrational purpose. Either the test of utility or that of reasonableness is, however, sufficient to show that fitness in the adaptation is not alone conclusive of intention. Many fortuitous assemblages of matter have all the fitness of adaptation which could be desired; but the resulting function not being a rational one, — that is, not such a result as we can conceive that an intelligent being would set before himself as an end to be attained, — we very properly decline to draw the inference that this result was intentional.

But, if the end must be a rational one, we cannot help begging the question. The major premise must be so framed that its subject designates, not merely a definite result, but a rational result, or else it is not true that the adaptation is intentional. We must not say, Complex structures well fitted to produce a definite result imply intelligence, but, Complex structures well fitted to produce a definite *rational* result imply intelligence, which is a bald truism. What is the trouble? Why is it that teleology cannot be freed from a fallacy in the statement of it? It is simply because teleologists have mistaken the true use and scope of this argument. They have employed it to prove the existence of God; and they have assumed — correctly, too, so far as this single point is concerned — that this proof must begin with a demonstration of intelligence in the universe. *But the mere existence of intelligence cannot be proved by means of teleology.* It cannot even be attempted without begging the question: the very first step is inevitably a fallacy.

This is obvious enough the moment we reflect upon the nature of the thing attempted. Teleology always has reference to an *end* selected and accomplished by suitable means. The essence of the attempt is therefore to prove the *existence* of intelligence by means of the definite *direction* given to intelligence. But its existence must be *assumed* in order to ascertain its direction.

Let us apply these statements to the classical watch-illustration. We are to prove an intelligent watch-maker from the fitness of the watch to mark the hours. The primary inference is simply intelligence. Other attributes of the watchmaker may be made out subsequently, but intelligence is the first conclusion aimed at. We first fix our attention upon the end contemplated, the marking-off of duration into definite and equal portions. That, in its very conception, not only implies intelligence, but the power of abstraction in a high degree. Any being who could contemplate such an end as that must be intelligent, no matter whether the means he employs are suitable or not. Regarding the means actually employed, we may observe that they are as suitable as the end is rational. But is that the real ground of the conclusion that an intelligent being made the watch? By no means. The marks of mind are inscribed on every wheel and pin and lever, without any regard to what they are good for as parts of the watch, and without any regard to what the watch is good for as a whole. Intelligence bathes and permeates the whole structure like a subtile atmosphere. It is obvious from the very start; and to be obliged to go through the long and circuitous process of scrutinizing the end to see whether it is a rational one, determining the fitness of the means employed, and thence inferring intelligence, — going over a long and intricate road to reach at the end the very thing you started with, — that is a "most lame and impotent conclusion." Not only does it seem an utter waste of strength, but it is *necessarily* illogical. The attempt to prove the existence of mind teleogically involves a fallacy which can no more be escaped than the law of gravitation.

It appears, then, that the most radical vice of the old

teleology lies in the argument itself, and not in the word
"design." I have spoken of the abuse of that word in
one sense; that is, the loose and ambiguous use of it.
We may now see that it has been *abused* in another
sense. It has been held responsible for fallacies which
are inherent in teleology whenever that argument is
employed as a primary proof of the existence of God.
The application of it in nature yields similar results to
those which are shown in the illustration of the watch.
Suppose we are to prove an intelligent author of nature
from the fitness of the eye for vision. The result is
rational, the means suitable: therefore the result was
intentional, and hence the eye was formed by an intelligent being. Such is the circuitous road we must travel
in order to prove *teleologically* that the eye was formed
by an intelligent being. We must first infer *intention*,
and thence infer *intelligence;* but the latter is more obvious than the former. As every wheel, pin, and lever
in the watch bears the marks of mind, so every rod,
cone, and humor of the eye is written all over with the
same marks. But the queer thing about it is, that the
very copiousness of the tokens of intelligence prevents
us from a *logical* inference of intelligence. It constantly
results in reducing our syllogism to the form A is A,
B is A: therefore B is A. The eye, as well as the watch,
is brimful of the marks of mind; and yet *teleology* is
incompetent to infer intelligence from either without
a fallacy.

This paradox is not merely a curious one. It is more
instructive than curious if carefully studied: it shows
plainly that teleology has been turned wrong end foremost. Its true use is not to prove the *existence* of mind
from its *direction*, but, *vice versa*, to prove the intentional
exercise of an intelligence whose existence has been pre-

viously established. Eutaxiology is the proper argument to employ for proving the *existence* of mind ; and, from that as a starting-point for teleology, it may be possible to prove something higher and farther on towards a demonstration of God's existence. The radical vice in the treatment of teleology hitherto has been to use it as a primary and independent argument. It can never take the first step towards a demonstration of God's existence without a fallacy. The end cannot be ascertained without assuming intelligence : hence we can never logically infer mere intelligence from the adaptation of means to an end.

Before passing to consider the true use of teleology, let us note that our examination ·has already disclosed the grounds and reasons of some curious facts brought out by the historical review. We found that the old teleologists were never disturbed by the discovery that a wrong function had been assigned to a particular organ. The mistaken adaptation was to them an evidence of wisdom, but the new adaptation was equally an evidence of widsom. The reason of this complacency under a change of base was, that their inference did not really depend upon the function at all, though they thought it did. An eye would imply intelligence in its structure if it had no function whatever.

A writer in " The Westminster Review " for July, 1875, on " Design in Nature," notes this as one of the fallacies of teleology. He cites the case of the lungs, which have been at different periods supposed to perform two or three distinct offices; and under each mistaken view of the case the teleologist was ready with his inference of divine wisdom from the nice adaptation of the organ to its supposed function. If a given adaptation was an evidence of wisdom, any other adaptation ought to be taken as an evidence of folly, says this reviewer. It is a poor rule that will not work both ways. But all the erroneous adaptations, as well as the true one of respiration, have been employed as good teleological material.

There is certainly ground for suspecting a fallacy in this facile inference of divine wisdom from every possible turn things may happen to take ; but the fallacy is not precisely of the nature claimed by this writer. It consisted in a wrong method, rather than a wrong conclusion. The inference of intelligence in each case was perfectly sound. But the evidence of intelligence lay in the orderly disposition of the tissues, without any reference to the function to be performed by the organ. If one should make a journey to Mars, and find people there who made watches for toys, just for the fun of "seeing the hands go round," he would not give up the belief that intelligence was concerned in their manufacture, simply because they were not intended to serve any useful purpose. The evidence of intelligence does not depend upon the adaptation to an end, and remains intact under a mistaken view of what the end is, or even upon the supposition that no purpose at all was contemplated. So that the old teleologists were right in their conclusion. Their only mistake was in placing the inference upon false grounds, — making it teleological instead of eutaxiological.

Another remarkable fact brought out in the historical review finds its explanation at this point. We found considerable differences both in the theory and practice of teleologists respecting the proper use of their argument, and a great deal of vacillation and vibration from one view to another in the case of individual authors. Shall we use teleology to prove God's existence, or assume his existence in order to establish teleology? That has been the standing problem, never yet fairly resolved, lying obscurely in the consciousness of all the old teleologists, and sometimes carrying them over to one view, sometimes to the other. Cicero used teleology, only to prove that the gods "care for man in particular," thus making it an argument for a special providence. Boyle argued for teleology on the assumption of God's existence, as did Ray also; but both these writers, and more notably the latter, turn about and argue for the existence of God from teleology, unconscious of the vicious circle in which they are moving. Dugald Stewart uses teleology, not as an argument at all, but for the purpose of illustrating the divine attributes. He held that the divine existence was intuitively perceived, and of course it would be folly to attempt to prove an intuition. Professor Cooke seems to have the same notion of the true function of design-arguments as illustrations of the attributes of God, though it does not appear that he had the same ground for it. He speaks of the possibility of demonstrating God's existence as clearly as any of the higher principles of science can be proved, which implies that he does not agree with Stewart that this fundamental truth is intuitive.

The authors I have mentioned appear to have settled opinions about the true use of teleology, though they are not all consistent with themselves in the practical treatment of their theme. Another class of writers seem to be in doubt which is the correct view of the case, and consequently vibrate from one side to the other. Now they are arguing for the existence of teleology upon grounds which involve the assumption that there is a God, and presently they are demonstrating God's existence by means of teleology. I conceive that the explanation of this vacillating course upon the part of individuals, and of the striking differences of opinion entertained by different writers as well, lies in the peculiar and paradoxical character of teleology as exhibited in this critique. It looks like a very promising line of demonstration, and yet it cannot be used as a primary and independent argument for the existence of God. Some suspicion of this difficulty seems to have mingled with a consciousness of real strength and soundness of the argument in the minds of its advocates, and to have produced these differences and vacillations.

But the third and largest class of the old teleologists had no suspicion that any thing was wrong. They plunge headlong into a teleological demonstration of God's existence; and, so far from suspecting that they are attempting the impossible, they think that their task is an *easy* one. Invariably, and without a solitary exception, we find them begging the question. Such a long list of fallacious attempts seems to argue a lamentable weakness, at least, if not a total atrophy of the logical faculty. But its true explanation lies in the remarkably deceptive character of teleology. It looks so strong and easy to handle, while in fact — regarding it, as they did, as a primary and direct proof of divine intelligence — it is really so weak and impossible to manage. There is, in the first place, the confusion of *function* and *purpose*, which forms the flimsy basis of its popular strength; and then there is the baffling paradox, that in an argument which, so to speak, floats in an atmosphere of intelligence, we cannot reach intelligence as a conclusion without a logical *faux pas*. The weakness exhibited by so many false attempts, extending over so many centuries, is certainly remarkable, but it had a remarkable cause.' The fault was, not that teleologists were guilty of a fallacy in the progress of their reasoning, for that was strictly unavoidable from the nature of the argument and the use to which it was applied; but the evidence of a weakness of logical insight is, that they suffered themselves first to be entrapped by the delusive popular strength of teleology, and then to be bound hand and foot in the coils of that remarkable paradox mentioned above.

Is there any such thing as teleology? and, if so, what use can be made of it? According to what has been already advanced, it is futile and fallacious to undertake to prove the existence of mind from its direction to a certain end. That is inverting the natural order of things. We must perceive its existence before we can even raise the question of its direction, much more before we can determine that direction. But can we determine the latter in any case? If so, there is such a thing as teleology, and we shall probably find some good and rational use for it if it really exists. There is no doubt but that we can often reach a conclusion which is practically satisfactory in respect to the direction of *human* intelligence. Right or wrong, we are constantly making inferences of this kind. When we see efforts intelligently guided to a rational issue, — to the attainment of a definite object, — we have no hesitation in concluding that this object is an end, and that these efforts were *intentionally* guided to its accomplishment. We may make wrong inferences, for men's intentions and motives are the most hidden and recondite of mental phenomena. Hence appears once more the folly of using teleology to prove intelligence. You select the most secret and difficult thing as the means of proving one of the plainest. You will not accept any tokens of the existence of mind till you have determined precisely what it is aiming at. If we are quite liable to mistake human intentions, how much less probable is it that we can fathom divine purposes! and how extremely hazardous to rest the proof of God's existence primarily upon our judgment that he *intended* this or that result of the action of natural forces!

Can we in any case decipher creative intentions? There is plainly a teleology of human motives. It is this which the courts employ in determining the vital question of previous intention in the commission of crime; and, with all the difficulties which beset the determination of motives, our judgments respecting them are quite reliable in ordinary affairs. But teleology, as it is commonly understood, does not refer to the deciphering of human, but of divine, intentions. Unless it is possible to discover the latter, there is no such thing as teleology in the strict and proper sense. Now, some of the results wrought out in nature bear such strong marks of purpose, that I, for one, have not the least doubt that they have been intentionally wrought out. I am free to say, without any fear of Huxley before my eyes, that I suppose eyes were made "for the purpose of enabling the animal which possesses them to see." This, however, is not the place to defend this belief, nor shall I make any set defence of it anywhere in this volume. My task at present is not to stand as the champion of teleology, but to determine its true use and its logical *status*. I have declared my belief that certain creative purposes may be deciphered, simply by way of answering the question, Is there any such thing as teleology?

Granting an affirmative answer to this question, in order that we may proceed to the next one, the true use of teleology is not hard to discover. By the light of the principles established in this chapter and the last, it is obvious that teleology must be used as a supplement to cutaxiology. The latter argument establishes the existence of intelligence in the universe, thus laying the first plank of the argument for the existence of God. It is possible that teleology, standing upon that as a foundation, may be able to show that this intelligence has been directed to particular and definite results, thus proving *volition*. If *intellect* and *will* can be shown to exist supreme over nature, the proof of a personal Supreme Being is not indeed complete, but some real advance towards it will have been made.

The moment we change the aim of teleology from the proof of intelligence to the proof of intention, it is relieved of the radical difficulty which beset its initial steps in the old form. The difference is precisely that between grasping a weapon by the blade, and grasping it by the handle. Starting as we now do with intelligence as an established fact in nature, and wishing to reach the conclusion that this intelligence has been purposely directed to a particular result, we are no longer obliged to exclude all terms implying intelligence from the subject of our major premise. The predicate has been changed so as to read *volition* instead of *intelligence ;* and we shall not have an identical proposition, although terms implying intelligence may be inserted in our subject. Circumstances, forces, or agencies converging to a definite rational result imply volition ; that is, imply that this result is *intended*, is an *end*. Such would be the character of the major premise in the new teleology.

The opinion of Dugald Stewart, that teleology should be used simply to illustrate the divine attributes was occasioned by his notion of the intuitive perception of

the divine existence ; but it is worthy of further notice in
this discussion of the true use of teleology, entirely aside
from the peculiar view which first inspired it. There
is one point of view which tends to throw teleology just
where he placed it, or where Cicero placed it ; that is, to
make it simply the means of illustrating the attributes
or the providence of God, at all events to exclude it
from any share in the demonstration of divine existence.
To many persons it may appear inexpedient — possibly
they may even view it as fallacious in logic and un-
sound in psychology — to separate the proof of intelligence from that of volition. We are so accustomed
to the co-existence of intellect and will in personality, that we with difficulty conceive of their separate
existence, or of the existence of either apart from a
person. So that, if cutaxiology is competent to prove
intelligence in the universe, it may seem that volition is
included in this demonstration, and that nothing is left
for teleology but some such function as that indicated
by Stewart or Cicero.

There is a degree of plausibility in this view, and yet
it is not sound on the whole. It would be a rash claim
to maintain that the proof of intelligence includes that
of volition, because the two must be associated in personality. We might as well put in the further claim,
that the affections are also demonstrated in the demonstration of intelligence, because they constitute the third
element of personality. On the other hand, there may
be a suspicion of unsoundness in the cutaxiological inference, because it is content to assert simply the existence of intelligence without volition, because these are
always associated in our experience. This suspicion
would be without just grounds, as we must readily
admit when we consider that the *separate existence* and

the *separate proof* of intellect and will are two entirely distinct things. The eutaxiologist by no means asserts their separate existence by making the demonstration of intelligence a distinct argument. Volition may necessarily accompany every movement of intellect, and yet it may be necessary to establish each faculty by a different and independent line of evidence. In this event teleology is unquestionably the proper form of demonstration to establish volition ; and, even if this may be proved in some other way, still teleology will furnish the best and strongest demonstration of it.

It is possible to prove volition by means of eutaxiology, — not, however, by claiming that it is included in the demonstration of intelligence. The course of the argument would be somewhat like this : We infer intelligence from the indications that matter has been adjusted in cornformity to a *plan ;* as, for instance, the bodies of animals exhibit a morphological type. But this type is a mere *idea*, and powerless in itself to shape any thing : hence volition must have been exercised in causing matter to assume the forms prefigured in the intellctual conception of the type.

This argument seems clear and sound enough, but it is not really strong against the attack of the fatalists. They would assert that a fatal necessity impelled natural forces to produce the given results, and even that the Creator was not free to do otherwise than he has done. I have already shown that this attack is powerless against the inference of intelligence : but it is fatal, unless fairly met and answered, to the inference of volition ; and it is not clear how a good answer can be framed upon the grounds and principles of eutaxiology. Teleology looks more promising at this point. Its principles of flexibility and specialty, and its facts of adaptation, may be wielded against the fatalists with better effect than those elements of stern, unbending, universal law which characterize eutaxiology. So that, upon the whole, I cannot agree with those who would exclude teleology from any place in the demonstration of God's existence.

The proposition which constitutes the major premise of teleology is an induction. Experience of our own methods of procedure, and observation of the actions and avowed purposes of other intelligent beings, lead us to connect actions and motives. We frame for ourselves some general principle like this : Certain lines of action all tending to a specific result imply a purpose ; and we use this in unravelling concealed intentions. This is all perfectly legitimate as applied to human conduct. The method is sound. If inaccurate results are occasionally exhibited, it is because of insufficient data, or a mistaken use of what might be competent to lead to a just conclusion if rightly applied. The vital question is, whether we may safely apply this method to similar indications of a purpose in nature. That there are such indications is the substance of our minor premise, and this will hardly be disputed. Long trains of agencies have converged to such a definite and rational result as the production of a given species, — the horse, for example, — or the production of a complex and useful organ, as the eye. The flexibility of nature is no less striking than its uniformity. The general plans of the cosmos are not more conspicuous than its special adaptations ; so that the inference of volition — the conclusion that the definite and rational results which are from time to time wrought out in nature are *intentional* results — seems not unreasonable. At all events, it is not illogical, and that is the point mainly insisted upon

here. I wish to show that teleology may be so constructed and applied that all its logical processes shall
be sound and legitimate. The truth of its premises,
and consequently of its conclusion, is another matter.

This argument does not, any more than eutaxiology,
depend upon the law of causation. Volition is indeed
causally related to the direction imparted to natural
forces, from which we infer the existence of volition.
But the validity of the inference is not determined by
the principle that every event has a cause. That law
can never lead to any thing more than a *general* conclusion, while the teleological inference is *specific*. From
the law of causation we know that the convergence of
forces to a definite and rational result has *some* cause;
but that is all we can possibly do by means of that
principle. By induction, however, we connect such
appearances with the exertion of will-power, and thus
reach a specific inference of volition, to which the law
of causation is wholly incompetent to conduct us. It
is clear and certain, that both of the design-arguments
are independent of the argument for a First Cause,
notwithstanding the high authority of those who have
maintained the opposite opinion.

The new teleology harmonizes entirely with the theory of evolution. At the same time the modifications
which distinguish it from the old doctrine have been
framed to meet the requirements of sound logic rather
than the requirements of evolution. It aspires to be
independent of any particular theory of nature. The
co-operation of natural forces to produce rational results is a fact, no matter whether evolution be true or
false. Undoubtedly a broader view of such converging lines of action may be obtained from the standpoint of evolution. Long trains of orderly sequences

may be observed, not only pointing to some one end worthy to be chosen and intended by a rational being, but accomplishing multiplied ends all along the course of progressive development. So that I entirely concur with those who hold that teleology is stronger upon the ground of evolution than upon the ground of special creation; but it may be placed upon a safe foundation, which is independent of either hypothesis.

Some general considerations respecting both of the design-arguments and their relation to other arguments for the existence of God, may be appropriately introduced at this point.

We have seen, that an impression prevailed among the old teleologists that it was an easy thing to make a book on natural theology. Derham excused the tendency to repetition, upon the ground that in this line of writing "the observations were obvious." It is true, that, without any dangerous mental strain, a deal of plausible and shallow discussion may be produced under the caption of "design." But both eutaxiology and teleology are in fact somewhat difficult. Any just or profound view of them discloses a wide, deep, and somewhat misty sea. A very delightful voyage may be made about the outskirts of this sea, keeping always within hailing distance of the shore in anticipation of rough weather. That is the way to make a popular book on such a subject. But, while it is not necessary to keep always to the deep water, no argument can be highly esteemed which has not shown itself to be sea-worthy.

While both of the design-arguments are to an unexpected degree difficult, there is yet a considerable difference in the character of the difficulties which beset each argument. Broadly speaking, we may say that the dangers of eutaxiology are metaphysical; of teleology, logical. The order-argument presents no such fallacy-traps as teleology; but it does conduct us into a realm where fate and necessity are words of ominous import. But, fortunately, each argument stands ready to re-enforce the weak points of the other. Eutaxiology, by its conclusion of the existence of a supreme intelligence, rescues teleology from its most dangerous fallacy; and the fatalistic aspects of eutaxiology are best answered by the facts of teleology. Here we see the importance of holding both of these arguments, as it were, in the same leash. Not only is each an aid and a corrective to the other, but each is competent to make a distinct and specific contribution to the general proof of the existence of a Supreme Being.

But when we speak of proving the existence of a *being*, meaning thereby a *person*, we are travelling far beyond the primary conclusions which may be legitimately reached by means of eutaxiology and teleology. Granting that the former is competent to prove an all-pervading intelligence in the cosmos, and that the latter is able to show the domination of a supreme will, the demonstration of a personal God is yet incomplete. The unity of the cosmos disclosed by modern science, the uniformity and universality of law, and the persistence of force, furnish a good foundation for the proof of unity in the mind and will which dominate nature. But respecting the possibility of proving from nature the benevolence of the Deity, and thus completing the list of attributes of personality, there are wide differences of opinion. The majority of the authors whose works I have reviewed are of the opinion that it can be done, and many of them have made the attempt. But Professor Cooke and Mr. Irons are positive that it cannot be done, while Mr. Henslow's method of doing it is a considerable remove from optimism. He thinks the evils of this life are themselves an evidence of divine benevolence, because they are a part of the general scheme of surrounding man with "unideal circumstances" in order to make his probation complete. The very badness of the world convinces him that God is good. There is a good deal.to be said for this view, but it would hardly come under the head of natural theology.

Some materials undoubtedly exist in the universe out of which to manufacture the blackest sort of pessimism, and other materials exist for the construction of the most extreme and brilliant-hued optimism.

This may account for the radical divergence of opinions on this point. Not only do authors differ in their conclusions, but individuals in daily life differ from each other, and from themselves at different times. The fact is, that one's view of this life is influenced by the state of his digestion, his bank-account, and other trifles of that sort, far more than is consistent with sound philosophy. Business reverses and dyspepsia are more fruitful of pessimistic views than all the speculations of Schopenhauer and Hartmann; on the other hand, a sound condition of the digestive apparatus and a handsome balance in bank enable us to see a deal of benevolence in the present system of things. The average sentiment of mankind is probably a compromise between the two extremes, but not an even compromise. It is optimism toned down, — a mild, rose-colored variety of optimism; and this comfortable average is very likely to be somewhere near the truth.

I infer this, not only because it is the average sentiment of humanity, but because the same conclusion may, I think, fairly be extracted from nature. But the proper way to reach it is not by attempting to sum up the evils and the beneficences of this sublunary existence, and then striking a balance, but by a generalized view of the system as a whole. In trying to read the riddle of nature in this way, and to determine whether its meaning is sinister or beneficent, I maintain that the theory of evolution is of great assistance. Not only does it lead us to observe the operation of general laws instead of isolated cases, and afford the opportunity of viewing the cosmos more at large as a compact unit with a general expression of benevolence : it has the further advantage of weaving in the evils themselves as a part of the scheme of progress, — a necessary incident of the struggle for existence.

But, supposing that we can establish all of the elements of personality on natural grounds, another problem is to prove that these attributes are *infinite*. Nature does not furnish the data for this demonstration. The power possessed by that Being who is supreme over nature must be adequate to produce all the effects which we behold ; but, since all these effects and the whole material universe are finite, we cannot thence infer infinite power, or infinite attributes of any kind. Neither of the three cosmological arguments — the eutaxiological, the teleological, or the causal — can establish the infiniteness of any divine attribute.

Is it not possible that some other theistic argument may fill this gap? It has been too much the fashion for the theologian to select a particular argument, stake his all upon it, and lose no opportunity of disparaging and sneering at the other arguments. Descartes' partiality to the ontological proof, and contempt of teleology, is a case in point, and by no means the only one. His pet argument has in turn been more scouted of late than any other. But perhaps these same despised *à priori* conceptions of a Being infinite in all perfections may be just the thing to supplement the conclusions of the three cosmological arguments. It is no doubt absurd to argue the existence of a perfect being, simply because we have the conception of such a being; but it is possible that this conception may enable us to round out to infinity the attributes of a being whose existence has been otherwise established.

May not all of the theistic arguments be combined into one, as suggested by the Rev. R. A. Thompson? They have hitherto been handled too much like partisan troops, each making his own fight without regard to the rest. The massing of them into a solid phalanx would be more effective. Possibly it cannot be done, but it is worth attempting. No line of work more inviting, or more hopeful of fertile results, could. as it seems to me, offer itself to the theologian than this of investigating what definite thing each argument is competent to do, in what form it is most effective, and especially how they may all be marshalled and combined into a single connected and logical demonstration. In the mean time let us rejoice that the practical human reason is already amply persuaded that there is a God. Mankind has not been obliged to wait for a logical demonstration of that fact. Faith has walked securely where Reason stumbled : the child and the peasant have believed and worshipped while the philosopher groped in doubt and mystery.

CHAPTER XVIII.

JANET ON FINAL CAUSES.

SEVERAL very recent works on natural theology have appeared, all of which contain more or less matter for criticism, provided the conclusions of this work are of any value. I had intended to review all of them, and point out minutely their merits and demerits as they appear to me in the light of those principles to which my investigation of the subject has led; but upon mature reflection I have determined not to undertake this task. The number of these books all told, great and small, including those which touch upon design-arguments as incidental to their main theme, is considerable; and I know not how much it may be increased by new publications before the appearance of my own. It seems a well-nigh hopeless attempt, therefore, to make my review exhaustive. Besides, there is considerable similarity in the style of treatment adopted by all these late writers, so that a good deal of repetition would be involved in a detailed examination of each of them. Hence I have concluded to select one of the most important of them, and to present it as a sample both of the excellences and defects of natural theology as it stands to-day. "Final Causes," by Paul Janet, translated from the French by William Affleck,[1] is

---

[1] An American edition has recently been published by Charles Scribner's Sons.

facile princeps among these recent works. It is almost the only one which is exclusively devoted to design-arguments: the rest treat of theistic arguments in general, or insert their discussion of teleology into the body of a treatise mainly devoted to some other topic. This alone would justify my selection of Janet as the type of existing teleologists. It would be impossible to leave him out, if later teleology is to have any notice at all; and a careful review of his work will, on the other hand, cover all the necessary points.

Janet's preliminary chapter is entitled "The Problem;" and his summary of it is, that "the final cause cannot be laid down *à priori* as a necessary condition of thought: it must be sought and established by analysis and discussion. That will be the object of this work. This inquiry divides itself into two problems, — 1st, Is finality a law of nature? 2d, What is the cause of that law? These two questions are quite distinct, and much obscurity arises from having confounded them. We will treat them separately in two different books."

It will be observed that he uses "*finality*" instead of teleology; but, as appears in the sequel, he gives it a much wider and looser sense.

In chapter first he reaches, by his method of "analysis and discussion," "the *principle of teleological concordance*, or principle of final causes." It is stated thus: —

" When a certain coincidence of phenomena is determined, not only by its relation to the past, but also by its relation to the future, we will not have done justice to the principle of causality, if, in supposing a cause for this coincidence, we neglect to explain, besides, its precise relation to the future phenomenon. In other words, the agreement of several phenomena, bound together with a future determinate phenomenon, supposes a cause in which that future phenomenon is ideally represented ; and the probability of this presumption increases with the complexity of the concordant phenomena, and the number of the relations which unite them to the final phenomenon."

Nearly half of "The Facts" in chapter second consists of a fresh discussion of that classical example, the eye ; and the other half, of an enumeration of remarkable cases of *instinct*.

Chapter third, on "The Industry of Man, and the Industry of Nature," is a very important one : —

"By a course of analogical inductions we have tried to prove : 1st, That our fellow-men act for an end ; 2d, That the animals, when they obey intelligence and feeling, act for an end ; 3d, That instinctive actions are directed towards an end ; 4th, That the functions themselves, so analogous to the instincts, are equally directed towards an end."

Such is the outline of his demonstration that "finality is a law of nature."

Chapter fourth, "Organ and Function," is a careful and extremely valuable *résumé* of the latest physiological researches : —

"To sum up : There is no contradiction between our principles and the most recent scientific conceptions."

In his fifth chapter, "The Contrary Facts," M. Janet frames clever explanations of a large number of facts which have been supposed to be hostile to teleology.

In the next chapter, on "Mechanism and Finality," he refutes the mechanical theory of nature by an admirable use of the method of *reductio ad absurdum :* —

"To sum up : It follows from the preceding discussion, that the mechanical hypothesis fully carried out leads, — 1st, To the violation of all the laws of analogical reasoning, by forcing us even to call in question the existence of intelligence in other men; 2d, To a violation of all the laws of science, by forcing us to acknowledge an absolute hiatus between all the phenomena of nature and the intelligence of man; 3d, To a contradiction, because it is forcibly arrested in the presence of a last case, the human intelligence."

He then proceeds to show that the teleological hypothesis is the only adequate one at those points where the mechanical hypothesis breaks down, and that it even covers the ground of the physical and inorganic, where mechanism is strongest. Thus he advances the argument a stage beyond the point reached in chapter third; that is, having shown in that chapter that there is a law of finality running through the realm of life, he now extends that law over dead matter.

The last three chapters of Book I. are devoted to "Evolution in General," and to the several forms of it advocated by Lamarck, Darwin, and Spencer: —

" Transformism, then, under whatever form it is presented, shakes none of the reasons we have given above in favor of natural finality; for, on the one hand, it is not irreconcilable with it, and, on the other, it is inexplicable without it."

Book II. is a prolonged tussle with German metaphysics and mysticism. He wrestles manfully with Kant, with Schopenhauer and Hartmann, with Fortlage, and last, but not least, with Hegel. Some of these he differs from *toto cœlo*, and challenges to mortal combat; in others he finds much to commend, as well as somewhat to criticise. In the latter category Kant naturally takes the highest place. Janet seems to have drawn more from him than from any other author on natural theology, unless it be Leibnitz, whom he always quotes with approval.

In the last chapter he concludes, that "The Supreme End of Nature" is morality. "Morality is, therefore, at once the accomplishment and the ultimate proof of the law of finality."

Such is the outline of this somewhat famous book, — M. Janet's "great work on 'Final Causes.'" Given a perspicuous and admirable style, thorough literary training, and free access to the best materials, and the reader can imagine how such an outline has been filled up. It is unquestionably done with great ability, so far as the matter of the argument is concerned.

With such an acknowledgment it would be a graceful and fitting thing to bring this notice to a close. It would certainly be far more grateful and agreeable to my own feelings to do so, for I have read this author with much pleasure and profit. But it would furnish just ground for a suspicion of timidity not to apply to a living author the same rigid canons of criticism which I have used unsparingly in estimating the works of the illustrious departed. I am constrained to say, therefore, that, while the matter of the argument is handled with signal ability, the logical form of it is lamentably at fault. Inasmuch as I believe that this is chiefly the result of a faulty nomenclature, I will discuss this matter first.

Janet retains the phrase "final cause," and even glories in it, since he makes it the title of his book. At the same time he makes a notable change in the meaning of it. Whewell, and the old teleologists generally, struggled to maintain a broad distinction between final and efficient causes, although they did not all, or any of them always, succeed in this laudable effort.

. "The idea of final cause, of end, purpose, design, intention, is altogether different from the idea of cause as efficient cause. But, if the idea be clearly entertained and steadily applied, the word is a question of subordinate importance. The term *final cause* has long been familiarly used, and appears not likely to lead to confusion." [1]

Once admit the term *final cause*, however, it is evident that the struggle to keep it clear of entanglements with efficient causes will be a losing game from the start, and will become more and more hopeless with the lapse of time. In confirmation of this it is interesting to note that Janet, and with him the whole group of recent design-advocates, has surrendered bodily and unconditionally to *efficient cause*. When they say *cause* they mean invariably *efficient* cause; for the final cause has been, in their understanding and employment of it, merged into the efficient, and become a *species* of it. Thus Janet says (489),—

"No one denies that the final cause may be reduced to the efficient cause, if in the efficient cause itself the final cause be introduced ; namely, the desire and idea, — in other words, the anticipation of the effect. And *it matters little whether the cause, thus analyzed into its elements, is called final or efficient.*"

To justify such notions the nomenclature ought to be enlarged. Causes are all efficient; but in the *genus* efficient cause there are two *species*, which may be distinguished as *efficient* efficient causes and *final* efficient causes. However, the difference between these two species does not amount to much anyhow, so that. in any given case "it matters little whether the cause is called" *final* efficient or *efficient* efficient!

Now, one or the other of these two things must be true: either there is more difference than that in-

dicated above between the notion of *efficient cause*
and the notion intended to be conveyed by the phrase
final cause, or else all teleology is in vain, all the books
and all the preaching on natural theology have been in
vain, and the world is destined to flounder along in
dense ignorance of its Author so far as any help from
final causes is concerned. For if they are only a species
of efficient causes, and so faintly distinguished from
"efficient causes properly so called" (one of Janet's
expressions which implies some degree of impropriety
in his own nomenclature) as to render it a matter
of indifference whether a given cause is called final or
efficient, then all the learned treatises about them are
a pure and prodigious waste of ink and paper. They
have too much "finality" in them to be good for any
thing in a theory of efficient causation, and too little
distinctiveness to be good for any thing by themselves.

It is the first of these alternative propositions that is
the true one. The difference between the two notions
in question is not a shadowy difference between species
or varieties of the same genus: it is radical and generic,
so much so that it is wholly inadmissible to call them
by the same name, or to include them in the same
genus. *The end is not a cause at all:* it is a *motive.*
Men act in view of ends as motives, but the efficient
cause lies in the determinations of the will. The characteristic element of a cause is *its power to produce the
phenomenon* which is its proper effect. Ends have no
such power. The will may choose them or set them
aside, unless you deny freedom to the will; for that
you virtually do if you attribute to ends the power of
producing phenomena. If the motive is all-powerful
and cannot be resisted, then the will is powerless, and
a blank fatalism alone remains to us.

It is true, nevertheless, — and this is what gives the semblance of a cause to ends, and makes it dangerous to juggle with them under the name of causes, — that an end having once been perceived and chosen, the anticipation of it, or its representation in the thought of the agent, thenceforth exerts a *regulative* force upon the whole train of agencies set in motion for its realization. It has the power of determining the means to be *these*, and not *those*. But at every point in the train of agencies the end is merely a motive, and lacks the power of producing the means, because at every step a new determination of the will may intervene to stop the whole process. For example, if health be the end in view, the mental conception of that end has the power of determining the means to be the exercise of walking in the open air, rather than sitting in a damp cellar; but this motive of gaining health has not the power to produce a single step. All that depends upon the will, provided the will is free.

Another characteristic of ends which gives them the semblance of causes is, that they are conditional notions. The conception of them is a customary condition to the action of the will as an efficient cause. Then, since the cause includes all the conditions, it is strictly true that the end, as a mental conception, is included in the efficient cause. But, instead of this circumstance being any justification for the phrase *final cause*, it constitutes a new reason for rejecting it. The very close relation of the end, as a motive and as a condition, to the efficient cause, is the precise reason why it breeds endless confusion to call them both *causes*. Janet is right in saying that the former is included in the latter, and may in a sense be resolved into it. But what follows? Why, that, without making any account of the physical causes, there are *two* mental efficient causes of every phenomenon! There can be no less in any case of acting for an end, provided you call the latter a cause at all. For the true efficient cause, the volition, is never absent; and, if the end is also a cause, it is in reality another efficient cause, giving us two mental efficient causes in each case. How much simpler and safer to call the end just *an end*, and so make an end at once of it, and of the dreary mass of confusion engendered by that fag-end of scholasticism, the phrase *final cause!*

Such is the true analysis of the nature of ends in human action. But all teleologists agree, that human acting for ends presents the best approximate model of divine acting for ends; and none of them is more emphatic upon this point than M. Janet. No more, then, in creative than in human thought can the conception of an end be the cause of its realization. If God is a free agent, then he acts in view of ends as motives; but these are not the cause of his action. He can choose or refuse to produce a given result. One difference there may be: we cannot conceive that he, like man, should once choose an end, and then abandon it. But this does not change the essential character of divine ends in any such sense as to convert them into efficient causes. The original determination of the divine will, and the steady persistence of that determination founded upon its wisdom, unlike the vacillating purposes of men, is the efficient cause of the whole train of physical agencies employed to produce the end.

This is true, no matter what theory we adopt respecting the relation of God's will to physical forces. If these are the direct expression of that will, as some suppose, then it is emphatically true; if they have some virtue in themselves aside from immediate volitions of the Deity, then it is still true, for they are subject to his will.

But, lest this should seem to be a mere dispute about words, let us see if any specially injurious consequences have resulted from Janet's retention of a scholastic phrase. Referring to the first page of his preliminary chapter, the first consequence we notice is the infelicitous paradox, that health is both "the *cause* and the *effect* of walking," — a slight infelicity, indeed, but an infelicity nevertheless. Such expressions give color and substance to the criticism of Spinoza, that teleologists "regard as cause what is effect." Thus far our author is leaning upon Aristotle, and has no chance to develop any latent confusion of ideas which is the inevitable product of a misapplication of terms. But turn over to his second page, where he essays to construct an example of his own, and you perceive that even so early in his first chapter he is caught in the toils of a faulty nomenclature : —

"A man kills another. In a sense the death of the latter had as a cause the action of killing, — that is to say, the action of plunging a poniard into a living body, a mechanical cause, without which there would have been no death ; but reciprocally this action of killing had as a determining cause the will to kill, and the death of the victim, foreseen and willed beforehand by the criminal, was the determining cause of the crime. Thus a final cause is a fact which may be in some sort considered *as the cause of its own cause*. [Most astonishing jugglery of words ! Either there is something very profound in it, or else it is what it appears to be on its face, — mere nonsense.] But, as it is impossible for it to be a cause before it exists, the true cause is not the fact itself, but its *idea*."

Setting aside, as comparatively trivial in importance, the improbability that death in itself should be the motive of any killing, or that any one should commit murder merely for the pleasure of it, and not with some such end in view as robbery, or the gratification of hate, or the defence of his own life, let us subject to analysis the several points of this example. 1st, Death is caused by stabbing; 2d, Stabbing is caused by "the will to kill;" 3d, Stabbing is caused, and consequently death is caused, "by the death of the victim," not as a realized fact, but as a preconceived *idea*. Thus the death of the victim is caused by the death of the victim, or the final cause (death) is the cause of its own cause (stabbing). The first difficulty about this is, that stabbing appears to have *two* causes, and both of them final; for it is apparent, that, in leading up to his brilliant paradox, "A cause is the cause of its own cause," M. Janet regarded stabbing as the efficient, and "the will to kill" as the final cause. Then subsequently he brings in the ideal death of the victim as the final cause. And, since it is quite inadmissible to suppose that our accomplished *membre de l'Institute* would reduce to one and the same thing the *will* of the criminal and his *idea* of the death of the victim, it follows that we have two final causes of the stabbing.

The second and most radical difficulty is to comprehend how an *idea* can be a cause in the sense of having power to produce the effect of stabbing and death. It is easy to see how it might be a *motive* in view of which the murderous purpose was formed. But the will was free to reject this motive.

However, suppose we grant that the idea of death was the cause of the killing. It was really an efficient cause according to M. Janet; although he amuses himself by calling it a final cause for a while, until, closely pressed in the last analysis, he at length concedes that it is at bottom efficient. The will to kill is also an efficient cause without any question. It is such in the true analysis of this example; and it is such in reality, even according to M. Janet, though he plainly considers it as *final* efficient rather than *efficient* efficient. So that the third difficulty about this example is, that the death of the poor victim has, including the stabbing, undoubtedly a *very* efficient sort of an *efficient* efficient, — no less than *three* efficient causes instead of two final causes.

There seems to be quite an advantage in point of simplicity, as well as of truth, in saying that stabbing was the proximate cause of death, and the will to kill the ultimate cause of it. Other elements of the case were not causes at all. The end in view, whether it was death for its own sake, or some ulterior purpose, was the motive of the killing, but not the cause of it in any proper sense of the word "cause."

It may possibly be doubted whether Janet regarded the will to kill as a final cause. Even if he did not, this will not rid his example of confusion. But that he did so regard it appears probable from the manner in which he contrasts it with the "*mechanical*" cause; viz., "the action of plunging a poniard into a living body." This probability rises into moral certainty when we observe how constantly he sets up the antithesis of the final cause and mechanical or physical causes.[1] Nor is he singular in maintaining this antithesis. We have observed a tendency among the old teleologists, notably Cudworth, to make all *mental* causality final, and to set this in sharp contrast with "secondary," "physical," "mechanical," and "blind" efficient causes. This tendency is one of several sorts of confusion arising from the doctrine of

[1] See pp. xvii., 52, 128; also the title of ch. vi., Book I., Mechanism and Finality.

final causes. It is surprising to see it perpetuated in the recent writings of able and generally clear-headed men. Thus Professor Noah Porter, D.D., says, "The relations under which this axiom (i.e., the necessary relation of means and ends) requires that objects should be connected, is higher than that by which they are united under the category of efficient or blind causative force." [1] The Rev. G. F. Wright says, "The doctrine of second causes involves difficulties analogous to those in the doctrine of final causes;" [2] and in another place he speaks of "secondary or efficient causation," as if secondary and efficient were equivalent terms, — as if God were not the Great Efficient. So Porter's expressions imply that efficient causative force is the same as "blind" causative force. Nor are these solitary examples: the works of recent teleologists are full of such expressions. This may possibly be explained by their disposition to magnify their office as teleologists, and to disparage efficient causes; but it is much more likely to be the consequence of a bad nomenclature. When you call the *end* a *final cause*, and invoke it as a higher and diviner explanation of things than mere mechanism, you are pretty sure to glide unconsciously into a vague and shadowy mental tendency to contrast the two things broadly, and to draw in, under the category of *final*, all mental and divine causation. That it was some vague tendency, rather than conscious and deliberate choice, which led these writers to use such expressions, appears from the fact that they would be among the foremost to admit

---

[1] Human Intellect, § 609, p. 595. Porter resolves the final into the efficient cause in these terms: "The end. . . . may be conceived of as an efficient force carried back from the end to the beginning of the series of causes and effects, which drives them to their issue by a constant energy" (§ 615).

[2] Studies in Science and Religion, 186.

that the human will is free, and therefore is a veritable efficient cause ; and also that God, as the First Cause, is an efficient cause.

Since I have alluded to the opinions and language of other recent writers, in order to illustrate some points of Janet's book, I will conclude this digression by an example from a famous logician, Mr. J. S. Mill, which exhibits very much the same confusion as the *criminal case* of M. Janet : —

"Sight, being a fact not precedent but subsequent to the putting together of the organic structure of the eye, can only be connected with the production of that structure in the character of a final, not an efficient cause ; that is, it is not sight itself, but an antecedent idea of it, that must be the efficient cause. But this at once marks the origin as proceeding from an intelligent will." [1]

Here we have "sight" for the final cause, and "the antecedent idea of it" for the efficient cause ; but what then is the "intelligent will"? Is it another final cause, or another efficient cause, or no cause at all? There seems to be an awkward plurality of causes in all these cases, wherever either the end or the antecedent idea of it is reckoned as a cause. Some need of Occam's razor (*Entia non multiplicanda sunt*, etc.) to shear away the superfluous causes. I would say the intelligent will is the efficient cause, sight is the end, and the antecedent idea of it is the motive in view of which the will acts.

A further evidence of confusion of ideas is, that, when M. Janet is arguing against the doctrine that finality may be laid down *à priori* as a necessary condition of thought, he maintains a very broad distinction between

[1] Three Essays on Religion, 171.

it and causality; but in answering Spinoza's criticism he approximates them so closely as to declare that "it matters little whether the cause thus analyzed into its elements is called final or efficient."

Again, on p. 419, he says, "The word 'end' may signi fy two things, — either the *motive* of the creative act, or the *terminus* of that act." But in the note on p. 440, "I know not whether it is admissible to confound the final cause with the motive." Now, the end and the final cause are one and the same thing in the unanimous opinion and usage of all teleologists, not excepting Janet, as appears both from the sentence following the one last quoted, and from the second sentence of his first chapter. In one place, therefore, he is positive that the end is a motive, but later he is in doubt about it. It would appear, that the true nature of the end constrained him in the heat of discussion to say that it is a motive instead of a cause; but, upon reflection, some obscure percep- tion that this was inconsistent with the scholastic no- menclature dawned upon him, and he expresses a doubt whether the end may be called a motive. Probably the same feeling led him to relegate to a note one of Lesage's best definitions: "The final cause is the *motive* that determines an intelligent being to will an end."

Upon the whole, it appears that Janet has been too compliant in the acceptance of a teleological nomencla- ture already formed. He would have prospered better if he had relied more upon his own penetration and power of keen discriminations, of which he gives abundant evi- dence in most of his work. So much for the latest sad example of the consequences of propagating a piece of scholastic word-juggling in modern scholarship.

A sort of succedaneum to the phrase "final cause" is the term "finality," which Janet habitually employs instead of teleology. But he makes it wider than the latter, inasmuch as he recognizes a " finality of *plan*," as well as of *adaptation ;* and this is the only recognition he gives to eutaxiology. He resolves the whole of physico-theology into teleology by making order an end in itself. This confusion of two distinct arguments, together with his loose employment of the word " finality," makes his Book II. peculiarly disappointing. One feels, that, instead of a close logical relation to Book I., we have here a free and diffuse dissertation upon the general question of an intelligent Author of nature, in which the writer seems content to overthrow certain errors of the German school, without much direct or positive argument of his own.

But the greatest blemish of this book, otherwise so excellent, is to be found in the logical form into which Janet has cast his teleology : " This proof, as is known, has been reduced to a syllogism, whose major is, that all order, or, strictly speaking, all adaptation of means to ends, supposes an intelligence ; and whose minor is, that nature presents order, and an adaptation of means to ends " (p. 290). The conclusion would be, that nature supposes an intelligence.

Leaving out the word *order*, because that belongs to a line of argument wholly distinct (namely, to eutaxiology), and because, " strictly speaking," it is adaptation alone that Janet relies upon, we have the syllogism, — Adaptation of means to ends supposes an intelligence ; nature presents an adaptation of means to ends : therefore nature supposes an intelligence.

I have shown above (Chap. XVII.) that teleology cannot be employed as a primary and direct argument for the *existence* of intelligence ; and this attempt of Janet's forms a fine commentary upon my Critique of Teleology.

Every teleologist who makes the attempt encounters this dilemma : Either *his major premise is an identical proposition*, or, if he frames it so as to avoid that difficulty, *it is no longer true.* The old teleologists were quite oblivious to this fallacy-trap ; and so we might suppose the author now under review to be, if we regarded his syllogism alone. Its major premise is clearly an identical proposition. But he states this syllogism in a casual, indifferent manner, not as his own chosen form of the argument; so that we must look to the body of his work, rather than to this syllogism, for the real logic of his argument. We then perceive that he has struggled manfully to impart a valid logical form to teleology ; and, if he has failed, it is only because failure is strictly unavoidable whenever *intelligence* is made the direct teleological conclusion.

Before proceeding to examine the course of his argument in detail, let us look once more at this syllogism. While it is true that his logic of teleology is not to be judged by it alone, still his statement of the syllogism with evident approval stands as a fact which must enter into our estimation of the logical validity of his work. That the major premise, " Adaptation of means to ends supposes an intelligence," is identical in its subject and predicate, is plain enough according to the uniform sense given to the word *end* by all the English teleologists, and by myself throughout this work ; namely, that an end is a result foreseen, chosen and accomplished by an *intelligent* agent. Such being the definition of "end," it is mere tautology to say that "the adaptation of means to ends supposes an intelligence." But the usage of English teleologists must not be appealed to against M. Janet, unless he himself sanctions and adopts that usage. But it appears that he does. He says

(p. 440), " Lesage defines the *end* nearly as we have ourselves done at the beginning of this work, — ' The effect of an *intelligent* cause, considered in so far as it has known and willed it, is called the end of that cause.' " Intelligence being thus included in the end by definition, once more we remark that it is pure tautology and a bald truism to say that " the adaptation of means to ends supposes an intelligence." Even if Janet did not thus define and use the word " end," he might fairly be held and judged by the uniform usage of teleologists, unless he distinctly renounced it.

But is there any such uniform usage? Do we not hear from the German thinkers a great deal about " unconscious finality," instead of a foreseeing, consciously intelligent adaptation of means to ends? Many have, without question, maintained that nature reaches her ends by a blind, groping tendency, rather than intelligent choice. It cannot be maintained that the usage has been uniform in respect to the including of intelligence in the definition of *the end*. This makes it clear, that to judge Janet simply from his syllogistic statement of the argument would be unjust and superficial. We are thrown back, therefore, upon the body of his work for a detailed examination of his logical processes.

Our author is not quite so shallow as to make finality include intelligence by definition, and thus assume at the start what he has written the whole of Book II. to prove. The *petitio principii* would be too gross and palpable. That definition may be regarded as merely the statement of his " problem," indicating what is to be proved instead of assuming it. Although he does describe the end in his " Preliminary Chapter " as a "*foreseen effect*," or an " idea," still he is very careful to exclude from Book I. any consideration of the cause of finality. His cautions are manifold and constant. He is laboring simply to prove the existence of the principle of finality without any reference to an intelligent cause of it, or any cause of it whatever.

As an evidence of his logical scrupulousness, study the following qotations : —

" We do not set out from the idea of an end to conclude from it that the combinations which conduct to it are means ; but, on the contrary, those combinations only appear intelligible to us when viewed as means, and this is why the effect becomes an end. We set out, in short, from a *fixed point*, which is given us in experience as an effect; but, this effect only being possible by an incalculable mass of *coincidences*, it is this agreement between so many coincidences and a certain effect which constitutes precisely the proof of finality. . . . It is evident we do not start at all from the hypothesis that sight is an end ; for that is what we wish to demonstrate. No more do we set out from the adaptation of the means to the end ; for, if there is no end, there is no adaptation, and there would be here again a vicious circle. We set out from an effect as an effect. Then, remarking that such an effect has only been possible if millions of causes have *agreed* to produce it, we see in this agreement the criterion which transforms the effect into an *end*, and the cause into *means*. . . . Now, how would so many diverse causes happen to converge to the self-same point if there were not some cause which directed them towards that point? " [1]

Here we see how careful he is not to take any thing for granted ; and we see also what is his criterion of finality. It is the *coincidence* of causes in a given effect; it is their *agreement* to produce this effect; it is their mutual *convergence* to the self-same point. Further light is thrown upon this criterion of finality in the *prin-*

[1] Pp. 40, 41, and 42.

ciple of teleological concordance quoted at the beginning of this review (p. 391). In all this we see that he is careful to exclude intelligence as a necessary element of his definition of the end, or of his criterion of finality.

It is all-important for us to know precisely what he means by "finality," when he concludes, as the result of the "analogical inductions" of Book I., that finality is a law of nature. In order to attain this knowledge of his meaning we certainly cannot do better than to apply the criterion which he himself furnishes. Accordingly we conclude that the end is a "determinate phenomenon" bound together with several antecedent phenomena which have conspired together to produce it by a manifest "coincidence," "agreement," and "convergence."

Now, if this is the true definition of "finality" as that word is used in Book I., we may insert it into the major premise of the syllogism at the beginning of Book II. Instead of saying, "The adaptation of means to ends supposes an intelligence," — a form of statement condemned by Janet himself,[1] although he uses it here, — we shall say, "The agreement of several phenomena, bound together with a future determinate phenomenon," "supposes an intelligence;" or the coincidence, agreement, or convergence of many causes to one definite and the self-same point supposes an intelligence. But we have already examined this species of teleological major premise in the beginning of our Critique of Teleology. We there found, that, while it had dodged one horn of the dilemma since it was no longer an identical proposition, it was firmly transfixed upon the other since it was no longer true. A garbage-heap breeding stench presents an unexceptionable example of coincidence, agreement, and convergence of phenomena bound

---

[1] See above the passage quoted from p. 41 of his first chapter.

together with a future determinate phenomenon. Who knows how many "Biddies" and "Chinese cheap Johns" have been concerned in this accumulation of kitchen-offal and what not? Who knows what peculations of city officials have absorbed the funds, and left the streets unswept? Causes enough there are in all conscience: they have perfectly "agreed" too, and the "effect" upon the nostrils is a very "determinate" one. Still, this example of "the agreement of several phenomena, bound together with a future determinate phenomenon," does not somehow exactly "suppose an intelligence," but rather the want of it. The simple truth is, that Janet has made his *finality* so broad that it is nothing but *causality*. It includes all sorts of effects without any relation to intelligence whatever. With such a range of meaning as that for his key-word, it ought not to have taken nearly three hundred pages for him to prove that "finality is a law of nature."

It seems, indeed, that he has himself discovered this weak point. In the preface to his second edition he inserts some notable amendments into his criterion of *finality:* "Now what is the distinctive character of these facts in which we recognize the necessity of an entirely new order of things, namely, of the final cause? That character is *adaptation to the future*." So far he is merely reciting his old criterion. But he immediately, in effect, admits that this criterion applies to "all causality without exception," and hence will not answer at all as *the* criterion of finality.

"That is the difficulty: here is the solution. Without doubt, given a certain number of causes that act together, they must produce a certain effect; and it is no way astonishing that they be appropriate to that effect. But that effect, so far as it is only a result, can only be an effect *what-*

soever, having no relation to the *interest* of the being that is the subject of it, supposing that there are beings that have an interest in such phenomena, rather than in others; but that is the property of living beings. Suppose now that such an interest exists, it is then evident that we no longer have to do with whatsoever effects, but with determined effects, having a precise relation to the conservation of the being. The unlimited field of undetermined effects is restrained. An infinitude of effects are found to be set aside as indifferent or contrary to the conservation of the being. Those only must be produced that are in harmony with life; but these phenomena are still in the future, when the organization is formed. That organization, in place of being called to produce whatsoever effects, is circumscribed in its work by the necessity to produce such a given effect, and not another. This is what we call adaptation to the future. [He would have us believe that he is only explaining his old criterion of finality, whereas, in fact, he has made an entirely new one.] For that there must be an *arrangement* of causes, not merely a confused and any rencounter, but a precise and limited rencounter. It is this precision, limitation, and circumscription in the arrangement of causes that is not explained, and that consequently, in the mechanist hypothesis, is without cause."[1]

Well did Maupertuis say that the end must be a *rational* one! Janet is forced at length to frame his criterion of finality in such terms as to *assume* intelligence after all! He *must* do it: otherwise he cannot distinguish finality from causality. The end has now become a *determined* effect, instead of a "whatsoever" (?) effect. The causes are *arranged with precision!* The organization is so circumscribed as "to produce such a given effect, and not another." Only *that* effect must be produced which is in harmony with life, and for the "*interest* of the being that is the subject of it." Truly,

---

[1] P. xviii.

nothing but *intelligence* can attend to all these points, and secure their realization.

Let us then insert this new criterion of finality into the teleological major premise. *The precise, limited, and circumscribed rencounter of causes so* ARRANGED *as to produce a* DETERMINED *effect for the* INTEREST *and* CONSERVATION *of some living being, supposes an intelligence.* Of course it does. No one would be likely to deny the *truth* of the proposition in this form. It is so true that it is a truism, an identical proposition once more. Intelligence has been assumed as the test of what an end is; and indeed it is impossible to define the end, or to distinguish it from a simple effect, without assuming intelligence in the statement of the criterion. In short, our author has now impaled himself upon the first horn of the teleological dilemma, instead of the second.

This may serve to illustrate the truth of the military maxim, that it is dangerous to change front under fire; and a further disadvantage of this change is, that much of Book I. would have to be rewritten to make it conform to the new criterion of finality. M. Janet would find the task of proving that finality is a law of nature much more onerous than he has, if it is understood that this finality is not merely an "adaptation to the future," but a principle or force which *arranges* causes in precise, limited, and circumscribed lines, for the production of *determined* effects in harmony with the organization, and for the interest and conservation of living beings.

Janet's work, including his last preface, serves most admirably to illustrate the inherent difficulties of the old teleology, which has the *existence* of intelligence for its direct conclusion. He has labored more diligently to overcome these difficulties, and with a keener insig't of their true nature, than any of the old writers. In the first place, we see him guarding his first book so sedulously against the assumption of intelligence, that he runs his finality into mere causality. He seems to have perceived the first horn of the teleological dilemma; and, in steering clear of that, he ran plump against the second. Such a finality as his old criterion described did not "suppose intelligence." His major premise was no longer true; and he himself plainly felt that something was wrong: so he proceeded to frame his new criterion of finality. This does undoubtedly distinguish it from causality. Truth is restored to his major premise. But, in thus wriggling away from the second horn of the teleological dilemma, he falls once more square upon the first. He has assumed an intelligent arrangement of causes as a criterion of the end. His major premise has again become an identical proposition. He has only two terms, instead of three, out of which to construct his syllogism; and, finally, he has begged the whole question.

What a pity that he did not perceive how useless all his efforts were, and must be, so long as he, in common with the whole company of design-advocates, was trying to force teleology to a conclusion which it will not bear! That is the whole cause of the trouble. His last criterion of finality, — and the only one which serves to discriminate between it and causality, — in which he speaks of the *precise arrangement* of causes to produce determined and rational effects, clearly shows that it is impossible, without the assumption of intelligence, to determine the *existence* of ends: hence that we cannot in any case infer from ends the *existence* of intelligence. That inference flows from order, and belongs to eutaxiology. But in the legitimate province of teleology we may infer, from the existence of ends, the *direction* of intelligence; we may infer that it has been concentrated in a *purpose* to be accomplished; we may infer that a divine *volition* has gone forth.   This is the true function of telcology; this is its proper conclusion; this is to take it by the handle, and not by the blade.

INDEX.

415